"Genghis Khan may have stormed across the steppes seven centuries ago but Michael Kohn has probably covered nearly as many miles around one of the world's most remote and untamed nations. That he's managed to explore Mongolia from Ulaanbaatar to the Gobi Desert and from frozen winters to baking summers on a salary of just 50,000 tögrögs a month (that's 60 dollars if your calculator isn't at hand) as editor of *The Mongol Messenger* makes his tale of strange places and even stranger people all the more remarkable."

— *Tony Wheeler*
founder, Lonely Planet guidebooks

"Michael Kohn simultaneously informs and delights the reader in his adventurous romp across the frozen steppes of the planet's most isolated and mysterious country. He writes with the fast-paced timing of a reporter who senses the global impact of minute issues; yet at the same time, he paints vivid pictures of the Mongolian landscape and people with the skill of a portrait painter. He offers a picture filled with information, where even the most bizarre characters are treated with dignity without avoiding the irony in their lives."

—*Jack Weatherford*
author of Ghengis Khan and the Making of the Modern World

"Here is a vivid account of post-Communist Mongolia that reveals much about the traditional culture while at the same time describing the challenges and problems that the country has faced since 1990. The author, a journalist who lived for three years in Mongolia and served as an editor of an English-language newspaper, traveled throughout the country and was a keen observer of tradition and innovations. His anecdotal style offers the reader a unique perspective on a little-known society."

—*Morris Rossabi*
author of Khubilai Khan: His Life and Times

DATELINE MONGOLIA

An American Journalist
in Nomad's Land

Michael Kohn

RDR Books
Muskegon, Michigan ~ Berkeley, California

Dateline Mongolia

RDR Books
1487 Glen Ave.
Muskegon, MI 49441
Phone: (510) 595-0595
Fax: (510) 228-0300
E-mail: read@rdrbooks.com

Text and Photos Copyright 2006 by Michael Kohn
All Rights Reserved
ISBN: 1-57143-155-1
After Jan. 1, 2007: 978-1-57143-155-4

Library of Congress Control Number: 2006930433

Design and Production: Richard Harris

Distributed in the United Kingdom and Europe by
Roundhouse Publishing Ltd., Millstone, Limers Lane, Northam,
North Devon EX39 2RG, United Kingdom

Printed in the United States of America

CONTENTS

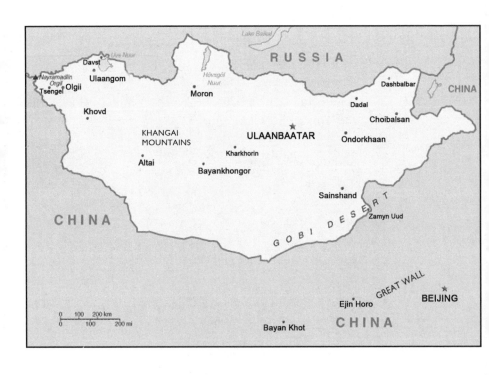

June 17, 1997

Dear Michael,

Thanks for your interest in *The Mongol Messenger*. Unfortunately Otgongerel is no longer editor—our new chief is Ariunbold, who speaks little English.

Established in 1991, *The Mongol Messenger* was the country's first English language newspaper and at present remains under state ownership. However, since the fall of communism, property privatization has been all the rage and I have no doubt that one day (not in my time!) the media will become privately run.

That's the good news! The bad news is that because it's still a state entity, all staff receive wages of about 30,000 tögrögs a month (US$40). In fact, whether you're a neurosurgeon or a cleaner you'll still only earn Tg30,000 a month!

Since the democratic revolution of 1990, the Mongolian economy has taken a beating. However, in 1996 Mongolians elected their first "democratic" government, finishing 75 years of rule for the communist party. Some people are optimistic, but with roughly half the country living in poverty, many have given up. This feeling was reflected in last month's Presidential elections when the communist party candidate was elected.

The wages are poor and the conditions basic compared to that of a Western publication. However, the office is more than adequate and thanks to the British Embassy we paginate on two fairly new

Apple Mac computers. I have spoken to the News Agency's general director and he says my replacement position would come with accommodation and you would be free to freelance. Official working hours are 9am-6pm Monday to Friday and half a day Saturday. However, things here are pretty relaxed and most of the staff don't get to work until about 11am and they rarely work Saturdays! The communist work ethic is alive and well!

The general state of life in Ulaanbaatar is pretty rough. Accommodation is basic and there are frequently hot water and power shortages. The sky is blue for 260 days of the year, but nine months of the year it's bloody cold. During the most intense winter months the temperature can drop to minus 30°C during the day. Most things are available here now, but they usually require a lot of searching. You'll need things like a flashlight (none of the dirty apartment stairwells are lit), lip balm (UB is at a high altitude and the climate is extremely dry) and don't forget a US-Mongolian power adaptor.

I'll leave you my herbs and spices, multi vitamins and some basic medical stuff (gastro bugs are pretty common). Would recommend you get vaccinated for Meningitis, Hep A and B and Rabies, although I must admit I only had half of these and seem to have survived. There may be a chance the embassy will demand an AIDS test.

Good luck with your visa application and don't hesitate to contact me with any further questions.

Kind regards
Jenni Storey

PROLOGUE

THE FOUR HOUR VISITOR

The greatest joy a man can know is to conquer his enemies and drive them before him . . . to clasp their wives and daughters in his arms.

—Chingis Khan

IN THE SPRING OF 2003 a chic London restaurant offered free lunch to any customer who tested positive for Chingis (Ghengis) Khan chromosomes following a DNA mouth-swab test. This was not quite as safe a bet as it may have appeared. Recent findings by British and Chinese scientists estimated that 17 million people across Eurasia are bona fide descendants of Chingis Khan, carrying his signature Y-chromosome. The research, conducted over 10 years, included 16 different populations from China to the Black Sea, all lands that Chingis Khan and his sons once ruled. Not bad when you realize they accomplished this feat on horseback.

While the 17 million figure is only an estimate, it could be higher; Chingis Khan's determination to embrace the wives and daughters of his enemies was no idle boast. History's ultimate alpha male, he founded an empire that stretched from the Pacific across Persia to the heart of the European continent.

The year 2006 promises to commemorate this remarkable achievement. It was 800 years ago, by the shores of eastern Mongolia's Blue Lake, that Chingis Khan brought together the Mongol tribes and united them, ending 25 years of civil war. That momentous event in 1206 marked the foundation of the state of Mongolia, a nation that still today fascinates scientists, politicians, filmmakers and students of history.

For centuries Europeans disregarded the Mongols as sub-human beasts that had sprung from hell (they were known as Tartars, a reference to the Greek version of hell, Tartarus), but America had long been enamored with their barbaric past. Teddy Roosevelt lovingly referred to his Rough Riders as the "wildest bad-ass regiment since the Mongols rode across the steppes." More recently, academic and cultural exchange has bridged the geographic gap. New biographies portray Chingis Khan as a strong military leader and an astute politician. The Washington Post enshrined his legacy by naming him the "Man of the Millennium"

Chingis was the man in so many ways that it is hard to believe that it took more than two centuries for an American president to pay tribute to the medieval superpower. On a chilly November day in 2005, Air Force 1 swept down from the Siberian skies and landed in Outer Mongolia, the region that is now one of the world's most important new democracies. Although part of the land Chingis Khan once ruled, Inner Mongolia, now belongs to China, the former Outer Mongolia is an independent country ruled from the capital of Ulaanbaatar.

Stepping off his plane at Buyant-Ukhaa Airport (since renamed Chingis Khan International Airport), President Bush began a four hour drive-by. The visit was not without purpose. For 15 years Mongolia had survived a white knuckle ride on the roller coaster of democracy and stayed the course. While other Central Asian countries like Kazakhstan, Uzbekistan and Turkmenistan had escaped communism only to make a 180 degree turn back to totalitarianism, Mongolia chose freedom, human rights and fair elections. The Bush visit was a pat on the shoulder, a reward from the only superpower certain to stick by this fledgling democracy.

After thanking Mongolia for its financial contributions to New Orleans following Hurricane Katrina and acknowledging its fierce commitment to democracy, Bush applauded the Parliament for Mongolia's contribution to Operation Iraqi Freedom. This of course was not the first time Mongolians had fought for Baghdad. Back in 1258 distant ancestors of the 160 Mongolian soldiers posted in Iraq won the same capital under the leadership of Chingis Khan's grandson Hulegu.

While Mongolia's emergence as a democracy had required no investment from America, the tab for achieving the same goal in Iraq is running into the hundreds of billions, not to mention the tens of thousands of soldiers and civilians dead on both sides. For the United States, invading Bagdhad and achieving its political ends has been far more difficult than it had been for Hulegu Khan. George Bush must have felt some relief in visiting a country that deserted totalitarianism for democracy without a shot being fired.

Per capita, Mongolia's contribution to the Iraqi combat coalition put them third behind the United States and the United Kingdom. And this was not Mongolia's lone token battle on the world stage. Mongolian peacekeepers have been deployed to Afghanistan, the Congo, Ivory Coast and the Balkans. Remote, tiny Mongolia has proven time and again that its voice will be heard on distant battlefields, fighting for the kind of geopolitical goals vital to preserving the presidency of men like George W. Bush.

Bush wrapped up his visit by drinking salty milk tea with nomads, posing for pictures with Chingis Khan look-alikes, and getting up close and personal with a yak. But as you'll learn in these pages, Mongolia is more than a passing photo opportunity. Ulaanbaatar and beyond comprise one of the most unique political, cultural, environmental, religious and human interest stories of our times; as much a spiritual story as it is a civics lesson.

Going inside Outer Mongolia takes more than the White House travel office, a tour company or even a good guidebook can offer. If George Bush had asked I would have been glad to take him beyond the wagon circle of Ulaanbaatar to the frozen steppes. I would have shown him the hunters and nomads, the remote rail lines, the mystic shamans, the ruins of Chingis Khan's capital, the glorious sunsets, the secret monasteries that survived Stalin's purge, the collapsible felt *gers* that the Mongols call home and the most beautiful mountains and valleys in this far off land—the most sparsely populated nation on the earth.

As the English language editor of a local newspaper, *The Mongol Messenger*, I had a chance to witness Mongolia's remarkable transformation. I spoke with goat herders and prime ministers, outlaws and ambassadors. I traveled thousands of kilometers of trackless steppe, camped with nomads and raced to meet deadlines for 156 weeks. In many instances I was breaking new ground—visiting lost temples, witnessing the revival of ancient rites, and uncovering stories and historical events hitherto unknown in Mongolia or abroad.

Mongolia taught me much, not just about its grand history and culture, but about the warmth, kindness and generosity of the human spirit. In Mongolia, I came to understand, anything good is possible. I hope these pages will lend some insight into what life is like there, and how the human experience can be powerful in even the most distant lands.

Michael Kohn
San Francisco, 2006

~ 1 ~

THE FROZEN CAPITAL

It seemed that here in Mongolia we had discovered an American frontier outpost of the Indian fighting days. Every house and shop was protected by high stockades of unpeeled timbers, and there was hardly a trace of Oriental architecture save where a temple roof gleamed above the palisades.

—Roy Chapman Andrews

Roy Chapman Andrews' words resonated loudly in my head as my train approached the Mongolian capital, Ulaanbaatar. It was true that eighty years separated his arrival and mine, but I wanted to believe that the timbers had not yet peeled and the temple roofs still gleamed with gold. As the train rounded the final bend and began rolling through the outskirts of Ulaanbaatar I pressed my face to the glass of the cabin window and watched as gray buildings marched past. Heavenly skies mingled with a hellish horizon as satanic factories belched smoke in the distance. Wire grew from the earth like weeds. Romantic images—an entire Asian fairy tale—vanished, as I found the old Mongolia buried under industrial estates and hideous housing blocks.

7

The Wisconsin-born Andrews, one of the greatest explorers of the 20th century, spoke of the "dizzying chaos" he experienced upon entering the city. Red-robed monks, swarthy old nomads, and richly dressed noblewomen with outrageous headgear amazed him. My view was more apocalyptic and I could not shake the feeling that the idea to come here had been a mistake.

At last the train jolted to a halt at Ulaanbaatar's Central Station. The carriage emptied quickly as passengers scrambled to unload their huge boxes, crates and bags onto the platform. I too hauled my luggage down the grated metal steps and onto the icy concrete, pulling my wool hat tight over my ears as workers furiously shuttled cargo around me. Families emerged from the gloom to greet their newly arrived relatives. Within moments I could feel Mongolia's famed cold settling in, biting into my cheeks and nose, loosening my sinuses and freezing my feet. The mercury in my key chain/thermometer had bottomed out and miniature icicles were forming on my eyelashes.

Steam welled up from under the train as I hauled my duffel bags to one side. I had lugged more than 150 pounds of gear from China, mostly food, as recommended to me by Beijing expats who testified to shortages and barren shops in Ulaanbaatar. This was far less than the 38 tons of gear Andrews hauled into the Gobi Desert for his 1925 Central Asiatic Expedition, but an impressive load nonetheless.

Moments later I was approached by a Caucasian woman in a large black corduroy hat and a long brown coat with furry lapels. We made eye contact and read each others thoughts. I knew it was Jenni.

Jenni Storey, an Australian journalist living in Mongolia for the past two years, had hired me to work for a local newspaper, *The Mongol Messenger*. She planned to leave in January and took me on as her replacement. We knew little of each other, having only corresponded by irregular snail mail over the past three months.

Trailing behind Jenni was a group of Mongols in heavy black boots, large button-down coats and Russian-style fur hats. Somewhere along the tracks a train let off an apropos whistle, signaling the start of a journey.

"Michael?" Jenni asked, dusting some snow from her shoulders.

"Hello Jenni."

She smiled and removed her glove to shake my hand. Flecks of coal dust sparked in the air as she turned to introduce me to the Brobdingnagian cast of Asians standing behind her, my new co-workers at the newspaper. They looked expectant, seeming as anxious as I was about our first encounter.

They each stated their names and I fumbled along, trying to repeat them. Like the Mongols I had met on the train, they were all imposing in size, much larger than the Chinese I had left behind in Beijing. While I was sure that their winter clothing expanded them several sizes, it was impossible to ignore their broad, dark faces, all molded with high, prominent cheekbones, and formidable black eyes.

Each of them extended their hands to shake mine, but recognizing the severity of the cold, we did not linger long on the platform. Jenni and my new co-workers lugged my baggage out to a slippery parking lot and stopped behind a blue Ford Explorer. A hulking figure named "Bold" unlatched the trunk and swung the doors open, revealing the bloody carcass of a wolf. The animal was pushed aside to make room for my bags.

"Welcome gift?"

"Sorry, it's mine," announced Bold in perfect English. "Just back from a hunting trip."

Bold slammed the trunk shut and we climbed into the car. Jenni got comfortable in back as Bold gunned the engine and barreled out of the parking lot. The streets were covered in a thin layer of oil-caked black ice, but there were few others using it, save the odd black Lada and trundling horse cart.

The ride to my apartment would only take a few minutes, they said, but that was all that was needed to get acquainted. Jenni, a confident and experienced journalist in her mid-30s, thanked me for coming from so far to relieve her from her post. She had enjoyed her time here, she said, but after 24 months of dark stairwells, mutton-fragranced banknotes and the vexations of a post-communist country, she was ready to return to the warm beaches of Perth from whence she had come.

Jenni had been dispatched here by the Australian Volunteer Association to work for *The Mongol Messenger*, a weekly newspaper with a circulation of 1500 copies, designed to serve Ulaanbaatar's small expatriate community. Now it was time to go home. She had been looking for a successor, and responded favorably when I had inquired about a job the summer before.

Mongolia seemed like an unlikely place to break into the field of journalism. I had been hoping to land a job in a bigger Asian market like Tokyo, Singapore or Hong Kong, but I had limited experience in the field, having only written for my college newspaper and a few small travel magazines. Competition for foreign correspondent jobs was tough; I learned this quickly after receiving a dozen rejection letters from the biggest daily newspapers in East Asia. When my options seemed to have run their course, a brown envelope postmarked "Ulaanbaatar" arrived at my house in California; beguiling stamps on the outside featured warlords atop shaggy horses. Inside, an application asked for little more than my name, date of birth and signature. It appeared that I had a job. I signed it, sent it back, and hoped for the best.

As Bold wrestled with the wheel, Jenni passed me a copy of that week's newspaper. *The Mongol Messenger*, I soon learned, was launched in 1991 by the state news agency Montsame as a government mouthpiece for the benefit of Western embassies and foreign investors. Its brainchild was an English-speaking reporter at Montsame, Burenbayar, who now worked as the official interpreter to the President. In the absence of his leadership, Jenni had been hired to keep the English up to scratch and train the reporters.

The paper was tabloid-sized and grainy, but at first glance did not strike me as a weak-willed, good-news-only piece of propaganda. The lead story was a seriously aggressive piece of reporting:

Foreigners Treat Mongols Like Dogs: MP

Americans like to talk about human rights, but at the same time they are the most serious violators of human rights in Mongolia. We shall not allow foreigners to treat Mongolians like dogs. Disrespect will be met with destruction—we will blow up their planes and hotels. Over the last seven years we have come to understand that democracy and human rights are ignored when it comes to justice.

The quote was from Member of Parliament O. Dashbalbar, a frowning, square-jawed man with jet black hair falling over broad shoulders. The MP's outrage was triggered by an American business manager who had allegedly shot one of his own employees a few days earlier in northern Mongolia. In connection with the story, Dashbalbar had organized an anti-foreigner rally where the demonstrators vowed to kick Americans out of the country.

As Bold dodged and weaved his way through traffic, I flipped through the rest of the paper. A police blotter described how two Cameroonian con-men who had swindled a total of $30,000 out of local money changers, assuring them that they had a "magic chemical" that would triple their money. There was a classified section ("Money offered for real Martian meteorites" and "Free bible postal course" were but a few of the ads). Page eight contained an Arts Diary ("The Barber of Seville" was playing at the Drama Theater) and a story about a notoriously fickle analog clock that loomed above the Cultural Center. The clock had recently stopped functioning because the city could no longer afford to replace the bulbs illuminating its numbers. To say that time literally stood still in Mongolia was more than just a cliché.

Light bulbs, I would soon discover, were not the only commodity in short supply. Running water, electricity, petrol, hospitals and paved roads were also badly needed. Mongolia is one of Asia's poorest countries, with a third of its 2.5 million inhabitants living on a dollar a day. And in an overcrowded world, it even lacks people—roughly the size of Alaska, but with less than 2 people per square kilometer, Mongolia has the lowest population density of any country on Earth.

But Mongolia was also Central Asia's best young democracy. Peaceful protests in 1990, led by a young political science teacher named Zorig, had ushered in multi-party elections and free market reforms. They had also ushered in seven years of hyper-inflation and snowballing job losses. But free and fair elections had also taken place; a recent one had knocked out the Communist party and brought Zorig and his fellow Democrats to power.

I looked up from the newspaper as Bold accelerated past Sükhbaatar Square, the central plaza where Zorig had led the 1990 Democratic Revolution. It was vast and gray, the ugly step-sister of Moscow's Red Square. Instead of St. Basil's Cathedral, the huge colonnaded Parliament House dominated its northern end. It was flanked by the Cultural Palace, National Museum, Opera Theater and City Hall (which had a big neon sign above it that read: "Mongolia Will Prosper in Its Renaissance"). A statue of Lenin, with his obligatory furrowed brow, stood nearby.

As my *Lonely Planet* guidebook explained, the Square was named after Damdin Sükhbaatar, the young revolutionary who enlisted Soviet aid to free Mongolia of White Russian occupation back in 1921. Thanks to Sükhbaatar and his comrades, Mongolia became the world's second Communist country. Sükhbaatar mysteriously died shortly after the Revolution (allegedly poisoned) and was subsequently spun by Soviet propaganda teams at the "Mongolian Lenin." His stern, boyish face, still adorns Mongolian currency, stamps and portraits that hang in the Government halls.

Sükhbaatar and I had one thing in common; we were both civil servants. He had worked on the east side of the Square as a typesetter in the National Printing House. My office, I soon discovered, was on the opposite side of the Square in the state-owned Montsame News Agency. Montsame was short for *Mongoliin Tsakhilgan Medee,* which is something akin to "Mongolian Wire Service." After a brief stop at my temporary apartment to unload luggage, Bold drove me to the agency, a white-washed, Victorian-style building that sat ominously next to the headquarters of the Mongolian KGB.

Jenni led me through the blue glass doors and into the marble atrium. A guard in green fatigues and medals on his chest stood at attention as Jenni flashed him a red-colored Montsame ID card. The guard stopped me but Jenni mumbled something to him in Mongolian and he let me pass.

We climbed the marble staircase to the fourth floor where a threadbare rug covered the baseboards. The floor undulated beneath my feet as Jenni led me to the door at the end of the hall, room 401. I stepped inside my new office and found a large, well-lit room. There were seven or eight desks, a few battered wooden chairs and a coat rack full of enormous jackets, each made of fur, down, wool or leather. There was a balcony, and I looked out the window to catch a glimpse of the Government House to one side, and to the other, the sacred mountain known as Bogd Khan—the massif Andrews had called the "gigantic guardian of the Holy City."

Several staff members lingered about, having beaten us back from the train station. I was introduced first to the Editor-in-Chief, Ariunbold, a tall, well-built man who nervously shook my hand and greeted me with a halting "How do you do?" As Jenni had indicated in her letter, Ariunbold was fairly new on the job, a recent appointee of the Montsame General Manager and his close friend, Mr. Amarsanaa. Ariunbold moved to one side as Jenni resumed the introductions.

One of the office translators, Bayarmaa, a pretty young woman with a lanky frame, dimples and shoulder-length hair, was busy pecking away at an Apple Macintosh keyboard. She had a beautiful smile and I was instantly attracted to her.

The computer was donated, she said, by the British embassy after the office had suffered a fire two years earlier. Meanwhile, two older journalists, Indra and Baatarbeel, were busy pounding on tank-like Russian typewriters that had clearly survived the blaze. Jenni explained that Ariunbold had a laissez-faire approach to management. Most reporters came and went as they pleased and wrote whatever they wished. Communist work ethics prevailed and some reporters went days without turning in any material. While I found this thought a little worrying, Jenni promised I would get used to it.

"Here is where the wire stories come in," said Jenni, pointing out an adjacent room that held huge yellow machines spitting out reels of white tape. Dour women in technicians' smocks sat close by, mechanically tearing the tape from the machines and decoding the little dots into actual words and stories.

The clacking typewriters, reels of white tape and the buzzing Bakelite telephones stirred visions of *Citizen Kane*. I spent the next hour or so going over some logistics with Jenni, before we parted ways so that I could go home and get some sleep.

As I discovered in the next few days, the obsolete state of the agency was on par with other government offices across the city. The disappearance of Soviet subsidies had resulted in an overnight failure not unlike the 1929 crash on Wall Street. Yet I didn't mind, the agency actually exceeded my expectations. It was a comfortable, welcoming place and I found the Mongolians that worked there to be a sociable, friendly lot. They were neither the grim communist stalwarts I had expected nor were they the wolf-like barbarians of medieval lore. The 13th century chronicler Roger Bacon called the Mongols the anti-Christ, but my new colleagues seemed surprisingly laid-back and open-minded. It was this attitude that made for a fairly easy entry into my new life at the agency.

After Jenni left I moved into her old apartment, located behind the State Department Store. (This was a department store owned by the state, not, as one friend from California suggested, a store for the US State Department). The neighborhood was called *Doochin Myang*, the 40,000s, because of the 40,000 units built by Chinese laborers in the 1950s. It was considered an affluent area (by Mongolian standards), centrally located and sought after by speculators and entrepreneurs trying to bank on new laws that allowed private ownership.

The apartment was simply furnished with a desk, pull-out couch and a chair. Bare floorboards were painted bright orange and the faded flowery wallpaper and pink curtains epitomized 1970s Soviet chic. The kitchen included a hot plate, a Russian stove and more cockroaches than I cared to count. There was no washing machine so I scrubbed my clothes in a red bucket, and hung them over the radiator.

Every morning I was woken up by an itinerant milk seller who stood in the plaza below shouting at the top of his lungs: *"Suu-arooo! Suu-arooo!"* ("Miiiilk! Miiiiilk")

He'd yell until my neighbors trundled into the freezing cold and bought a liter of milk for 50 cents. Rising stiffly, I'd migrate to the bathroom to check the water pressure. Nine times out of ten it did little more that dribble cold water. I boiled pots of water on my electric range, and washed in the tub as though I were in a Japanese bathhouse. Having been brought up in a Jewish household in Hillsborough, a fairly well-to-do suburb of San Francisco, *Doochin Myang* Apartment Block 8b felt a long way from home. Yet I had come to the country with fairly low expectations and the fact that the apartment had a solid roof over head was enough to put my mind at ease.

In the afternoons, after work, I'd visit the public library, a behemoth of a building, built by Japanese POWs after World War II. It contained more than a million books, plus the largest collection of sutras anywhere in the world. There were Manchu-era government documents, Russian diaries and antiquarian novellas. It was here that I gave myself a crash course in Mongolian history and culture. Besides my Lonely Planet guide, the only other significant source of information I had read on Mongolia came two years earlier in the form of a Peace Corps acceptance packet.

During my senior year of college at UC Santa Barbara I had entertained the thought of joining the Peace Corps, hoping to be assigned to an exotic island in the South Seas, where I'd live in a bamboo hut with a coral reef as my backyard. Someone in a Washington DC office seemed to think I was better suited for a landlocked country in Asia. The packet included detailed notes on Mongolia's political structure, geography and economy. Among its standard advisories about the lack of hygiene and scarcity of goods was a warning that recovering alcoholics not accept this assignment "due to the high prevalence of vodka and social pressure to drink."

I pondered the possibilities, and the sanctity of my liver, for some time, before finally passing on the Peace Corps in favor of a more financially viable option—teaching English in Japan. Still, the Mongolian seed had been planted in my mind, and when the completely unrelated job opportunity at *The Messenger* came up two years later, I had to accept.

Among the books at the Ulaanbaatar library, my favorites were those written by Roy Chapman Andrews, who had come to Central Asia to find the missing link but instead uncovered huge quarries of dinosaur bones. He was a brash, swashbuckling character; fending off attacks by hostile bandits, digging fossils, and schmoozing with New York socialites, all with equal aplomb.

Andrews spoke mostly about the Gobi Desert, but that was not my home. I was living the life of the urban Mongol, and one day Amarbat, a colleague from the *Messenger*, offered to show me around town.

Amarbat arrived at my apartment dressed in a thick overcoat and cap, his hands buried deep in his pockets. Like me, Amarbat was 24, but he was very shy; in the office he went about his business in silence, never speaking to anyone. He had been hired as a translator and was now essentially a gopher—his duties included developing film, buying supplies, delivering papers, bringing the proofs to the printer and occasionally picking up lunch for the other staff members.

I learned that he had spent most of his life in Zavkhan, a remote western province, where his family followed their herds of cattle, horse sheep and goat. He was now married and had a three month old son. His childhood memories were filled with romantic scenes of charging across the steppes on horseback, rounding up wayward animals and delivering fresh milk to market.

He had been lured to Ulaanbaatar a few years earlier with the promise of a good education followed by a furnished downtown flat and a high paying job in the private sector. But economies-in-transition being what they are, he had to settle for a $40 a month gig at *The Mongol Messenger* and a *ger* (yurt) in a tumbledown suburb two miles and several worlds away from downtown.

Together we meandered between Stalinist apartment blocks, past smoldering trash bins, and across open plazas where day laborers chipped ice from the concrete. We eventually reached Gandan Monastery, the biggest monastery in the country and the reason for the city's existence. Since the city was settled here nearly 200 years earlier, Gandan had stood at the center of all religious and social activity, but after 70 years of communism, most Mongolians were now atheist. We found only a few elderly folks mumbling prayers, thumbing their rosaries and walking the pilgrims' path around the temples.

I tried hard to get something out of Amarbat. I knew he spoke English because he had studied it for four years in college. But whenever I asked a question about Mongolia's history or culture he just smiled broadly, gave a shy laugh and uttered *"Medekhgui"* ("I don't know").

Amarbat and I walked back toward the news agency. We passed through *ger* districts whose inhabitants stood patiently, somberly, in the freezing cold, waiting to collect icy well water and rations of coal like characters from a Charles Dickens plot. While they do have electricity, the districts lack paved roads, running water and most other services associated with urban life. Alcoholism is rampant as are breakouts of tuberculosis. Unemployment runs to 50 percent and theft is a part of life.

Within these districts, each family owns a plot of land (about the size of a basketball court) that is surrounded by a *hashaa* (a word that means both wood fence and property). Within the *hashaa* is the *ger* itself and oftentimes a small house made of wood or concrete. (The warmer *ger* is used in winter and the house is used in summer). The *hashaa* will also contain a pit toilet (not the easiest things to negotiate in winter) as well as a cow or two, plus a ferocious (sometimes rabid) guard dog.

The *ger* districts have a temporary feel; a gold rush tent city at best, a shantytown at worst. It felt as though the residents might just pack up their *gers* and move back to the countryside at any moment; which certainly happens when work opportunities are low. Until the 1830s, old Huree really was a nomadic city, packing up its *ger*-homes, *ger*-shops and *ger*-temples, and moving when the livestock depleted the surrounding grasslands. By the middle of 19th century, permanent buildings were put down, and the modern city started to take shape.

Amarbat resided in a *ger* district like this one but said nothing when I asked him what it was like to live there. I thought maybe he'd been instructed not to answer any of my prying questions, but really it was just the overwhelming shyness of a country boy not at all adapted to urban life.

We trudged through the icy streets together—my jabbering English filling in the blanks of Amarbat's Mongolian silence—while the daylight quickly faded away. Back in the city proper we ducked into a *guanze* (canteen) for a meal. These late night eateries, especially the ones around the bus stand by the Ulaanbaatar Hotel, attracted a horde of woebegone souls. Like us, they had come in to escape the cold, but many just stayed there all night, passing around bottles of moonshine. As I stepped gingerly over a man passed out on the muddy floor, Amarbat ordered our diner.

"*Zurgaan khuushuur,*" he said to the waitress. ("Six mutton pancakes, please.") "*Khoyer undaa.*" ("Two drinks.") It was the most I had heard from him all day.

As we ate, two homeless boys, unimaginably filthy, poked their heads inside and extended scabby fingers from torn jackets. I passed them each a mutton flapjack and they charged out the door with their meal. When we finished, Amarbat and I parted ways with a "*Bayartai,*" (goodbye) and I returned home, the howls of a thousand mongrel dogs accompanying me on my way.

Come daylight, I'd start my routine all over again. My main concern in those early days was how I was actually going to put out a newspaper. The job requirements ranged from grammar and fact checking to writing, photography, layout production and finally sending it all off to the printing house. What I quickly found was that most of the stories needed to be completely re-written, which is what occupied most of my time. This was much more than I had signed up for but I had always been something of a workaholic and didn't mind putting in the extra hours if it meant a better looking paper. Layout also occupied a lot of my time as I had never done it before. Jenni had given me a crash course in Page maker when I first arrived but it took a few more weeks before I finally found a rhythm for it.

Getting accustomed to Mongolia-style journalism and local business-acumen was another cup of tea. The concept of an advertising department, for example, had not yet arrived in Mongolia, and when I suggested starting one I was received with a wall of disparaging faces. My colleagues considered the $6000 we made per year from our 120 international subscribers sufficient enough, and there seemed something profane, unethical, and revoltingly capitalistic about including the ads of local businesses, as if we might be unfairly taking sides.

As a revenue loser, we had to tighten our belts, which included distributing the paper ourselves. Every Tuesday afternoon each member on the staff would roll up a stack of papers, shove it under their arms, trudge out into the snow and deliver them to news stands on the way home. For all this, I was paid $60 a month, twice that of my colleagues, plus the rent for my apartment.

Reporting and writing was another area of culture clash. There were two kinds of writers: the first group included the older journalists who had trained during Soviet times. They reported with great accuracy, frequently handing in the complete transcript of a press conference as their story. Quotes from other sources were frowned upon, as were elements of analysis. They preferred factory production numbers, livestock population figures and other statistics. It was bland, uninspired reportage that dated from the School of Stalin: don't ask, don't tell.

The second class of journalists included those that had grown in the post-communist-era. These young reporters were free-thinking, opinionated, scandal-seeking and often downright reckless, giving no regard to common journalist ethics of privacy, honesty or accuracy. They reflected the generally lawlessness that came in the wake of communism.

Most of the younger journalists were employed by any number of tabloid newspapers that had popped up in recent years. These papers were usually found piled high on street side magazine racks; I could not read any of them but Bayarmaa, the young translator at *The Messenger,* offered to read me the headlines.

An uncomplicated girl with freckles, razor-sharp bangs and a full wardrobe of homemade ankle-length dresses, Bayarmaa had only left the city a couple of times in her life. She had recently finished university with a degree in English and landed a job translating at *The Messenger,* but now doubled as the staff secretary; taking notes, answering phone calls and running errands for the senior journalists.

Down at the newsstand one day, a quick review of the tabloid papers had Bayarmaa blushing. She skimmed one paper and then quickly put it down, covering her mouth with her hand.

"What's it about?" I asked.

Giggling, she opened up the paper, revealing pictures of naked women and small crude drawings of stick figures in various kama sutra positions.

"It's called *Hot Blanket,*" she said, her cheeks growing redder by the moment.

A crowd gathered around us, staring with wide eyes.

"And this one?" I asked, pointing to a colorful paper with photos of Russian *GQ* men posing with Mongolian *Cosmo* women.

"*Binoculars,*" she said, "It's about the rich and famous."

The number of onlookers had grown. They hovered over us, huddled up against the cold, eating up all the raunchy details. Mongolians are insatiably curious people by nature and these tabloids helped to feed their fix. Collectively, Bayarmaa said, the papers were known as *Shar Sonin,* the Yellow Press.

If Bayarmaa represented the suburban innocence commonplace among families living in the *ger* districts, another friend from the news agency, Ariuna, portrayed the other half of Ulaanbaatar—a savvy, streetwise attitude that only came from growing up in downtown wealth and urban sophistication. Ariuna, a girl with knockout looks, purple streaked hair and a different color of lip gloss for each day of the week, was always looking for another gig to help pay for her cigarette and alcohol habit. She probably should have gone into modeling but had an insatiable curiosity that steered her toward journalism and part time work at a yellow press paper called *Disgusting Crimes.*

Ariuna and I went out on a few dates, unbeknownst to her co-workers and mine, and once while walking down Peace Avenue we stopped at a news stand so that she could show me the latest issue of *Disgusting Crimes.* The lead story featured pictures of a man lying by the side of the road, curled up in a pool of blood. A hitch-hiker had bludgeoned his driver to death with a crowbar, raped the driver's wife, and run off into the mountains.

"How did you get the pictures?" I asked.

"Oh that man is just our office driver," she chirped. "Our editor mocked up the whole photo sketch and story."

The daily papers were only slightly more reliable. Alien sightings, Bayarmaa told me at the office, had recently featured in the country's top newspaper. One article, titled "UFO Lands in Sükhbaatar Square," was published in *People's Right* the day after the grand opening of the Manhattan Night Club. The event featured high-powered searchlights that waved across the night sky. An intrepid journalist took this to be an alien invasion and ran a full page story on the coming "war of the worlds."

We didn't have any of those freewheeling writers at Montsame. The state news agency was the last resting place of the old guard. Although their feelings about communism had changed, their writing style hadn't. I wrestled with this. Young, ambitious and naïve, I thought I could waltz in and apply a code of Western journalist ethics and make it stick. I tried mini-workshops and skills sessions with the journalists. I went over their stories, discussed format changes and encouraged them to develop interesting paragraphs. It was not easy. I was too young and inexperienced to change their work habits. I questioned how I could deal with the alcoholism around me, half-baked stories and a financial department that barely had enough money to buy ink for the printer. How would I cope with colleagues who didn't have enough to eat, some so desperate they took home our back issues papers and burned them in the fire to keep warm at night? I had trouble drawing a line between the needs of the paper and the hard facts on the ground.

Yet through these early hardships came small personal victories. I started to notice engaging leads and improved story lines. A trickle of paid advertisements seeped through without too much backlash (the proceeds going toward film and much needed printer ink). There was more content coming from junior staffers (Amarbat and Bayarmaa) as their confidence improved. There were challenges ahead and we were still a long way from a Pulitzer, but it was certainly a start.

~ 2 ~

THE CONQUEROR
AND THE COMMUNISTS

BEFORE LEAVING CALIFORNIA, I went to a video shop to search for movies about Mongolia, hoping to find something that would enlighten my coming adventure (Chingis Khan's cameo in Bill and *Ted's Excellent Adventure* having fallen short of expectations). After some rummaging through his video archives, the shop owner uncovered an old John Wayne film, *The Conqueror*. In the 1956 film, John Wayne plays Chingis Khan the early years, a role originally scripted for Marlon Brando. The scrappy Mongol wages war on two fronts, the first to defeat the rival clan that killed his father, and the second to win the heart of the beautiful red-head Bortai, played by Susan Hayward.

Temujin (as Chingis was known in his youth) discovers that the ferocity of his enemies and the callousness of his love-to-be are of equal strength. "You are beautiful in your wrath," he tells Bortai. Later, she flings a sword at Temujin while belly dancing in the palace of a local chieftain. It is a love story after all.

When all seems lost Temujin turns to the gods for direction. "Eternal skies, Yesugai my father! Summon the spirits of heaven

24

to my aid!" The Duke calls out in his best Shakespearian English. "This day I have long awaited and now I am beset with weaklings and traitors... Do not desert me in this fateful hour. Let treachery not prevail!"

The gods hear his cries and send their favor. Temujin's war machine is unstoppable and his manly charm irresistible, soon his enemies are vanquished and Bortai is his. In the final scene, Temujin and his men ride triumphantly into the sunset, prepared to sink the Asian landmass into flames and dust.

Despite backing from Howard Hughes, the film never really got off the ground. Much of the trouble came as a result of the shooting location—in the canyonlands near the town of St. George, Utah. During production, the actors suffered 120°F heat, a flash flood and a feisty black panther that nearly took a bite out of Ms. Hayward. The site was also downwind from 11 atomic bomb tests in nearby Yucca Flats, Nevada. Over the years, nearly half of the film crew would be diagnosed with some form of cancer and a number would die from the disease, including John Wayne, Susan Hayward and Director Dick Powell. Burdened by guilt, Hughes withdrew *The Conqueror* from circulation and watched it night after night, alone, in his final paranoid years.

Some 800 years after his death, the name "Ghengis Khan" still sends a tingle down our spine, as if it were etched into our genetic code. Somehow, the name only evokes images of death and destruction; yet for the Mongols, there is a different tale to tell. In this land of nomads, Ghengis Khan is the founding father, a great unifier, giver of laws and a brilliant military strategist. He is George Washington, Abraham Lincoln and Douglas McArthur rolled into one man. Just how Chingis and his grandsons rose from obscurity to become a superpower merits careful study.

Mongols claim descent from the Huns, a vast nation of nomadic tribesman that spread out from Inner Asia in the fourth and fifth centuries to reach India and Europe. Modern historians link the Mongols to other loose confederations, including the Tartars and the Khitan who lived in eastern Mongolia and the Manchus who lived further east. Culturally and linguistically, the Mongols could also be grouped with Turkic tribes of Central Asia.

These predecessors underwent similar cycles of warfare with the settled nations that lay to the south and west (ie China). Over the course of several thousand years, a pattern developed whereby these nomads from the north would occasionally race off the steppes, pillage Chinese lands to the south, and retreat when their enemies were able to repulse the attacks. The Great Wall of China, begun in the third century AD, was designed to keep these barbarians out of China. The wall slowed the attacks, but ultimately the raiders from the north found their way through the gaps and continued their plundering ways.

According to the *Secret History of the Mongols,* written by an unknown author in 1228 (or possibly 1240), a young woman named Hoelun of the Olkhunuud tribe was kidnapped and taken away by Yesugai of the Mongol tribe. The story tells how, several years later, their first son Temujin (later Chingis Khan) entered the world clutching a large clot of blood in his fist. His name meant iron.

Life was harsh. At the age of nine Temujin's father was poisoned. Fatherless, the clan banished Temujin's family to the forests. Temujin later killed a half-brother in cold blood and was forced to wear a cangue (yoke) for his crime. Then his wife was kidnapped and impregnated by a rival warrior.

But as he grew up, Tenujin's charisma and leadership won him both friends and followers. He enjoyed success on the battlefield against rival clans and in 1189 was crowned "Chingis Khan" (Universal Ruler). Civil war raged for another 17 years, but in 1206 the violence came to an end and Chingis declared himself the leader of a unified Mongolia. With a supply base in Avarga (modern day Khentii Province), Chingis headed south to secure his border lands.

After wiping out his southern rivals, the Tangut, Jin and Khitan dynasties, Chingis' territory bordered on the great Khwarazmian Empire, a vast inland territory that covered much of Central Asia. Seeking to establish relations, Chingis dispatched 400 merchants to Otrar, now part of Kazakhstan. The local governor condemned them as spies and they were executed. Ambassadors sent to receive an apology were also killed. In return, Chingis destroyed Otrar and put the local governor to death by pouring melted gold into his mouth. He subsequently laid waste to Samarkand, Bukhara, Gurganj, Merv, Herat and Ghazni, cities now located in modern-day Uzbekistan and Afghanistan. City-states that surrendered were spared, those that resisted were leveled and their soldiers slaughtered. People of use—craftsmen, doctors, translators, clerks, merchants, musicians, carpenters and others were taken prisoner and pressed into service for the new Mongol empire, which now stretched from China to the Caspian Sea.

Having conquered all of Inner Asia, Chingis assumed the role of statesman and invited wise men from around his empire to provide council. He set up a code of ethics, the *yasaq,* which called for discipline and religious tolerance. He re-established trade links between East and West and created a pony express that sent information across his empire at record speeds. He also commissioned a Uighur scholar to develop the first written language and alphabet for the Mongols—until then their history had only been recorded orally.

Chingis Khan probably did not know where he was going when he set off for Central Asia. World domination was not on his mind. His reason for conquering so many people was fuelled by his desire for justice and perhaps a belief (issued by his shamans), that he was an agent of the sky gods. After conquering Bukhara (Uzbekistan) in the year 1220, Chingis rode through the city gates and entered the great mosque. Calling the city leaders, he stood on the pulpit and told them he was the scourge of God, sent to cleanse them of their sins. Outside the mosque, Chingis stood before the magnificent Minaret of Kalon and wept in humility. He ordered it spared, considering this monument too remarkable to crush. It's still there today.

Chingis' death in 1227 did not slow the Mongol conquests. Under the reign of his son Ögödei, the Mongols marched west again, trouncing the cities of Russia until they reached Europe. Led by a brilliant general named Subodei, the Mongol soldiers easily outmatched their European counterparts. Assembled in teams of ten, the lightly armored Mongol cavalry, experts in the saddle and skilled with the bow, swarmed over disorganized European brigades, exposed in large groups and burdened by heavy steel armor.

In their march across Poland, the Mongols were finally met on the battlefield of Wahlstatt (the Chosen Place) by Duke Henry II of Silesia and 30,000 Teutonic knights from Germany, France and Poland. After an initial attack the Mongols strangely feigned retreat. Sensing victory, the knights broke ranks and pursued them across the plain. It was in this state of chaos that the Mongols launched a surprise counter attack, complete with explosives, fire and flames. The disorientated European soldiers were cut to pieces; an estimated 25,000 men were either killed or captured.

After Wahlstatt, Polish and German cities fell like dominoes to the Mongol army. Still today, tourists stand below the tower of St. Mary's Church in Krakow where a trumpeters' signal ends abruptly in mid-bar, a tribute to the 13th century bugler whose alarm ended when a Mongol arrow was shot through his throat.

The Mongols veered south to Hungary, home to vast grasslands prized by Mongol horsemen. Here they were met at the Plain of Mohi, by King Bela IV and tens of thousands of Hungarian soldiers. The Mongol generals were amazed to witness the Hungarians assemble their camp in a tightly formed circle, fortified by a heavy chain. They looked like sitting ducks and the Mongols attacked with flaming oil and gunpowder launched with catapults. The Hungarians attempted to flee back to Pest but were slaughtered to the man;

an estimated 70,000 people died in the short battle. The Mongols continued their march, put Pest to the torch and chased King Bela to the Adriatic, en route taking Zagreb, Split and Dubrovnik.

"We have the heavenly consolation that, should these Tartars come, we shall either be able to send them back to Tartarus whence they have emerged, or else shall ourselves enter Heaven to enjoy the rapture that awaits the elect," King Louis of France told his mother when it appeared that the Mongols were headed his way.

Panic gripped Europe as the "demons" stood at the gates of Vienna. Soon a rumor emerged that they were in fact humans, actually a lost tribe of Jews recently escaped from Babylon. Christian Chroniclers noted that 1241 was actually the year 5000 according to the Hebrew calendar and deduced that a holy apocalypse was at hand. Church leaders responded by declaring war on the Jews or their cities. Mobs went round burning them out of their homes from Austria to England and Jewish refugees were forced to wear special emblems on their clothing. Unaware of this, the Mongols were busy preparing for their next battle when news arrived of Ögödei's death on December 11, 1241. The grandsons of Chingis were recalled to Karakorum to vote for a new leader. This disruption put an end to the western campaign—Europe was saved.

Mongol leadership changed hands frequently for the next decade, but the army remained unstoppable, next crushing Persia and the Middle East. A grandson of Chingis, Hulegu was dispatched to Persia to destroy Baghdad, Damascus and Cairo. En route he defeated the Assassins, a heretical Muslim sect of Shiites, and by January 1258 had circled the fortified city of Baghdad. When the Caliph refused to surrender, the Mongols attacked. Debris and flaming oil were catapulted into the city. Explosives were used to destroy the city walls. Dams on the Tigris were broken to flood camps used by Caliph's army. On February 5, the Mongols entered the city and sacked it over 17 days. When the Caliph was located he was unceremoniously rolled up in a carpet and trampled by horses. When the dust cleared, a reported 800,000 people had been put to the sword. Whether of not the figure is correct no one will ever know, but if true it would certainly go down as one of the single largest massacres in human history.

Baghdad was set alight as mosques and tombs were destroyed, although Christians and churches were spared. The Armenian chronicler Kirakos of Ganja, a Christian, wrote: "Five hundred and fifteen years had passed since the founding of this city. Throughout its supremacy, like an insatiable leech, it had swallowed up the entire world. Now it restored all that had been taken. It was punished for the blood it had shed and the evil it had done; the measure of its iniquity was full. The Muslim tyranny last 647 years."

Hulegu's dynasty in the Middle East was the last time infidels would rule Baghdad, until an American named Paul Bremer took control of the city 745 years later.

The Mongol Empire lasted for another 100 years. During that time, the famed Khublai Khan rose to power, built Xanadu, conquered southern China and invaded Burma and Java. It was the empire explored by Marco Polo and described in his book, *The Travels*. Although this was the largest land empire ever created it was doomed to fail. The Mongols fell into a sedentary lifestyle, influenced by the populations around them. No longer conquerors, they had lost the ability to fight the mobile wars that had been so successful for Chingis Khan. Local populations rose up and sent the vanquished army back to the steppes of Mongolia where they resumed sporadic bouts of tribal warfare.

The centuries passed until finally a Mongol leader named Altan was able to unify the clans, not by war but with religion. In 1578, Altan Khan met with Tibet's spiritual leader Sodnomjampts, and bestowed upon him a new honorific name—Dalai Lama (Ocean of Wisdom). In exchange, Sodnomjampts sent in a wave of monks to convert and pacify the heathen Mongols, a method Altan believed would keep them under his control. From a political standpoint, the result was disastrous. The Mongol army enjoyed some early success in defending Sodnomjampts' Yellow sect against the rival Red Hats. But the number of conscripts dwindled as the growing church required more monks. Armies disbanded and nomads took up a sedentary lifestyle around the monasteries. The descendents of Chingis Khan had become peaceniks. It was in this state of weakness, that China, now ruled by Manchus as the Qing Dynasty, over ran Mongolia during the 17th century.

China's occupation of Mongolia lasted over 200 years until the fall of the Qing Dynasty in 1911. Tenuous times followed. The Chinese tried to make a comeback, as did a brigade of White Russian (anti-communist) soldiers. But it was Red Russians, the communists, who eventually made inroads. At last, in 1921, Mongolia declared independence. In 1924, a communist government, the Mongolian People's Revolutionary Party (MPRP) was installed, abolished the monarchy and declared the country a republic.

A new era of socialism was ushered in as the Communists swept away the feudal establishment. The process of collectivizing nomads, however, failed in most areas, resulting in mass famine. The new regime also determined that its rule must be absolute and decided to eliminate its biggest rival—the Buddhist clergy. This totalitarian ideology spelled death and persecution for thousands of Buddhist monks and intellectuals. Those that survived the storm spent the next seven decades stripped of their rights, fated to be unwilling participants of the great Soviet experiment.

The years of repression never received much publicity. Even after democracy, it took more than ten years for the MPRP to acknowledge its roll in the massacres that took the lives of some 27,000 people. Whenever I asked about it people shrugged their shoulders and turned away, many of them not even aware that the genocide had occurred. The more I nosed around the subject the more I wanted to learn—I wasn't unraveling any great mystery, the facts were already there, but it seemed like so many personal stories had been unaccounted for. I felt like there was work to be done here and after talking it over with Ariunbold, I decided to launch a series of articles about the repression years for the paper.

The story began at a new museum that chronicled the repression years. Skipping out of the office one day to pay a visit, I walked across a windblown Sükhbaatar Square, between the grim government blocks at the other end, and down a side street to an incongruous pre-WWII home with a steep roof and warped clapboards. The door creaked loudly when I swung it open and, peering inside, I was greeted by an enormous painting that revealed the horrors of the purge—torched monasteries, mass graves and figures being executed by firing squad. The floorboards shifted uneasily under my feet as I moved into adjoining rooms, each filled with artifacts salvaged from the destroyed monasteries—half-burnt sutras and battered Buddhas. Skulls with bullet holes in them lined the walls. Old photographs of lamas glared accusingly down upon me. As I contemplated a large hall filled with the names of the purge victims, an elderly curator in a brown camel-wool jumper approached.

The curator, Tserendulam, showed me the inscribed name of her father, P. Genden, a former Mongolian prime minister. He had been exiled, tried and shot at Stalin's order back in the 1930s. This had been his house. Tserendulam, his only daughter, said she had opened the museum to honor her father and teach Mongolians about the "lost years" of their history.

"My father was considered an enemy of the state," she lamented, a look of sorrow spreading across her wrinkled face. "Stalin and Choibalsan called him a Japanese spy. He wasn't, of course. He was killed because he refused to purge the monks."

Tserendulam said the communist era was so secretive that she didn't learn the fate of her father until 1989, when a journalist showed her declassified documents. Her mother died still thinking that Genden might come home. Further investigation revealed that Genden was not an "enemy" of Mongolia. He was, in fact, one of the few people to stand up to Stalin.

Stalin and Genden had a longtime disagreement over the issue of Mongolia's monastic class. Communism and Buddhism, Stalin warned, could not co-exist and eventually one would eliminate the other. Stalin urged his protégé to destroy Buddhism before it was too late. Genden refused, and in one particular meeting he lost his temper and started throwing chairs across the room. According to witnesses, Genden, presumably drunk, then snatched Stalin's beloved pipe from his lips and smashed it on the floor. His fate was sealed. He lost all his titles before being exiled with his family to Sochi on the Black Sea.

"He really missed Mongolia," said Tserendulam. "He had no news or information and was not allowed to meet other Mongolians. He was worried I would forget how to speak our native tongue. He said he would do anything to return, even if it meant being exiled to the Gobi."

The family was held captive in Sochi for over a year until Genden was put on trial in Moscow. He was found guilty of counter-revolutionary activities and executed by firing squad on November 26, 1937.

"We didn't know what had happened. They just said my father was being held in Moscow and that we would have to go back to Mongolia alone. They sent us back in a cattle car and we stayed in my grandmother's *ger.*" Tserendulam said. "My mother couldn't get a job and I was banished from school. No one was allowed to speak to us."

With Genden finally out of the way, Mongolia's new leader Choibalsan finally launched the purge at Stalin's directive. Eight hundred monasteries were torched as monks were led away, never to be seen again. Fifty years went by before this genocide was finally made public.

* * *

I wrote an article about the museum, and then one about Choibalsan and the legacy he left behind. He had died in 1953 and the occasion seemed to mark the close of a very dark period of Mongolia's history. The years of repression, however, were not entirely over. For the next 42 years the country suffered more human rights abuses under the leadership of one Yu. Tsedenbal. Tsedenbal was a different kind of tyrant. Rather than executing his rivals he exiled them to the desert. Rather than burning the holy temples, he just issued a new set of regulations. Tsedenbal ran his country not with an iron fist, but with mind-numbing boredom.

Tsedenbal urged his compatriots to follow the Russian lead, to eat Russian food, to speak the Russian language, to watch Russian ballet, to read Russian novels and to wear Russian clothes. Communism was all the rage while Mongol customs, traditional script and Chingis Khan became taboo territory.

Over time, Tsedenbal became more reclusive, leaving the country in the hands of his wife Filatova, an uneducated Russian peasant woman, appointed by the Soviet secret service. She ran her husband's affairs like an overprotective mother worried that her children might run with the wrong crowd. Under the rule of the Tsedenbals, hundreds of regulations and rules were enacted to keep people in line. History prior to 1921 was erased from school curriculums and every effort was made to make the Mongols forget that they were a race who once upon a time had ruled half the known world. It was only in the privacy of remote *gers* where elders secretly regaled their grandchildren with stories of their glorious past.

Filatova loathed Mongolian culture and convinced her husband that Mongolia would be much better place if it was more like Russia. Soon Tsedenbal was reading his speeches in Russian and professors were teaching their classes in Russian. Filatova's major personal achievement was the laundering of a million roubles out of a children's summer camp, which she used to build a dacha in a

Moscow suburb. For holidays, she escaped with her family to the Black Sea.

"Tsedenbal did not like Chingis Khan," Ariunbold, my counterpart, said to me one day. "He was not a patriot, he was an internationalist. He always talked about the proletariat of the world. Whenever he gave a speech he only talked about Russia. But Filatova was worse. Everywhere she went she complained or tried to change things without asking people what they wanted."

"The students at my university didn't like communism," he added. "But in public we had to show our love for it. We weren't really afraid to speak for ourselves but we knew that our families would be punished, so we said nothing. It was difficult at that time. Most people didn't know any better, they thought they were defending the country."

There was little Mongolia could do but wait for better times. I asked Ariunbold if the opportunity for change ever presented itself. Rarely, he said. But some dissidents, like Tumor-Ochir, never gave up trying to reform the state.

Tumor-Ochir was a Politburo member at a time when the Soviet Union was starting to rehabilitate the victims of Stalin's purge. Following Khrushchev's lead, Tumor-Ochir decided to do the same. The year was 1962, eight hundred years after the birth of Chingis Khan, and Tumor-Ochir saw this anniversary as the perfect opportunity to see just how far the reform-minded Soviets were willing to bend.

It had been decades since anyone had publicly uttered Chingis Khan's name but Tumor-Ochir went ahead and organized a Chingis Khan birthday bash. A commemorative stamp and postcard series was printed. Then a monument was erected in Dadal, the legendary site of Chingis' birth.

Next Tumor-Ochir organized a "Chingis Khan Symposium" for scholars and academics. The event was meant to be a serious affair but things got out of control and it ended with thunderous rounds of applause, cheers and Chingis Khan chants. Plain-clothed KGB informants in the crowd singled out Tumor-Ochir as the ringleader and had him expelled from the Party and sent into internal exile.

Tumor-Ochir was later brought back to Ulaanbaatar, at which time he began secretly investigating economic reports that he believed had been falsified to maintain the public's good faith in communism. KGB agents uncovered the plot and exiled Tumor-Ochir again, this time to the northern Mongolian city of Darkhan where he was assigned to work as the curator of a local museum.

Tumor-Ochir might have lived to see a free and democratic Mongolia had his life not been cut short by assassins. On October 2, 1985, henchmen broke into his home and hacked him to death with an axe. The killers were never found and a motive never announced. Family members still blame the KGB.

Although Tumor-Ochir never experienced a free Mongolia, it was his rebel spirit that carried over to the next group of dissidents. When the Soviet Union showed signs of weakening in the late 1980s, Mongolia's young and restless rose out of the shadows and proved that dissent, though dormant for 25 years, was still strong and about to strike.

~ 3 ~

THE WINDS OF CHANGE

IN 1989 A GROUP OF MONGOLIAN STUDENTS got hold of a Russian edition of *Playboy* magazine, featuring an interview with Gary Kasparov. Asked how the USSR could solve its financial woes, the chess champion said the country should sell the Kuril Islands to Japan, East Germany to West Germany and Mongolia to China. Insulted Mongol artists sent Kasparov a group letter explaining that Mongolia was an independent country and not for sale. They advised him to "stick to chess, not politics."

Ironically, Kasparov's remarks came in the midst of a political thaw that was opening Mongolia up to the world. Under the careful watch of President Batmönkh (Mongolia's version of Gorbachev), *glastnost* (*il tod* in Mongolia) ushered in renewed nationalism. Professors slowly re-introduced the deeds of Chingis Khan to their classes. Little books called *Zarlig*, which contained words of wisdom of the Khan, started popping up in Ulaanbaatar shops. Calls were made to restore the traditional script. Western influences made their first appearance in Ulaanbaatar—rock and roll bands belting out odes to Chingis Khan enjoyed great popularity. After seven decades of tyrannical rule, the Soviet grip was finally losing strength.

These small triumphs, however, were coming at a price. During the hot summer of 1989, the economy suffered setbacks after the USSR withheld aid to Mongolia. There were petrol shortages, factory closures and worker layoffs. The government apologized for the temporary inconvenience but skepticism was at an all-time high.

In November there were radio reports of a momentous event occurring on the other end of the Iron Curtain—the destruction of the Berlin Wall. Demonstrations erupted across Eastern Europe and Mongolians watched with wonder as Soviet hegemony in the region collapsed. Until then, Mongolian dissent had been limited to anti-communist poster pin ups that appeared mysterious around Ulaanbaatar during the night. It was revealed later that three young men had been responsible for the "Liberate Mongolia" posters, one of whom was a journalist named Amarsanaa (who would later become my boss, the Director at Montsame).

"I hated the Communists. They murdered my family!" Amarsanaa would bellow when he entered my office after hours, his face red with rage and alcohol. His grandfather, a lama, had died in the purges. His mother's side, all wealthy aristocrats, was ruined when communists confiscated their livestock and possessions. Another relative was executed for supporting the White Russians.

Amarsanaa was joined on his late night poster pin ups by a physics teacher named Bat-Uul and a radio DJ called Tsogtsaikhan.

"Somehow they traced us," he said. "One night I was in my home when KGB agents came and arrested me. They interrogated us and threatened our families, so we had to stop."

But others had democracy on their minds too. One was Enkhee, a former journalist at *Unen*. He was a tall bespectacled man with bushy, disco-style sideburns, and by the time I met him, a receding hairline.

Enkhee had come from a long line of scholars and even his father had been a close advisor of Marshal Choibalsan. In 1988, Enkhee wrote an article about Mongolia's staggering economy. The article shocked his editors.

"Anyone who wrote negatively about the government was arrested," he said. "There was a show trial and they convicted me of spying for China."

Enkhee was released from prison a year later, just in time for a cultural fair that brought together Ulaanbaatar's musicians, artists and journalists. During the meeting, one group of young men got together and talked about change, real change, in Mongolia. They felt they were on to something and continued to meet underground. Enkhee emerged as one of the group's early leaders but another key member was Zorig, a young university lecturer who organized the secret meetings at his office in the National University.

Zorig, an Isaac Asimov fan and former rugby player in college, had an unusual bloodline. His grandfather was Andrei Simikov, a Russian explorer who had been part of the Kozlov expeditions in the 1920s. Simikov stayed in Mongolia after the rest of his team went home and went to work as a geographer with the Academy of Sciences. He married a Russian woman but tragedy befell the couple when their 3-year- old son Alec died of scarlet fever. After the birth of their second child, Natasha, Simikov sent his wife and daughter to Moscow. He remained in Mongolia and acquired a German mistress, whose own husband (an ethnic Buriat) was in jail. Together Simikov and the German woman had a daughter named Dorjpalam—Zorig's mother. The German woman gave Dorjpalam to Simikov, who might have raised his daughter had he not become a victim of Choibalsan's purge. Sensing danger, he gave Dorjpalam to a local couple—a Mongolian woman and her Chinese husband who owned a photography studio in Ulaanbaatar. Growing up in this household, Dorjpalam learned Mongolian and Chinese.

Fast forward 20 years and Dorjpalam, a student at the medical college, was cast into a movie called *Serelt* (Awakening) where she played a Russian doctor sent to rural Mongolia to establish a country hospital. This classic is still shown on Mongol TV during the holidays. Sanjasuren, one of the professors at the medical college, took a liking to Dorjpalam after seeing the movie and the two were soon married—Zorig was the second of their three children.

Fast forward another 25 years to Zorig the young university lecturer. A recent graduate of Moscow State University, Zorig thrilled his peers with an impressive report on scientific communism at the meeting of artists in Ulaanbaatar. He was the most politically minded of the group so the young artists elected him their leader (he would later be dubbed the "Golden Magpie of Democracy").

Zorig was a leader for a time when Mongolia needed its own Velvet Revolution. He did not crave money and authority. Like Chingis Khan, Zorig wanted something more valuable; he wanted justice for his people.

Zorig's university curriculum included Communist studies, Western philosophy and history. During the *glastnost* years he read the works by the anti-totalitarian philosopher Karl Popper, which cast doubt over Mongolian-style socialism. According to his students, Zorig often strayed from his regular syllabus on Scientific Communism and lectured on philosophy and politics outside the Soviet world, explaining that communism as they knew it was obsolete.

Zorig's group staged their first public meeting on December 10, 1989, United Nations Human Rights Day. It was freezing cold outside and about 200 people stood shuffling around on the ice. A list of their objectives included multi-party elections and liberalization of the economy. The government ignored them.

Another month went by and the Democrats seemed to disappear, but like the rest of Mongolia, they were just hibernating during the darkest days of winter. Secretly they continued to meet in Zorig's apartment. Zorig was not married so his younger sister Oyun, an English-language student at the university, took care of the household, cleaning up and serving tea and coffee to Zorig's guests. They sometimes came ten at a time and when they left the phone would ring, calls from supporters in the countryside wanting instructions on how to organize themselves.

By the end of January 1990 the Democrats were back on the street. The first weekend protests in Sükhbaatar Square were small and went unnoticed. But the winds of spring swept in the crowds—by late February the square was choc-a-bloc with protesters brandishing banners and demanding freedom.

With the protests proceeding at breakneck speed, conflict arose in the democratic camp. There was uncertainty about what demands should be made and what type of system they ought to strive for. Ekhee started to distance himself from their squabbles. Zorig and Bat-Uul took charge and formed the core of the protesters. Joining them was Elbegdorj—a 26-year-old journalist who wrote for the military newspaper *Red Star*.

"They were wary of capitalism," Enkhee recalled. "They wanted to abolish Stalinism and build genuine Marxism. I advocated for a multi-party system. It took some time, but eventually they agreed that democracy was the only way."

The old guard resisted. Batmönkh and his cronies launched a propaganda campaign to denounce the protestors. Newspapers filled up with letters by "citizens" who condemned them as criminals and drunks. Zorig was attacked in the press, which lamented how the son of a respected commissar was now running with radicals. Death threats were whispered through his phone line.

Down on the streets, the young democrats were trying to appeal to nationalistic sentiments. One of the rally cries was *"Moriin-doo!"* an old cavalry term that meant "Mongols! To your horses!" Tsogsaikhan's band whipped up a song called "The Sound of Bells," which was meant to "wake the masses from their long slumber." A friend of mine named Eddie (his real name was Enkhee) was with the protesters and loved describing the energy of the movement

"It was big and exciting, but scary. Any criminal could have just hit a soldier or thrown a rock and that would have been it. We were close to a riot, but it never came to that. That was the mark of our revolution. Not one stone was thrown. Not one shot was fired."

Eddie explained that among the dissidents, Zorig was the most trustworthy, intelligent and talented. Others lacked experience or natural leadership abilities. Some were just hooligans looking for a fight to pick. I asked Eddie if he had been afraid.

"At first many people were skeptical of democracy. My relatives were angry when I went to the Square. It was dangerous and they had grown accustomed to Communism. It was the only thing they knew."

It had only been a few months since the massacre in Tiananmen Square and some members of the Politburo suggested sending out tanks to disperse the crowd. One tense day there was a stand off. The crowd was scuffling with soldiers outside the Government House. With snipers on the nearby rooftops, Zorig mounted his friend's shoulders with a microphone and ordered everyone to back down. They relented and the bloodbath was avoided. This image became a symbol of the Revolution—appearing in books, on museum walls and postage stamps.

"There were so many foreign journalists," recalled Ariunbold. "At least 100 journalists came up from Beijing to watch what was happening. The Ulaanbaatar Hotel ran out of rooms so they slept inside the Foreign Ministry, there was no other place for them to go in those days. I remember how they just sprawled their bags across the floor and slept like gypsies!"

"We went down to the square to interview people," he continued. "It was really the first time we spoke with people on the streets. But we didn't understand how to cover the story or what questions to ask. So we watched the foreigners and read some of their stories. It was interesting to see how they reported the situation." Then he hit on a crucial point. "Some of them came to our office and asked for help. They even paid us US dollars! There was nothing in the shops then so I went to a Russian store and bought a bottle of whiskey."

Meanwhile, Bat-Uul and another man named Boshigt started a

hunger strike in the center of the Square. A former MPRP member, Boshigt changed sides and became an advisor to the Democrats. It was March 7 and the temperature was still well below zero, so the hunger-strikers sat huddled in wool cloaks near Sükhbaatar's statue. They drank water with a salt solution but nothing else.

"They announced that if they died it was the Politburo's responsibility," Ariunbold recalled. "We had never seen anything like it. We stood around and stared at them like it was a circus act."

"Each day the crowds grew larger. It really looked like it was going to get out of hand but at the last moment, Batmönkh made a dramatic announcement. He said he was going to resign with the rest of the Politburo. He said it was time for young people. Some of the Politburo wanted to bring tanks onto the streets but Batmönkh refused. He said 'these are our sons, our people.'"

The Politburo's peaceful resignation was the beginning of the end. On March 22 a 48-year-old minister and geologist named Ochirbat replaced Batmönkh. Assemblies were held and a campaign was launched to determine the future of the country. Before all else, Article 82 of the Constitution, which had previously provided the MPRP the right to rule, was deleted.

The end of one party rule saw an outpouring of emotion. Regional representatives voiced their needs and wants; herders demanded their livestock privatized; Buddhists called for freedom of religion; writers wanted freedom of speech and businessmen declared the start of private ownership.

Chingis Khan was resurrected and Tsedenbal was stripped of all his titles. In the middle of the night the statue of Stalin was removed from his plinth in front of the library and dumped in an empty field. (Stalin has since been recovered by a budding entrepreneur and placed inside a night club where go-go girls gyrate against his groin).

"Just after the government resigned everything changed. An editor came into our office one day and said we could write whatever we wanted. The censorship just ended in one night," said Ariunbold.

"Now people say that democracy made us poor. But it's not true. Democracy gave us freedom. The communists said, 'you will live in that apartment, you will do that job.' But now we can live wherever and do whatever we want. Our stomachs were full but our heads were empty," said Ariunbold.

With the whole of Mongolia on a democratic free-for-all, voters went to the polls in July to elect a new government. The MPRP, now known as the "ex-communists" won easily, having gerrymandered the constituencies to their benefit. The MPRP took 357 out of 430 seats in the Great Hural and 31 of 50 seats in the Small Hural. But given the wider implications of the election, the democrats still found personal victory.

In September, Ochirbat was sworn in as Mongolia's first elected President. Gonchigdorj, a well-groomed mathematician and the leader of the newly formed Social Democratic Party, was elected Vice President. Other democrats were given token positions of authority (only to be used as whipping boys when things started to go badly).

The new government set up a rudimentary plan for a free market economy. Advisors were brought in from all over the world to tell them how to do it. The foreign observers were delighted with the prospects and the Mongolians were left dizzy with the options set before them.

The new economy was set up from scratch, the brainchild of a 26-year-old economics whiz named Zoljargal. His voucher system entitled each Mongolian to buy stocks from a new Stock Exchange, located in a colonnaded building on Sükhbaatar Square. The savviest Mongols went around buying other people's vouchers, gathering enough to buy off whole companies. But not all went smoothly. Many were accused of corruption, including Zoljargal's older brother, who went to jail for allegedly losing Mongolia's gold reserves (US$150 million) while gambling in foreign stock markets. Many of these cases, of course, saw the wrong people going to jail.

In the case of Zoljargal's brother, it's believed that the government of the day sold the gold on the London Exchange, with help from the Russian KGB, and kept the earnings for themselves.

Corruption was one of many problems. Chronic alcoholism, domestic violence, homeless children and closed schools were also heavy burdens to bear. Ration tickets were issued to deal with food shortages. Lines snaked around buildings and it sometimes took three or four hours to pick up the government-issued bread loaves.

Meanwhile, anyone with money stashed away left the country as soon as possible. Eddie was one of the new rich—he scrambled to win a grant from the United Nations and was sent to Germany to train as an engineer. When he came back from Europe it occurred to him that what Mongolia needed more than another engineer was a good pizza parlor. So he launched a chain of successful restaurants called Pizza de la Casa and amassed a small fortune.

Another friend named Enki escaped Mongolia to work at a radio station in Hong Kong. He came back, opened a cultural exchange society and was last seen giving tours to the likes of Hollywood stars Stephen Segal and Julia Roberts.

And then there was Batsukh, a modest 41-year-old fellow with half-moon eye-glasses and a penchant for fast cars and young women. One day he invited me out for a night at his countryside *ger* camp, where he would celebrate his birthday with friends and his new 19-year-old bride. We drove out over the empty grasslands in his Jaguar, which made as much sense as driving a tank through Times Square, and he told me the story of how he made his fortune. He said in the late 1980s he had been able to get out of Mongolia because his brother worked for the Gobi Cashmere company in Berlin. Through this window to Germany, he was able to buy stolen BMWs and Mercedes-Benz cars, drive them back to the Mongolia and sell them for a profit.

"I had saved up about $20,000 by 1995 and took it with me to Istanbul," Batsukh explained. "I wanted to go into the leather business there. In Istanbul you could buy leather cheap and sell it for 10 times the price in Russia."

I asked him where he kept his money as credit cards were unheard of in those days.

"I just kept it my handbag," he said. "But it was pretty risky. One night I got in a bar brawl and nearly lost it. Then I was arrested, but fortunately the police didn't take it."

"So what happened to the leather business?"

"It never happened," he lamented. "A couple of weeks later I entered my first casino and got bit by the gambling bug. I lost everything."

Similar boom and bust stories were common in Mongolia in the early 1990s and instability was the norm. Yet overall the country was improving. Food shortages ended and the government developed trade relations across Asia.

Yet Mongolia didn't completely shut off its past. It was still one of North Korea's closest allies, emphasized in 1996 when high level North Koreans came to Ulaanbaatar, though one could not say the visit was entirely diplomatic. The Koreans spent thousands of dollars on imported whisky and caviar, paying for it all with counterfeit US dollars.

Despite the shortcomings of the new system, Mongolia's love for democracy, by the time of my arrival, had hardly waned. There were some who questioned it, but it seemed that for most of the population, no amount of poverty could sway their emotions away from the freedoms they had earned. The winning picture in a photo contest seemed to say it all—it showed a homeless man reading a newspaper next to the garbage bin. The photographer titled it, "knowledge overwhelms poverty."

I duly noted this enthusiasm throughout my stay, but I remember it most vividly at a reception held at the Democratic Union headquarters. Throngs of people arrived to see a photo exhibit that featured black and white images of the 1990 Revolution. As the masses pointed at Zorig's image high above the crowds, rowdy and intoxicated men-boys hugged each other. They drank for freedom. I saw Enkhee there and asked him how he thought his movement had turned out. Lamenting that progress was too slow and the country still mired in problems, he said Mongolia was not working hard enough to build real democracy. But as we spoke, the revolution song "The Sound of Bells" came piping through the PA sound system. A boisterous drunk in the back of the room crooned with delight. I noticed Enkhee's normally stiff face had softened into a smirk. Established democracy had not yet fully been realized and who knew if it ever would? Yet something special had been accomplished and he could smile for now. The real tests, however, were yet to come.

~ 4 ~

THE BOLD HUNTER

IT WAS ULAANBAATAR'S ROUGH-AND-TUMBLE SPIRIT that set it apart from the more glossy capitals of neighboring Asian countries; precisely the reason why Westerners found it so alluring. But it was also a façade, all you had to do was look around the back of the downtown buildings and you'd find what the rest of Mongolia looked like, a vast frozen steppe punctuated by rugged hills, forests and immense deserts. Signs of civilization—towns and roads—are generally absent, which makes getting lost the usual routine for any road trip. This is the sort of thing that travelers can only discover through experience and mine came soon enough.

The trip began in a casual manner. Bold, the same Bold who had picked me up from the train station on the day of my arrival, approached me in the Montsame café where I was having a mutton pancake lunch with Amarbat and Bayarmaa. Bold sat down with his own stack of fried flapjacks and announced that he was off to the countryside for a weekend wolf hunting trip. Amarbat noisily slurped tea while Bayarmaa helped translate Bold's halting English.

"I try to go a couple times a month in winter," he said. "My cousins have a *ger* in the woods."

"That must be amazing!" I said, thinking dreamily of the country-side.

"Why don't you come along?"

"Now? But it's 30 below outside. Shouldn't we wait until spring?"

"*Muur,*" ("Tracks,") Amarbat said in a rare moment of outspokenness.

I looked at Bayarmaa and raised an eyebrow. By now she could recognize this as a request for elaboration.

"He means it's easier to hunt wolves in winter because you can follow the *tracks.*"

"But winter is also the best time because the wolf's pelt is thick and warm," she continued. "If you shoot one I'll make you fur hat!"

She laughed and I smiled back.

"All right, that's it then. I bring a wolf to the office and you sew me a hat," I said, shaking her hand to seal the deal, "unless I don't come back!"

I would have asked Ariunbold for the weekend off, but he hadn't been seen for days. No one was particularly concerned, at least not enough to call his home. In any case, I had come to realize that Ariunbold's control of the paper was nominal at best. De facto leadership was in the hands of Indra and Undrakh, the two elder female staff members. Indra, a journalist in her late 40s, was a jolly extrovert with an irrepressible laugh and a mind to make her name known in the halls of Parliament. She attended every government press conference possible, hobnobbed at every banquet and had a Rolodex filled with the names and numbers of every prominent politician, entertainer and businessman in town. She was largely in charge of day to day administration—contacting advertisers, managing records, accounting. She was made for this kind of work.

Because age plays a major role in determining who wields power, Undrakh, in her 60s and with the paper since its inception, was a sort of backroom boss. She was a kindly woman, grandmotherly in her mannerisms, but tough when it came down to business. No major decision could really go ahead without her consultation. Of course, when problems arose, everyone would pass the buck. Eventually, blame would fall on Ariunbold. In his absence we all just shrugged our shoulders and went back to work.

When all was said and done, organizing a couple days off for the wolf hunt proved to be no problem at all. Indra excitedly provided me with story ideas while Undrakh quietly agreed with a nod of her head.

A couple of mornings later I found myself in a different world. I was no longer squashing cockroaches in my kitchen or blowing up electronic devices in the wall sockets of my apartment. I was no longer dodging out-of-control buses, wheezing on coal-choked air or grappling with last-minute layout decisions. I was no longer in civilization. I was under a mountain of blankets inside a nomad's *ger*, fending off temperatures that had fallen to 25°F below zero, wondering if I was dreaming.

It was the woman of the *ger* who first stirred from her winter's slumber. Swaddling herself against the cold with a sheepskin cloak, she moved toward the pot-bellied stove and built a fire from twigs and dried cow dung. Within minutes the *ger* was room temperature and the men rose, quickly shifting into hunting mode. Steaming cups of tea and mutton grease were ladled out and we sat there slurping until our bellies burned from the inside.

Next came the ritual dressing. I wore four pairs of long underwear, ski pants, several layers of fleece and my down-filled Himalayan North Face jacket. Three pair of socks and Raichle hiking boots covered my feet. A wool cap protected my head. Meanwhile, my Mongol companions donned *dels,* traditional one-piece cloaks that are cut just above the ankles, fastened at the shoulder with metal clasps, and tied at the waist with a long silk sash. The Mongol wardrobe generally consists of four *dels*—a sheep lined winter *del*, a lighter wool *del* for spring and autumn, a thin silk del for summer and a better quality silk or leather *del* (sometimes designed in a more modern fashion) for special occasions. Their foot gear came in two types: sturdy leather boots with soft felt lining and upturned toes (easy stirrup access), and humongous pressed-felt boots that looked like casts for broken legs.

Properly equipped, Bold, his friend Amar and myself, plus two cousins, Ganbaatar and Bayar, fell out of the tiny *ger* door and into the biting chill. A blue light fell over the frozen landscape around us as we moved quickly to pack up Bold's Ford Explorer. With each passenger holding tight to his rifle, Bold fired the ignition and we were off across the snowy trackless slopes, stopping every half mile to unload a passenger. At last it was just Bold and me, rumbling toward a ridge that overlooked a giant, pancake-flat plain of snow and ice. Bold eased the car to a halt and motioned for me to keep quiet. Stealthily we got out of the car, walked toward the edge of the ridge, and found a place to sit in the snow.

As a purple and orange dawn broke over snowy plains I made a mental note of the spectacular scenery. This was what we had missed the night before when Bold was driving aimlessly in the dark searching for his cousin's *ger*. We had spent a good two hours driving in circles, completely lost in the wilderness. I was rather worried that we would have to sleep out in the cold, although Bold seemed totally unfazed by the episode and somehow we managed to find the *ger*, well after midnight.

As we sat and waited on the hill the cold began creeping in. It was a bone-numbing cold, as if clamps were bearing down on my extremities. Having spent the first 22 years of my life in California, and the past year backpacking my way across balmy Southeast Asia and Australia, I wasn't quite acclimatized for this. My fidgeting so irritated Bold that he was probably regretting his decision to bring me out here at all. With every twitch of my body he narrowed his eyes, furrowed his brow and raised an index finger to his pursed lips.

We must have sat in that location for an hour, staring out into the white wastes, before Bold finally gave up and headed back to the car. My fidgeting probably scared away the wolves and I apologized to Bold. But he only laughed, his huge bright face looking unconcerned. "The wolf hunter must remain in good spirits," he said. The waiting game could be a long one.

Bold was an august figure, with enormous hands and a round, pale face underneath a fur hat. He was broad shouldered, thick skinned and looked the part of the hunter, although in real life he was a biologist, educated in Moscow back in the 1970s. Democracy and economic upheaval had forced a career change and Bold had recently started a successful tourist company. Realizing that Western clients would be most lucrative, Bold had picked up some English, certainly better than my halting Mongolian. Apparently, Bold was also weather resistant because the cold didn't seem to faze him at all. Without so much as a shiver, he slipped into the leather seat, set the car in gear and drove back toward our comrades.

Near a grove of pine trees, Bold's hunting partners waited with hand rolled cigarettes stuck between their lips. They made an imposing group—men sculpted by the wind and hardened by the sun, raised tough on meat and milk. Amar climbed in first, his smooth mahogany skin reflecting the daylight.

"Chon baikhgui," he said with a little laugh . . . No wolves.

Ganbaatar and Bayar piled in and the car soon swelled with excited chatter, each hunter calling out suggestions for where to find wolves. With Bold wrestling the steering wheel, we gained a ridge and stopped just short of the peak. The others got out for a look and I stayed in the car, pulling off my socks to massage some feeling back into my lifeless feet.

"You need Mongolian boots," Bold informed me while searching his glove compartment for bullets. "Those American boots are not warm enough."

Bold was right. I needed to get my hands on some local winter gear. Wearing hiking boots in these temperatures was asking for trouble. Thankfully, Bold's cousins managed to rustle up a spare pair of sheepskin boots when we returned to the *ger* for lunch.

Gers are small, one-room domiciles (about 18 feet around) with a lattice wood frame and 108 poles that support the roof. They are illuminated by sunlight which comes through a smoke hole in the center of the roof. The walls are insulated with large pieces of pressed felt while the outside is covered with a canvas sheet. Surprisingly plush inside, the furnishings include three beds, two dressers for clothing, plus a cabinet for kitchen utensils. For embellishment, most families line the interior walls with colorful carpets, often depicting idyllic countryside scenes or Buddhist themes.

As we sat down for lunch, Bold explained how life inside the *ger* follows an unwritten slate of rules. The male side, as you enter on the left, is the designated place for hunting gear, saddles and horse tack. The female side, to the right, is for pots, pans, dishes and other cooking utensils. The most honored portion is far end of the *ger* (opposite the door), where the oldest members of the family sit. The doorway is the domain of children. In the center is the all important hearth (nowadays a cast iron stove with a metal pipe sticking through the roof), and everything revolves around it.

I found *ger* decorum to be very relaxed, as it should be when a family or five or six is trying to co-habitat in a single room tent. *Ger* etiquette, however, dictated certain obligations. It is considered rude, Bold noted, to point your feet at the sacred hearth or the altar. Leaning against the support column is a definite no-no, as is stepping on the threshold. Touching or moving somebody's hat is a borderline criminal offense.

Bunched up like this, living without privacy, secrets, inhibitions, or even personal possessions, it was clear that it was the *ger* which truly shaped the Mongol character. It pacified them and made them tolerant of others. They were not individuals but a cohesive family unit, sharing everything. I was envious in some ways. Not that I could ever have lived this way myself, but it made me wonder about my own upbringing. Growing up in my own room with my own belongings in a large suburban house, I had more private space than any Mongolian could fathom. And yet when I compared our lives, I saw my own faults. I was materialistic and impatient. I came from a world ruled by money and self-ambition. It was refreshing to enter a society where money was an abstract concept and it was family bonds were so inherently important. I had come to improve a newspaper, but I wondered if it was me that would change even more.

Upon the stove, Ganbaatar's wife brewed up a heady cocktail of ingredients called *suutei tsai* (goat's milk, salt and tea stems). As she ladled out the drink, Ganbaatar described the recent move they had made from their autumn pastures, about five miles up a nearby valley. Contrary to popular belief, Mongolia's nomads do not roam aimlessly across mountain ranges. Most have particular pastures that they move to each season according to the climate and grass quality. Rarely do they move more than 15 miles from their wintering grounds.

Ganbaatar said his family would move the *ger* again in April. Their belongings would be moved by camels and setting up the new site would take about two hours. This move will mark the most difficult time of the year for Ganbaatar and his family as spring is notoriously dangerous in Mongolia. There will be little rain, poor grass, strong winds, flooding and the odd snowstorm.

By June, the worst of the weather will be behind them. This is the time to comb the goats for cashmere and sell it for a nice profit. June is also a good time to make dairy products like cheese, butter, cream and *airag* (fermented mares' milk).

July, Ganbaatar revealed, is holiday time. The entire country will take a mid-summer break to visit relatives and celebrate Naadam, the famed summer sports festival featuring horse racing, wrestling and archery. August will be marked by torrential rainstorms and green grass, allowing animals to fatten themselves for the coming winter. In September and October, Ganbaatar and his family will make their winter preparations—collecting dung for fuel and stocking up on foodstuffs like flour and potatoes. At last, winter returns, and the family will hibernate during the coldest, darkest months of the year.

Ganbaatar explained that the times had been different for his father, who grew up on Soviet built collective farm. The new generation was making a break from communism by reverting to traditional nomadic customs. My fingers now thawed, I started scribbling in my notebook as Ganbaatar's words inspired story ideas. Indra had advised that in the countryside nomads like to reminisce about the days of communism and I wanted to hear how they felt eight years after its demise.

"Communism was all about working together," said Ganbaatar, slurping his tea noisily. "In those days the government wanted to build some kind of collective paradise. But the Russians never understood Mongolians. They thought they could build camaraderie, but the nomads just wanted to go their own way."

This was the problem with collectivizing a people whose entire history had been one of movement. As soon as democracy allowed it, they gravitated back to the steppes. Ganbaatar said he had spent most of his childhood in the nearby (Soviet-built) village, but over the past eight years his generation had rediscovered their roots in the wide hills and valleys of central Mongolia. They had moved back to the land of their ancestors and they were free. I asked if there was any reason to go back to communism.

"My parents would like to go back, but not our generation. Those days are history, it's time to move on and take care of ourselves."

A few minutes later a steaming bowl of boiled sheep flesh and various other animal parts was laid in front of us. A few potatoes and wild onions were tossed in for variety, but there was nothing in the way of spices. Spices do not grow on the cold hard steppelands and Mongols never developed a taste for them. It was the fat that my comrades found most appetizing. Mutton, I found, was an uncomplicated dish with the purpose of providing sustenance rather than satisfaction. It was survival food.

We sat around a small orange table, decorated with blue curving lines that looked like the horns of an Argali (wild) sheep. Resting on footstools, we plunged our hands into the communal pot while Bold scooped up the bones with his fist. Taking his buck knife, he shaved slices of meat and fat back into the pot. While the grease dribbled down my fingers and the chunks of meat lodged themselves between the spaces of my teeth, I felt the shoulders of the men to my left and right close in. We huddled barbarian-like over the tub of meat until only bone and grease remained.

I had with me a copy of Marco Polo's book, *The Travels*, borrowed from the modest selection of books in *The Mongol Messenger* library. Polo never made it this far north, but he did go hunting with his Mongol hosts in China. The Venetian had traveled with men who hunted almost exclusively with raptors trained to capture prey.

"Those that are trained to take wolves are of immense size and power, for there is never a wolf so big that he escapes capture by one of these eagles," Polo wrote.

And while my hunting party consisted of just five men, Marco Polo witnessed up to 10,000 hunters setting off from the Khubilai Khan's Xanadu, the retinue including servants, bird keepers and concubines. The Khan observed all from a bamboo pavilion strapped between four elephants. For me, the view from the passenger seat of Bold's Ford Explorer was as good as it would get.

* * *

After the meal, the hunters leaned back and rubbed their bellies. I took the opportunity to snoop around my host's home, inspecting the photos and medals clipped to the dresser. Amid the jumble of ancient looking family photos there was a bronze medal emblazoned with a rifle.

"What is this one for?"

Bold translated to his hosts and there began some wild-eyed story telling on the part of Ganbaatar.

"He said he won the medal from a local hunting group after killing many wolves. You see, the nomads hate wolves because they kill their livestock. They kill wolves any chance they get."

"What do they do with the wolf?"

"They keep the pelt and hang it on their wall for decoration or use it to make a hat. Then they sell the organs for medicine."

"Medicine?"

"Sure," Bold said, counting off the medical advances that wolf parts provided. "The intestines aid digestion or, if you have gland problems, you can just hang a wolf tongue around your neck."

"I've heard that works."

"There is nothing that wolf organs cannot cure," Bold continued, "Even hemorrhoids; all you need is some powdered wolf rectum. But the blood is most important. To drink the blood of a freshly killed wolf is to take its spirit, to use its energy."

Later on in my stint in Mongolia, when I caught a bad cold that kept me home, Bold's wife gave me a plastic bag filled with wolf lungs and meat. She said that if the contents were cooked at a low temperature and eaten *without* onions I'd be back on my feet in no time. (Indeed, it seemed to have worked).

"But isn't the wolf also respected?" I asked.

"The wolf is the king of the forest," Bold said. "But to kill a wolf, a man proves himself a man. It is a sign of strength and leadership."

I asked about snow leopards. Weren't they a symbol of power, too? To this Bold agreed but lamented the difficulty in finding one.

"You have to trek many miles into the mountains to see a snow leopard. On the other hand, wolves are more common. They are all over the forests and steppes. Many drivers just go off road and try to run one down."

I had assumed that harassing wolves with motor vehicles was a sporting technique introduced by the Russians until I read an account of hunting written by Roy Chapman Andrews. He spent a good deal of his time in Mongolia chasing down wolves in his Dodge sedan (one of whom ran ahead of his car for 12 miles). But Andrews was less fond of wolves than his Mongol counterparts; after chasing one down in his car he wrote: "Had it been any animal except a wolf I should have felt a twinge of pity, but I had no sympathy for the skulking brute. There will be more antelope next year because of its death."

Although loathed, the wolf had at least managed to earn its rivals' respect. Images of wolves could be seen in the modern artwork displayed in Ulaanbaatar gift shops. A popular rock band was called Wolf, as well as a beer bar around the corner from my apartment. Later I would run into people who kept a wolf anklebone on their key chain for good luck.

The connection between the Mongols and the wolf is also interwoven with religion and folklore. In the Shamanic culture, the wolf is connected with mountain spirits. Children's fairy tales are often filled with references to the clever and mysterious wolf. With all these connections, I assumed it would make sense if Mongols had a bit of wolf blood in them. And perhaps they do. A legend is told about a blue wolf that mated with a red deer. It was their offspring that spawned the tribe of Chingis Khan. Since Chingis is considered the father of the nation, it's no wonder why the wolf is held in such awe.

I sleep poorly in the cold. I had been on many camping trips before, but nothing had prepared me for the winter freeze that my hosts endured so calmly night after night. An hour after we had all gone to bed on the orange floorboards of Ganbaatar's *ger*, the fire went out and the temperature inside the *ger* began to drop.

I slept fitfully, emerging from dreams as if coming to the surface of the ocean in desperate need of oxygen. Forced awake on several occasions, my body needed to relieve itself of the cups of tea I had drunk. Flipping on my Princeton Tec headlamp, I slunk into my hiking boots, stepped cautiously over the others who also slept on the floor, and ducked out the door. "Bathrooms" in rural Mongolia are pretty much any spot 50 feet or more from the *ger*. I crunched my way 20 paces into the blackness, and whizzed into the snow, staring up at the mind-boggling array of stars glinting against the jet black sky.

The break of dawn was followed again by hot cups of tea poured by Ganbaatar's wife. Warmed and with our muskets loaded, we trod outside for a second day of hunting. Our luck, however, had not changed, and the words *"Chon baikhgui,"* seemed to be the motto for our trip.

Furthermore, I came to the conclusion that rural news reporting had its limitations. I had become reliant on Mother Nature and there would be no story for *The Mongol Messenger* without her cooperation. Although the elusive wolf was failing to provide me with any semblance of drama, Bold and his friends remained undeterred. In Mongolia, where life is already hard enough, frustration over petty issues is an unnecessary hardship that they had learned to avoid. One thing we had on our side was time. In Mongolia there is time enough for everything.

It was around midday when Bold drove to the edge of a forest and let Ganbaatar and Bayar out. Their job, I now realized, was to walk though the woods and scare up game while the older hunters waited on the other side of the glen with their guns at the ready.

"Chon bain aa!" They promised. There will be wolves!

I joined them, hoping for a new angle to my story, and we quickly disappeared into the woods. Enveloped by the stand of pine, larch and fir trees, I suddenly felt small and disorientated. Out on the vast, open steppes, a man knows his place in nature. In here, I was momentarily lost, shuffling through the dry snow unsure of what lay ahead. I pulled my down jacket tightly around my body and quickened my pace to keep up with my companions.

The forest was silent and as we walked became less threatening. A cloud moved away from the sun and golden light came streaming through the eaves, igniting the green pine needles and the blue sky that hovered over the forest canopy.

My mind to wander absently but was suddenly shaken when Bayar let out a shrieking "KAAAAA!" like the sound of a cartoon pterodactyl. Ganbaatar joined in with his own ear-shattering calls, and the forest erupted into a chaotic den of zoological mimicry. The look on my face must have been one of disbelief because Bayar then tried explaining what they were up to.

"*Chon, chon,*" he said, waving his arm ahead of us and pretending to shoot his gun. The idea, it appeared, was that any wolves would bolt ahead of us, right into the path of Bold on the other end of the forest.

At some point Ganbaatar and Bayar set off in different directions and I followed Bayar up a densely forested hillside. We moved through the trees quietly now, the silence again overwhelming us. Ahead of us, the forest gave way to sunlight and a clearing. Bayar picked up a rock and tossed it onto the small *ovoo* (sacred rock cairn) in front of him, a token to the forest spirit. I was about to do the same when Bayar suddenly ducked down and motioned for me to join him. A shot of adrenaline ran through me as I crept low to his side. Did he see a wolf? Bayar pointed down the hillside. No, there was no wolf, but between the trees, about 100 yards away, I saw five brown deer quietly picking at the exposed grass. Bayar immediately lifted his old Russian .22 caliber rifle to his shoulder and released the safety. He squeezed one eye shut, took aim and pulled the trigger.

We watched as the deer leapt in all directions. They scattered, except for one deer that bucked into a dramatic back flip. Bayar and I were off, racing down the snowy ravine in our slick-bottomed sheepskin boots. Shouting wildly, we leapt over rocks and logs until we reached the fallen deer. Adrenaline coursing through our veins, we found the deer at the bottom of the slope barely alive. The shot had been perfect—right into the side of its head. It was amazing aim, considering the quality of the antique rifle and the distance the bullet had covered. I guessed that any shot to the body of this huge beast might only have wounded it and we probably would have lost our meal. I passed Bayar my knife and he plunged the blade deep into the deer's head, killing it instantly.

Soon we joined the others and set to work on skinning the deer. Incisions were made in strategic locations at the ankles and belly. Then the whole hide was peeled from the body like the rind of an orange. The deer, now a purple, sinewy hunk of meat, was hung upon a tree and gutted. Bayar then reached into the pan and pulled out the heart. A chill settled over us as he held the hot slimy organ in the palm of his hands. Borrowing my knife again, he pierced a hole in the side of the heart and spilled its blood into a ceramic cup.

Now came the *coup de grace*. As a finishing touch we drank the blood of the deer, taking in its spiritual power. A wolf would have been the ultimate prize, Bold said, but the blood of a deer would do.

One by one the cup went around until it was my turn. I accepted the cup of warm, salty blood, raised it to the others, and gulped it down in one go. I opened my eyes and looked around at my companions. In the cold crisp air, with signs of winter all around and blood on my lips, I knew I had found a new home.

~ 5 ~

CRIME AND PUNISHMENT

WHEN I ARRIVED IN MONGOLIA there were two major stories brewing in the news. The first involved George Risley, the American business man who had shot his employee and was being tried for murder. The incident had sparked anti-American demonstrations in the capital; all led by a firebrand politician O. Dashbalbar. The second story was another criminal case involving two con-men from Cameroon who had ripped off $30,000 from local money changers. Both were a mainstay in the *The Messenger* during my first season in Mongolia.

The case of the Cameroonian swindlers took the early lead, largely because it evolved into a story that had greater ramifications for our readers. It started out simply enough; the Cameroonians had tried conning local money changers out of their greenbacks, promising to triple their money with a "magic chemical" they themselves had developed. The Mongolians fell for it and naïvely handed over huge wads of cash. It seemed like easy money and the Cameroonians probably would have gotten away with it had they escaped sooner. But police soon caught up with them at their hotel and had them arrested. They were convicted of fraud and sentenced to five years in prison.

The story appeared to end here. But then it was announced that the Africans had been given a medical exam and tested positive for a rash of sexually transmitted diseases, including gonorrhea and syphilis. One tested HIV positive. This in itself was not particularly newsworthy, but when the Africans admitted to having unprotected sex with a bevy of Ulaanbaatar prostitutes, the importance of the story grew ten-fold.

We had to make some last minute layout changes when we heard the news. George Risley, who was being held in jail during his investigation, was moved further down page one to make room for expanded coverage of the Cameroonians. Until now, HIV/AIDS was really a non-issue in Mongolia (there was only one confirmed case in the entire country). But when the news story broke it became a landmark event in Mongolia, and was covered relentlessly by a news-starved media.

The city was gripped by an AIDS scare. Newspapers were filled with myths about the virus, how it was spread and where it came from; black expatriates suffered racial profiling; and police rounded up local sex workers and their clients for testing. When the dust started to settle a few days later, we learned that one of the prostitutes that had slept with the Africans had tested HIV positive. The number of known HIV cases instantly doubled from one to two.

Several pressure-filled days passed by before Montsame received a new update on the story. The police, it seemed, thought the best way to deal with this matter would be to deport the Cameroonians immediately, which is precisely what happened. According to the official response, police were not confident that the Africans would survive the winter in their jail. They added that releasing the men would save them money, not to mention protecting Mongolia from the further spread of disease. Just as the Cameroonians could not survive in a Mongolian jail, we knew that the government could not handle the psychological and physical challenges of this ground-breaking incident. Washing their hands of the entire affair was the only option. It seemed a strange sort of justice, letting these con men go free because they lacked the resources to properly punish them. But as we would soon see, lightning would strike twice. George Risley was right on their heels.

A middle-aged lumberjack from Woodland, Washington, Risley managed a Mongolian jail better than the Cameroonians, and was not sent home on account of illness. He would remain a fixture in the news well into spring.

Risley's story had its roots in 1997 when his employer, Pacific American Commercial (PACO) sent him to Mongolia to set up a new logging operation. He was posted to Khövsgöl Aimag, Mongolia's northernmost province, where PACO hoped the abundant pine forests would yield quick profits.

Khövsgöl is dominated by peaks that reach to 11,800 feet, not to mention the giant Khövsgöl Nuur, a lake that contains 2 percent of the world's fresh water. Bears roam the taiga, wild sheep scamper up the cliffs and among the population live a tribe of reindeer herders, hardened folk who dwell in teepees far away from any town or city.

Living off the land in remote areas was nothing new to Risley; PACO had dispatched him to set up logging mills in other parts of the world. He was a barrel-chested man of the woods, a hardened pioneer whose entire career had been spent sawing logs. George Risley and Khövsgöl seemed like a good match.

Risley had spent most of 1997 working hard to get the timber mill up and running. He had hired several men to work the mill, and a translator to help with logistics. There was a PACO office in Ulaanbaatar, but Risley preferred to stay in Mörön (which means river) where he could keep a tight reign on quality control. Aside from a few glitches and cultural differences, Risley had gotten along well, until one bitterly cold night in December.

It was December 9, 1997 and Risley was trying to keep warm by the fire. Suddenly, he heard strange noises coming from his sawmill. He stood up and opened the door, feeling the chill of the night immediately against his face. The sound was stronger now, a screeching, irritating sound, like someone clawing their fingernails against a chalkboard. He knew immediately something was wrong.

Climbing into his snow boots and hauling a big down jacket over his shoulders, Risley clomped out into the snow and headed for the timber mill. It was freezing outside, one of the coldest nights he had ever felt, but there was no time to worry about the weather. He jogged to the door of the mill and flung it open, lights from above swayed in the gloom. The sound of the machinery shrieked ominously in Risley's ears as he quickly located the problem. The saw blade in the major log-cutting apparatus was caught in the wood and straining mightily. Rivets holding the blade together were bending awkwardly and nearly at the point of breakage. If the machinery was not shut down immediately, Risley knew the blade could fly off its hinges, causing serious damage or injury.

Risley acted quickly and flipped the switch that powered the blade. Within seconds the horrible sounds dissipated as the machinery slowly came to a grinding halt. Relieved, Risley turned to see Bayarsaikhan coming in from the cold. Where had he been? Why had he not been watching over his post?

As Bayarsaikhan staggered forward Risley knew he had been drinking again. He had warned him before but this time Risley was furious. He scolded his worker in English but soon realized Bayarsaikhan was too drunk to care. Bayarsaikhan lashed back, lurching angrily toward his boss, kicking him in the leg and then hitting him with a stick. Bayarsaikhan appeared out of control and Risley wisely backed off and retreated to his log cabin. But Bayarsaikhan was not finished; he followed Risley into the snow and pounded his fists against the frozen door of the cabin. Terrified, Risley barricaded himself inside, praying that his worker would not break a window or set the cabin on fire.

Bayarsaikhan eventually grew weary and gave up. Risley's heart was pounding in his chest as he peered out the window, seeing Bayarsaikhan in the moonlight heading for a *ger* that doubled as a guard house.

Taking a deep breath, Risley decided he had to go back to the mill and lock it down before any more accidents or damage occurred. He was a dedicated worker and knew it was his responsibility if any of PACO's assets were lost. This time, Risley went outside carrying a flashlight and a loaded Marlin .22 caliber hunting rifle.

After locking down the mill, Risley went to the guard *ger* to tell Bayarsaikhan and the others to go home. He hoped his Mongolian employee had calmed down enough to make peace. But to Bayarsaikhan, the gun did not look like a peace offering. In his drunken eyes it must have looked like Risley had come for some pay back.

Bayarsaikhan responded to Risley by picking up a carving knife left on a table in the *ger*. The alcohol egging him on, Bayarsaikhan staggered outside after Risley. Risley held his ground, showing Bayarsaikhan that the gun was loaded. But Bayarsaikhan continued to stagger toward Risley, holding the knife aloft, swearing in Mongolian.

Risley yelled back in English, telling him to back down. He let off a warning shot, the blast from his gun piercing through the ink black sky. Bayarsaikhan responded by brandishing the knife above his head. He continued to cut the air with his knife, even after Risley let off a second warning shot.

Risley knew he was in trouble. The last thing he wanted to do was shoot his employee, but he found himself backed into a corner. He considered running, but his leg still ached from the kick he had received in the mill. Trying to escape might lead to a knife in his back. So he stood firm, aiming the gun squarely at the man before him.

At last Bayarsaikhan decided his own fate, charging toward Risley. Instinct for self-preservation took over and Risley squeezed the trigger, landing a bullet in Bayarsaikhan's shoulder. Amazingly, the shot seemed not to affect Bayarsaikhan at all. He charged a second time. Now there was no time to think. Risley shot again, firing off four more shots until the magazine was empty.

Bayarsaikhan staggered forward, his arms flailing, and collapsed face first in the snow.

The shooting death of J. Bayarsaikhan occurred at approximately 9:45 p.m. The location was five miles outside of Mörön, the capital of Khövsgöl Aimag and around 400 miles northwest of Ulaanbaatar. Within an hour, Risley was booked on a charge of murder.

News of the incident shook Mongolia to its core. First of all, Risley had come from the United States, the country that Mongolia lovingly referred to as its "third neighbor," and the country that had encouraged Mongolia to open up to trade and foreign investment. Now one of these "investors" had shot dead one of their own. Secondly, it was inconceivable that someone could be shot over an alcohol-fuelled dust up. Drinking and fighting was something of a national pastime, but it rarely led to such extreme violence. Risley had confirmed the belief (already promoted by Hollywood) that Americans are a violent people.

Following the incident, anti-American protests in Ulaanbaatar saw hundreds of people and politicians rallying to throw these unruly Americans out of the country. Dashbalbar, the MP leading the protests, warned foreigners that Bayarsaikhan's death would not pass without retribution. The US embassy posted standard warnings to Americans to avoid crowds, demonstrations and public transportation.

In response, Woodland, Washington rallied behind Risley. A local hangout called Jack's Diner served as an impromptu "Free George Risley HQ," with newspaper clippings and a map of Mongolia tacked up on its walls. A Washington state senator had gone through diplomatic channels to request that Mongolia release the prisoner. Newspaper offices in Seattle were calling me at the office every week or so, hoping for an update; rumors were rife that Risley would get the death penalty. I assured them this was not possible. The prosecutor for the case was seeking a charge of murder, which carried a 25- year term in prison, though for all intents and purposes, sending a 56-year-old man to a Mongolian jail for 25 years was a death sentence.

Immediately following the incident, Risley summoned his translator, drove into Mörön and gave himself up to the police. Following a night in the Mörön jail (which he later likened to a medieval dungeon) Risley was met by a United Nations volunteer living in town. Risley gave the volunteer the keys to his truck and told him to go to the market to buy food and clothing for Bayarsaikhan's family. Angry locals pelted the car with stones as the volunteer made his way through the snowy streets of Mörön.

After a week of questioning, Risley was brought to Ulaanbaatar in chains and thrown in Gants Hutag prison. I had already seen the inside of local schools and hospitals and did not want to contemplate about the conditions of a Mongolian jail in January.

In a letter sent to his family, Risley described being fed horsemeat and potatoes, served in a mop bucket. Prison guards had forced him to squat naked in a corner for hours at a time. "They did that to work on your mind," he said. Indeed, he was in no enviable spot; over 900 prisoners had died of starvation and tuberculosis in Mongolian prisons over the previous eight years.

The awful conditions in the jail had a bad impact on Risley's health. He was taken to the prison hospital and monitored for a case of bronchitis. Hospital staff fed him a steady diet of salty milk tea and mutton until PACO was allowed to bring him Western food.

George Risley's adventure in Mongolia had been reduced to a living hell, but the misery of a disease-ridden jail was nothing compared to the news he learned from home. Risley's son Bob had died in a car accident on a rural road in Washington state. Mongolians, strong believers in karmic principles, read deeply into this news. I dismissed the correlation between the deaths of Bayarsaikhan and Risley's son as an unfortunate coincidence, but my colleagues were convinced that higher powers had played a roll.

With the AIDS scare becoming yesterday's news, our attention was now firmly focused on George Risley. Sometime around February, the prosecutor summed up his side of the story with a version quite different from the one Risley told.

"Risley hit Bayarsaikhan over the head with a metal pipe and went after him with his gun, so Bayarsaikhan used a knife for self-defense purposes. There are other questions that were not answered—such as why five bullets were found in Bayarsaikhan's back," said the prosecutor in a statement to the press.

The trial was finally held in March. The prosecutor made sure it was held in the hostile environs of Mörön, which had never been known as a foreigner friendly place. The Mongol judicial system is based on the Russian model, so rather than a jury deciding Risley's fate, it would be three judges that would listen to the case and make a joint decision.

On the day of the trial, an official at the US embassy reported seeing an "angry mob" lingering outside the courthouse. Inside, the official added, the Mongolians in attendance groaned in protest when the verdict was read. The judges found Risley guilty of manslaughter. Risley was acquitted on a charge of intentional murder, which carried a penalty of 25 years in prison.

But Risley would not be going back to jail. He would have to serve an 18-month "corrective labor" sentence, which could mercifully be done from behind a desk at his office in Ulaanbaatar. PACO was required to compensate the family, but this amounted to little more than pennies—each of Bayarsaikhan's two sons was entitled to $60 per year until they reached the age of 18. This was far less than the $24,500 in compensation that Bayarsaikhan's wife was seeking.

The penalty also stated that Risley would also pay 25 percent of his salary to the Mongolian government for the next 18 months.

A *Mongol Messenger* straw poll revealed public dismay with the sentencing. Undrakh, our senior translator, was livid, telling me one morning that he ought to be locked up forever. I played the devil's advocate, saying the killing was, as the court ruled, an act of manslaughter. It was poor judgment to confront Bayarsaikhan while holding a gun; this had escalated the incident to the point where Bayarsaikhan had to respond with the knife. So in the end, I felt, Risley had to bear some responsibility for pushing the incident to the point of violence.

But for Undrakh the incident was more black and white. She didn't care about the events leading up to the shooting. For her, Bayarsaikhan was dead so Risley should endure the full penalty of the law. The real reason why Risley had gotten off easy, she said, was because the court had been bribed.

Our street interviews revealed similar disapproval for the ruling. Risley had gotten off too easily because of his nationality, people said. From their point of view, Mongolia had been pressured by the United States to issue a lenient sentence. The judges must have been bribed to order such a paltry fine.

Though quite different stories, both Risley and the Cameroonians had initiated a sense of xenophobia in Ulaanbaatar. Until now, many foreigners had come to Mongolia with good intentions, to set up aid agencies or businesses, but local faith in foreigners had been shaken.

The bottom line was that Mongolia needed allies—living between two countries not known for their philanthropic policy makes you want to go out into the world and win some friends. Trying not to ruffle any feathers had softened their approach to law and order, and frontier-style justice (which once meant rolling up a lawbreaker in a carpet and trampling him with horses) was no longer *en vogue*.

A week after the trial Bayarmaa and I flagged down an old Lada and gave the driver directions to the PACO head office. This is one of the joys of Ulaanbaatar—every car is a potential taxi for 25 cents a mile. The only problem is that Mongolians do not drive. They swerve. They dodge. They careen. When a pedestrian crosses the street they *speed up*. Driving had evolved from a means of transportation to a legitimate freestyle sport.

The car lurched across the icy streets and up a pot-holed road to the White House Hotel, which housed PACO's Western-style office. We were met in the lobby by Jim Ray, a PACO representative who had come to Mongolia to help Risley with the trial. Jim Ray was a mountain of a man with a checkered shirt and voice so deep it shook the walls. He had agreed to let me interview Risley. Bayarmaa came along because she wanted to meet Risley face to face, so I passed her off as my photographer.

Much to Bayarmaa's surprise, Risley was not the monster portrayed by the Mongolian media. He was soft-spoken and ordinary, a country boy with a ruddy pockmarked face and a gray crew cut. Red suspenders labeled Woodland Supply held up his blue jeans. He *looked* like a lumberjack.

Jim Ray directed us to two chairs behind a desk, opposite Risley and Risley's wife. Bayarmaa snapped a photo and set my tape recorder on the desk. Wiping a layer of sweat from his brow, Risley began to speak, first about the night of the murder and then about his experience in a Mongolian jail, and finally his reaction to the court decision. Surprisingly, he announced that he was upset with the court ruling. While the public thought he had gotten off too easy, Risley declared his innocence until the end.

"I was charged with manslaughter. If I was a Mongolian I would never have gone to jail," he told me. "They just want money and they think that since I am American I will pay them."

Risley's lack of remorse infuriated the public. Nobody believed, or wanted to believe, in his innocence and they could not understand his defense. Surprisingly Risley told me he wanted to serve his labor sentence back at the Mörön timber mill, not at the office in Ulaanbaatar.

"I wanna fix the mill and start sawing logs again, I'd like to work there until I retire." he told us. Jim Ray gave a nod of approval.

"Hasn't this whole incident changed your attitude toward working here?" I asked, amazed with his resolve to return.

"I know it won't be like before, I am still watching my backside. But I have an obligation to my workers and PACO; that's why I must return."

Risley appeared sincere and I began feeling sorry for him. He was not the brutal killer that the Mongolian press had made him out to be. He was a family man, and no longer young. His son had recently been killed in a car crash, but he had not been allowed to return for the funeral. This tragic sequence of events had clearly changed him, but he was not a broken man. Bayarmaa snapped her final photos and I turned off the recorder. We thanked Risley, wished him well, and set off back to the office.

While Risley may have wanted to return to Mörön, PACO had other plans. Jim Ray saw the danger in sending Risley back to the mill and three months later the company negotiated an early release with the court. Bayarsaikhan's wife received the full compensation owed to her children, about $1200, and Risley flew home almost unnoticed by the media. Woodland, Washington was blanketed with "Welcome Home" signs upon his return.

The story that had pre-occupied a nation soon drifted into the past tense and became just one episode in the daily soap opera of the frozen capital. George Risley had been lucky to escape this saga early on. Had the same tragedy occurred a few years earlier, or in neighboring China or Russia, he might still be in jail today.

~ 6 ~

ON TOP WITH OLD SMOKIE

IT HAD BECOME A FAMILIAR ROUTINE. In the wee hours of the night, while I sat mesmerized by my computer screen, I knew Baatarjav's approach was imminent. It was well past midnight, the rest of the agency had closed and Baatarjav, the night watchman, would be feeling lonely at his desk by the entryway downstairs. I re-focused my attention on the computer screen, transfixed by the columns of words before me. Then, in the midst of my trance, he was there— lunging forward, a giant exposed gold tooth and maniacal green eyes burning before me. He grunted something incomprehensible as I jumped out of my seat. He then leapt backwards into a song and dance routine.

"Bi sakhilikhgui jijuur bain aa!" ("I am a naughty watchman!"), he chanted, kicking up his heels and twirling his arms like a Bolshoi Ballet trouper. The only way to mollify Baatarjav's excitement was to accept his invitation for a wrestling match—my size (I had a good four inches and 20 pounds on him) and strength proving a fairly even match against his wit and experience.

On the surface, Baatarjav was the sixty-year-old door guard

at Montsame, assigned by the army to defend the national news agency. He had the physique of a tree trunk, a bulging square head and a trim crew cut. A career serviceman, he knew well how to put on a menacing look. But on the inside Baatarjav was a softie and a prankster. And he never missed an opportunity to play a joke or challenge me to a bout of wrestling.

His job was to keep order at the news agency, keep out vagrants and kick down office doors when the locks failed (a surprisingly common occurrence). One thing that Baatarjav never did was drink on the job. The same could not be said about my fellow correspondents. For the male reporters (women drank much less), a bottle of vodka was simply another tool of the trade.

"We journalists drink so we can think clearly. We need to free our minds," said Davaajav, the editor of the Foreign News Desk. In lieu of a reporter's lounge, Davaajav and his colleagues smoked cigarettes by a window at the end of the hall, near the director's office. At first I thought they were lined up for a meeting with our boss, Mr. Amarsanaa.

"What are they waiting for?" I once asked Moogie, a young translator who worked on the Foreign News Desk.

"They are just waiting until drinking time at four o'clock," Moogie explained.

"They aren't waiting for Amarsanaa?"

"No."

"But didn't the prime minister just announce that anyone caught drinking in a government office would be fired?"

"Yes, but that was *last* week. You know, laws in Mongolia are only good for three days, after that no one cares!"

Drinking was not condoned by everyone. People knew it was a bad habit but it was something that had come to be accepted as a societal norm. Ariunbold, as an example, was typical: a tipple or two in the morning and afternoon before a heavier bout of drinking in the evening.

"I think it's a tragedy that Mongolians drink so much," Ariunbold once told me. "It's a bigger tragedy than the economic collapse. My father didn't drink, old men don't drink, it's just our generation; we were influenced by the Russians. They would tell us, 'Why don't you drink? You are a man! Now get it down!' It became a habit for most of us. Many of my friends are still alcoholics."

Actually, Mongols had been hard drinkers long before the Russians arrived. Favorite drinks include a fizzy, yogurt-like brew called *airag* that is made from fermented mare's milk, and shimiin *arkhi,* an oily spirit made from distilled cow's milk. Eight hundred years earlier, Chingis Khan warned his subjects on the dangers of alcohol, but even his own son Ögödei did not heed this message. When an advisor suggested he save his health by halving the number of cups of wine he drank each day, Ögödei agreed, but then doubled the size of his cups. The Scottish missionary James Gilmour commented extensively on the Mongol love of *airag* and *arkhi* and noted how even the lamas failed to avoid it despite their vows.

Teetotalers they are not. Among many hundreds I have met (there was) only one who would not take spirits; the common run of lamas drink as much as they can get. I do not remember ever having met a layman who refused to drink; and drunkenness is common among all classes.

One afternoon I sat down with Davaajav and Moogie in their office. The other journalists joined us and a bottle of vodka suddenly appeared on a table already cluttered with newspapers and notebooks. Moogie translated bits and pieces of their conversation for me. I was still having difficulty with their devilishly hard language and tongue-twister names. Moogie tried helping, but most of the time I was lost in a veritable soup of guttural noises.

My language skills tended to improve with alcohol, so I took a swig of the Chingis Khan vodka offered to me by Davaajav. By now he was rather loose and, patting his round belly, started to reminisce about his childhood in the countryside.

"I moved to the city to become a Russian language teacher and then I started working for Montsame. But I don't consider myself a real journalist," he admitted. "I am just a common worker. Journalists must be very talented."

Despite his modesty, Davaajav had been a reporter for Montsame since 1970 and had spent many years doing radio broadcasts, as well as lectures to factory workers. "I used to tell them about life on the *outside*. I felt privileged because I was allowed to listen to the BBC and Voice of America."

Since he had been working in the field or journalism for so long, I asked him to tell me about the old days. Instead he told me a joke. "One day, Tsedenbal, Mao and Brezhnev were traveling by plane from China. But the plane started having engine problems. Mao jumped up and said that since they were flying over China, he should get one of the two parachutes on board. So Brezhnev gave him one and Mao leapt out of the plane. When they came over Mongolia, Tsedenbal became nervous and asked for the remaining parachute, since they were over his territory. Brezhnev said, 'Hey, don't worry, I just gave Mao my sack of groceries! There's still two left!'"

Davaajav's co-workers roared with laughter. "Oh, he has so many good jokes!" wailed Moogie.

"In those days we used to ridicule the system privately. Our reports supported the government but nobody believed that stuff," explained Davaajav. "Sometimes journalists were punished if they made a mistake. The party would take away their awards or salary. One had to be careful. A friend of mine who worked at *Unen* (Truth) newspaper was exiled to the Gobi because he was critical of the government."

The group continued to fraternize as a young woman reporter behind them diligently put fresh news reports up on the Montsame wire. I turned to Ariunbold and asked for his experiences during communism.

"My father was an ambassador, so we lived in Budapest when I was a teenager," he began. "Budapest was the best city in the world, all the foreigners said that. It had a great location on the Danube, with mountains and bridges nearby, a good climate and nice people. At night I went out with my friends to see soccer matches and concerts."

"Who played at the concerts?" I asked.

"Suzie Quatro and Boney M," he said.

"Everyone loved Boney M . . . Daddy. Daddy cool. Daddy, Daddy cooool . . ." he sang before erupting into laughter.

"Hungary was a communist country, but it was much more liberal than Mongolia. It felt like freedom. We went to bars and traveled in the countryside. There were no bars in Ulaanbaatar and if you wanted to travel to the countryside you needed special permits. We listened to Western music on Radio Luxembourg. There were things to buy in the shops. Some men wore their hair long. That was illegal in Mongolia. If any young person in Ulaanbaatar was found with long hair, the police would take them to a barber."

"I cried when I returned to Mongolia. Our country and people were good but we could not live normal lives. It was the Soviets who oppressed us; we were their slaves. Our leaders bowed down to them. I used to tell people this. I said Hungary was better. But the mentality was different then; people wanted to follow Russia because they gave us food, money, medicine and protection from the Chinese."

"Was there an alternative?" I wondered.

"We could have protested against the Soviets, but it wouldn't have done any good. As you know, we are just a small country in between two superpowers," Ariunbold said, underscoring one point Mongolians would never let me forget.

"Did you think that by becoming a journalist you would be able to raise awareness?"

"I never wanted to be a journalist. I wanted to be a biologist. But they assigned me to the School of Journalism. I studied in Leningrad. It was okay though not as good as Budapest, but still there were things to buy! Plus there were cinemas, theaters, museums and restaurants."

"What was it like at college?"

"I lived together with a Latvian and an Afghan named Abdul Malluk. Abdul was a big guy, very strong. We used to drink together and he cooked great food." Ariunbold stretched his hands in front of him as he described the Afghani culinary treats Abdul whipped up in their kitchen.

"That's when I started drinking. Every night we drank, every night we had women," he said chuckling. "It was fun, but I really didn't like all those communist classes—the history of the communist party and the study of Lenin's thesis." He shuddered at the thought. "They taught us about capitalism; they said it was bad. They said capitalist countries made slaves out of the poor and stole the resources of weaker nations. They said those countries have no morals and the people are sad. But secretly the students did not believe any of that."

"The "science of communism" was the worst class; I failed it twice. I was very angry and told the instructor that I believed in God. She was shocked and threatened to report me to the Mongolian Embassy."

"What did you do?" I asked, hoping his Mongol bravado would have made short shrift of the Soviet educator.

"I apologized," he said meekly. "In those days we could do nothing."

"And they sent you to Montsame as well?" I guessed.

"Yes, I started working in 1978. First I just worked for a desk that put together a bulletin of news for the embassies. It was very tedious work. We never went out to the street for reporting, we only attended official press conferences. We couldn't ask any controversial questions and if you wrote anything bad you'd get in trouble."

"What happened during *glasnost?* Did things get any better?"

"In 1986 our editors said that we could go out and organize our own interviews. That was a bit better. My first interview was with Bat-Erdene the famous wrestler. But he was just a teenager then. He was shy and didn't know what to say. He put his head down and said '*Medekh gui*' (I don't know) whenever I asked a question. Finally I said, 'Look, this is your first interview and this is my first interview. How can I write anything if you don't say anything to me?' So we helped each other out, but it wasn't a very good article."

"Really the most important thing was just getting to work on time," he continued. "If you came even one minute after nine a.m. you were in trouble; they could dock your pay. After getting to work we had to write out our schedule for the day and have it signed. They usually gave a lot of work and had strict deadlines. They would say 'Tomorrow morning, ON MY TABLE!' You could be fired for missing a deadline and then you would never get another job!"

"What about *The Messenger?* How did you get involved?"

"After the first elections in 1990 we had a change of management at Montsame. The new general director was Erdeni. He was intelligent but he had no management skills. The financial situation was a mess because one old man was stealing all the money."

"That's awful," I said. The other reporters nodded knowingly.

"But it was typical in those days. People became opportunists and took what they could. Anyway, Erdeni gave the go-ahead to start *The Mongol Messenger* and Burenbayar was the first editor. The news bulletin closed down so Undrakh and I went to work at *The Messenger.* I only worked there for a year before I left for a different job."

"Go on," I prodded.

"I needed money. My wife was in America at the time, she had a grant to study at the University of Wisconsin and I had to stay here and take care of our son. The times were bad then; the government issued ration tickets that we exchanged for sugar, flour, bread, milk and meat, but we had to wait three or four hours just to get the stuff. *That* was awful."

"So what did you do?"

"I started working for an import company that ordered beer from Singapore. I managed the orders and they paid me $100 a month. But the company eventually closed. There were no other jobs so I ran for public office."

"Really?" I had trouble imagining Ariunbold stumping for tax cuts and pension raises.

"Yeah, but I lost. It was close. After that I just came back to work at Montsame."

While the others drank in solemn appreciation, both to Ariunbold's stab at Parliament and to the agency for taking him back, a senior editor took a seat at the table.

Zorigt accepted a shot glass, flicked some of its contents into the air with his ring finger and smeared the rest onto his forehead (showing respect to the holy vodka). Old age had slowed Zorigt a little, but he was a dedicated agency worker and was the third man in charge. He had served three decades as a sports reporter and managed to cover several Olympics before becoming a Parliamentary correspondent.

"Mr. Michael, you are . . ." his voice trailed off.

"Sain bain, Noyon Zorigt." ("Very good sir"). "We have been reminiscing about the old days."

"Yesssssss," he said, as though the memories were already flooding into his mind.

"Didn't you report on the Olympics?" I asked. "What was that like?"

He said it was difficult to cover the Munich games; I thought perhaps Soviet censorship or the Palestinian terrorist attack had affected his work. But the real problem was the lack of Cyrillic typewriters. "I had to stay up all night learning how to type in Mongolian while using Latin letters. Mongolians are good at improvising though," he said.

"What else did you learn in your travels there?"

"Before I went to Munich I thought the Western athletes were the enemy, but I interviewed some of them and they were very nice. Even the wrestlers were well-mannered. They were not wild animals like I thought they would be.

"Munich was interesting because we were free to walk around and see things. The buildings were tall and the streets narrow. And the shops!" His eyes glittered. "The shops were incredible; you could buy anything! In Mongolia there was little choice. If you wanted to see a shirt at a shop you had to buy it; if the size was wrong you couldn't exchange it—everything was behind a glass counter so what you asked for you had to keep. (Things have improved since then, if only slightly).

Despite a botched plan to save the Israelis, Zorigt remained impressed with the German security. "The German police were very nice; they were orderly. Mongolian soldiers were rude, they pushed people away and ordered them around. It was not just the soldiers; during that time all Mongolians were rude to each other."

Listening to him, communist Mongolia sounded like jail—a reasonably safe place that slowly drove you insane. But some were nostalgic for the good old days.

"I think the old system was better," said Chuluun, a retired Montsame editor who had been standing silently, listening to our conversation. Chuluun was an old hand at Montsame, having worked here for over 35 years during the height of the Cold War. He had interviewed the Dalai Lama twice, and covered visits by Zhou Enlai, Brezhnev and Kim Il Sun.

"The free press is not so good because the news is always wrong."

He mused on this for a moment while a silence stung the room.

"During communism, the censor changed our stories but it was better because it set a standard!"

"Plus we used to work harder in those days," Chuluun continued, shifting his eyes back and forth at his juniors as they listened. "Journalists worked from morning to night. Now they are lazy, they don't like their jobs and they are not well-informed."

He raised a crooked finger in the air. "I used to do 15 or 20 assignments a day. Each day we had a strict plan of what to do; it was a good idea. We had no time to talk to friends on the phone or socialize; the editors would yell at us if we didn't do our work." He looked around again, "Yes, some people had their salaries cut and some were fired; some were even exiled to the Gobi. The system was very tough! But it gave us *self-respect.*"

Those last words hung in the air ominously and the disappointment in Chuluun's voice silenced all. The lack of discipline that had befallen the agency was a mere reflection of Mongolia, as its urgent need for personal freedom had led to national chaos. Mongolia had gone from the ultimate "we" society to the ultimate "me" society.

Compared to some other offices in Montsame, *The Mongol Messenger* was known for its rather subdued atmosphere. Indra was a single mom who lived a pedestrian lifestyle with her father and teenage son. Bayarmaa cut the image of a choir girl. Rather than hitting the clubs like other girls her age, she spent her time helping her parents sew together leather bags which they sold at the Central Market. Likewise, Amarbat was a model of integrity, an incredibly shy person with Buddha-like virtues.

Baatarbeel and Ariubold, on the other hand, could drink you under the table if you challenged them. But they usually drank with Davaajav and the others in the Foreign News department. This was all just as well as my liver would have dried up had I spent more time with them. *The Mongol Messenger* staff had become more like extended family. We enjoyed each other's companionship, occasionally went for dinner or a beer, but our closest friends were often disseminated amongst the other Montsame offices.

After *The Messenger* staff had gone home, and I settled in for my usual late night editing work, it was the staff at the Translation Desk down the hall that kept me company.

I knew their late night partying started when music floated through the hall, followed by woozy, red-faced translators. They would drift into my office with a glass of vodka in hand, throw an arm over my shoulders, and urge that I drink "to international friendship." (A phrase popularized by their Russian brethren)

These office parties either ended in folksong sing-a-longs or drunken brawls. I remember one night in particular when a normally passive secretary drank too much and sent a male co-worker to the hospital with a left hook to the jaw. Another night, I entered the Translation office to find a drunken reporter kicking an unconscious colleague in the gut as if he were a stubborn camel.

"What the *hell* are you doing?!" I shouted.

"He's a Russian, so I am beating him up. I will kick him out of my country." I believe the prostrate man was of Central Asian descent, perhaps a Mongolian-Kazakh, although I was never quite sure. In any case, with his occasional black eye and bruised body, he seemed to be the agency punching bag, and there was nothing anyone could do about it.

"Do you need some help?" I asked the man, who showed only the slightest bit of cognizance. He let out a groan. "He'll be okay," the reporter said, delivering another blow to the ribs. "I am done now."

The Montsame staff often celebrated in bars. They had plenty of choices; there was something like 600 bars across the city, mostly cheap drinking dens not worthy of mention. Some had dance floors and a few sported in-house go-go girls. The Five Star, one in my neighborhood, was a grungy little place that served beer in coffee pots. I went there one night with some co-workers—two translators named Batbayar and Shineh and a computer tech named Chuka.

We left our coats at the door, settled into big black seats near the dance floor, and ordered a round of drinks. The coffee pots arrived full and flat, and after a few moments the DJ ordered the patrons off the dance floor. When the next song cracked through the speakersk, a lanky woman in a furry green outfit stepped onto the dance floor. With slow, calculated dance steps she spun toward the crowd and delicately removed various articles of clothing until all that was left were a set of green lingerie and a bow tie. The bar patrons looked on with indifference. At last she took her top off, did a hurried lap dance and disappeared behind a curtain. A moment later the music resumed and the seated crowd took to the dance floor again as if nothing significant had occurred.

"We'll have another, umm, pot," I told the bartender, motioning toward the small kettles of beer he was slowly filling up on the counter. I paid him 1500 tögrög, about $1.50, and whisked the beer back to our table, where four newcomers had wedged themselves in.

"Looks like we're going to need another pot."

Chuka had apparently taken charge and invited over four plus-sized women, all school chums from the Economics University. The alcohol was taking effect and Batbayar fell over the table while trying to get acquainted. Soon all eight of us were on the dance floor, cautiously swaying to the beat of the Backstreet Boys.

There were a few other patrons, mostly college age kids, plus one bloke at the bar that everyone recognized as Mongolia's only cross dresser. He kept to himself, content to apply powder to his five o'clock shadow and touch up his lip gloss while everyone else mingled.

As the night wore on Batbayar became an increasing liability. He wobbled, spun around and then sent himself careening headlong into the bar. It seemed like an appropriate time to continue our bar-hop.

"We're out of here," whispered Shineh. We grabbed Batbayar, skirted quickly across the dance floor, past the cross-dresser, and out the door.

We had only managed about 20 paces, however, when a squadron of police, prowling the neighborhood for drunks, pounced on

Batbayar and tossed him into a wall. Eyes closed, Batbayar managed to get one of them in a chokehold while Chuka assisted with a karate chop. But our colleagues were no match for the truncheon-wielding policemen. Zorigt, the Montsame editor, saw that they were released from prison the following day.

Montsame proved to be more than a place of work for my colleagues. Perhaps because Ulaanbaatar lacked social opportunities, employees tended to view it as a second home, hanging around long after the bureau had closed; napping, knitting or enjoying a newspaper. Baatarbeel took up temporary residence at *The Mongol Messenger* when his wife ordered him out of the house; I'd find him there in the morning, asleep on a makeshift bed of back issues of our competitor the *UB Post*.

During communism, state agencies like Montsame doubled as monitoring facilities where work units were scrutinized and kept on file. Big Brother no longer existed but Montsame still viewed itself as a great provider for its employees. Social events and field trips were commonplace. Activities included volleyball Tuesdays and ping pong Thursdays. On weekend outings during winter they held soccer and sumo matches in the snow.

But the all-time favorite team sport was basketball, and there was a gym conveniently located across the street from Montsame. I joined them a few times but stopped playing because the games were simply too violent. There were no rules or strategy. The lone offensive maneuver was to charge up the court, hard and fast, swerving between defenders who thought nothing of tackling the ball carrier. It was more like rugby than basketball, which is fine if you play rugby.

Incidentally, Mongolia did have a professional basketball league. The six teams were sponsored and all played in Ulaanbaatar. One, backed by a Christian church, was called "1+11," in reference to Jesus and his disciples. "1+11" had a fair few fans among Ulaanbaatar's born again Christians, not the least of whom was my translator Bayarmaa.

My favorite team was the oddly named Business Devils. Bayarmaa and I once went to a Business Devils—1+11 game. I cheered for Satan's free-marketeers while Bayarmaa waved a pom-pom for the Christians. The quality of play was only a step above Montsame's, with the exception of one player. Sharavjampts, the seven-foot-tall star of "1+11," scored most of his team's points and blocked all the Business Devil shots. It was like watching Shaquile O'neil agains the local high school squad. (Sharavjampts' talent was eventually noticed by American scouts—he even spent a couple of years with the Harlem Globetrotters). After the game I interviewed the coach of the Business Devils for *The Messenger*. Bayarmaa translated, explaining that the coach had learned most of his plays by watching NBA games on satellite television. When the interview ended he offered me a job as his assistant coach, assuming that as an American I knew something about the sport.

I never did take the coaching job, and probably lost my one opportunity to become the Phil Jackson of the steppes, but there were other fringe benefits at *The Messenger*. As employees of the state-run English paper, we were often invited to ritzy government parties and social events where the caterers passed out bottles of vodka and served ox tongue hors d'overs. Sometimes we were sent tickets for concerts or theater events. I remember Indra rushing into the office one day to show us tickets for a rock concert.

"Look!" she yelped, "We got Chris Norman tickets!"

"Really? Let me see!" they all said, jumping out of their seats. I inspected the tickets; indeed we would all be seeing Chris Norman live and in concert.

One of the main initiations for any foreigner living in Mongolia was the barrage of music by a little-known 1970s British pop band called Smokie, whose frontman had once been Chris Norman. You would be forgiven if you haven't heard of them before. Ariunbold explained to me how Smokie had been big in Europe around the same time that Abba had peaked. They were known for their hit singles "Living Next Door to Alice" and "Stumblin' In," the latter song as a duet with Suzie Quatro.

Mongolian smugglers picked up on the sound and brought home contraband Smokie records. Yet few other albums made it through and Mongolia was stuck listening to Smokie for 20 years. Chris Norman's voice became so ingrained with youth culture that he was elevated to godlike status.

"We used to sit in the stairwells and play Smokie songs on the guitar," said Ariunbold. "We had competitions to see who could best impersonate Chris Norman."

"Well you were so young! And I was so free! . . ." sang Ariunbold, laughing at his own Chris Norman impersonation.

When communism collapsed, the Russians started asking about Chris Norman's whereabouts and he soon learned of his fame behind the Iron Curtain. Chris came out of retirement, dusted off his guitar, and rocked his way across Russia.

The concert had been announced two weeks earlier and the city was subjected to Smokie marathons on every local radio station. Tickets sold in the thousands and the mayor ordered 900 police in full riot gear to patrol the stadium grounds on the day of the show. Chris Norman arrived in the country, coincidentally, on the same flight as US Supreme Court Justice Sandra Day O'Connor. This presented a problem for Mongolia's Justice Minister Nyamdorj. Would he comply with diplomatic protocol and whisk the Supreme Court judge into her motorcade? Or would he live out his dreams and be the first to greet Chris Norman to Ulaanbaatar. In a classic moment of Mongolian diplomacy, Nyamdorj chose the latter; smoothly slipping past Justice O'Conner to welcome and pose for pictures with hero Chris Norman. While senior US diplomats turned a shade of raspberry, the minister became the envy of a nation.

A day later I also had the good fortune to hang out with Chris

Norman and the graying members of his band. Nice guy, but stuck in another age. I told him that he fell just below Ghengis Khan and the Dalai Lama in popularity here, and he gave a little nod of appreciation. A few minutes later he leaned over to his drummer's ear; "Oi," he said, "Who is the Dalai Lama?"

Knowledge (or lack thereof) goes both ways. While Chris Norman knew little of Tibet's spiritual leader, the concert organizers knew less about how to stage a rock and roll concert. Frightened by rowdy concert crowds they had seen on MTV, the organizers sent a battalion of shielded policemen to hold back the faithful at midfield. Seventy-five yards of empty soccer field lay between the fans and the stage.

"Unbelievable!" I said to Ariunbold. "We can't even see him! This is outrageous!"

"No, it's great! There he is!"

Ariunbold pointed to a giant TV screen that showed Chris Norman's wailing image. Nearby, Bayarmaa clasped her hands together and looked hopefully toward the stage. She grabbed Amarbat's hand, encouraging him to sway with the crowd.

The actual Chris Norman was a mere speck in the distance. After a few songs he asked for the spotlights to be shone on the crowd. When the lights went on he shielded his eyes and gave a futile search for his fans. I was hoping the crowd would revolt, but they were far too polite; they stood tamely at a distance and waved their glow sticks in welcoming admiration. Chris Norman had arrived and Mongolia would never be the same again.

That summer, during a rare heat wave, the entire news agency shut down for a camping trip. One journalist was left behind to cover breaking news that might transpire over the weekend, and the 50 or so other employees went bouncing out of the city in a cavalcade of battered buses, Russian Volgas, an army truck, and one Hyundai Sonata III (for Mr. Amarsanaa).

We arrived at a pristine spot along the Tuul River and proceeded to unload our gear. It was just a one night trip but this didn't stop my co-workers from transporting half their households: stereos, cast-iron stoves, small children, massive rugs, and crates of food, all spilled from the army supply truck. The tents were huge canvas shelters, furnished on the inside with sheep and bearskin rugs. It took three hours to get everything setup, and afterwards I had an itch to go for a hike.

Indra called me back. "Michaelah," she said, "cooking time!" And she bustled off into the woods to gather kindling for the fire.

Ten minutes later I heard shouts coming down a nearby hill and looked behind some trees to find three men in tracksuits herding goats our way. Our main entrée had arrived.

"You've got to be kidding me."

Each Montsame office received one goat. Ariunbold and Baatarbeel grabbed ours by the scruff of the neck and pinned it down to the grass. The small creature bleated loudly while its eyes looked close to exploding from their sockets. Amarbat, our only staff member to have grown up in the countryside, was summoned to do the slaughtering. He placed a knee on the goat and while it bucked and struggled he sliced a hole in its chest. With the swiftness of a cat, he slipped his hand inside the beast and severed the aorta. It was dead within 20 seconds.

Organs were removed from the goat and placed in a pot to be boiled. Next the meat was stripped away and dropped into a large metal container with vegetables, hot rocks and water. The severed head was left by the fire, the flames twinkling in its eyes.

While the sealed container was left to simmer over the open flames, the agency wrestling tournament began. I had had enough experience, with my daily match against Baatarjav, and felt primed for a win.

It is a rather simple sport: both contestants start on their feet and the first to fall to the ground loses. Whoever is unbeaten at the end of the day is rewarded with another adjective to add to his title. The national champion, Bat-Erdene, has won so many tournaments he is called "Renowned across Mongolia, Greatest of the Great, Invincible Titan."

I lasted two rounds. First was Baatarjav, whom I muscled to the grass. "You are a strong bastard, aren't you!" he said through clenched teeth. I gave my arms a little flap and hopped on one foot, my best attempt at the compulsory eagle dance. A computer technician named Gantamor, whom the others nicknamed "Tank," made quick work of me in the next round.

The final match was a David and Goliath contest between a young, athletic door guard against the obese editor of the Chinese newspaper. After great straining by the two protagonists, quickness and skill prevailed and the giant editor was toppled, much to the delight of my co-workers.

The desks then retired to their respective fires for dinner. Ariunbold opened our metal jug and fished out the scalding hot stones, which were passed around the group. Juggling one of these stones between your hands is said to improve blood circulation. Next the meat and potatoes were removed and left in a communal bowl.

"Have some fat," said Ariunbold, passing me a chunk of puffy goat fat and gristle. Mongolians don't particularly mind eating fat as it's said to boost energy levels. There is little worry about the pounds it can add as a bulge around the middle is a sign of robust health or even high social standing.

While sprawled out in the grass, enjoying the evening light, someone popped Boney M into the cassette player. Some of the journalists and translators got up and started dancing. Editors, technicians and cleaners joined in. Soon everyone was up, circling the bonfire, and skipping around it like elves, chanting "By the Rivers of Babylon." Next was Smokie, and everyone linked arms and sang along with Chris Norman. Eventually the batteries of the stereo wore out, and we slept.

* * *

Come morning, I stumbled to the dining area, where Baatarbeel was sitting by the smoldering fire, clasping a bottle of vodka in his right hand.

"Michael," he said with an outstretched cup, "Mongolian breakfast."

I accepted the vodka with an appreciative nod and fell into the same lackadaisical state as the others. Soon Ariunbold was up and, with a shot of vodka, looking lively.

"Anybody wanna go for a walk?" I asked, thinking it might be nice to explore the surrounding hills.

"Where?" asked Baatarbeel.

"How about that mountain up there," I said, pointing to a pine covered slope in the distance.

"Michael, we've come here to relax. What do you want to go up *there* for?"

"Hiking is relaxing. It's fun, it's exercise and we'll get a good view."

He just stared at me, not understanding why anyone would want to struggle uphill.

Baatarbeel was a fairly athletic fellow, trim and tall, and I thought he'd be up for it, but the agency had made a collective decision to remain comatose. It took me some time to crawl out of camp, but I did manage to climb that hill. Looking out from the peak I was once again mystified by Mongolia's stunning beauty. The emerald green valley, cut by a winding river, was home to tiny white *gers*. Herders idyllically grazed their sheep, horses and cattle. And we were only a few miles from Ulaanbaatar.

Returning to the camp I found Moogie leading the others in a game called Dembe. There was a lot of shouting, arm waving and singing—it was an advanced form of Rock, Paper, Scissors. Moogie, an extrovert and grand showman if there ever was one, was defeating the competition in style. They had not a care in the world. I looked at my watch, it was past 4pm and no one seemed the least bit interested in going back to town.

"What time do we go back?" I asked Moogie.

"You know we are journalists, but firstly we are Mongolians. Time is not so important," he said, throwing an arm around me. With a wink he hopped back into the frenzied game and started singing.

~ 7 ~

POLITICS AS USUAL

Its wickedness does not spring from one source, but the full tide of
the stream of iniquity that rolls through is fed by several tributaries,
which uniting make up the dark flood of its evil. Thus it happens
that the encampment of the Supreme Lama of Mongolia is reputed
to be the most wicked place in the whole of that wide country.

—James Gilmour, 1870

ON FRIDAY, OCTOBER 2, 1998, the pro-Democracy activist Zorig was
sitting inside the Government House, staring at a chess board. With
his spectacles glinting in the light, Zorig rubbed his stubbly chin and
pondered the alignment of chess pieces before him. Sure enough,
with a few brilliant moves, the game was over, once again in his
favor.

Zorig joked with his challenger, thanked him for the match, and
looked at his watch. It was nearly 10 p.m. and he knew his wife,
Bulgan, would start worrying about him if he didn't get home soon.
It had been a long day; the political crisis swirling around the city
had been taxing, but there was reason to relax even just a little.

93

Monday would mark a new beginning—he would be nominated as Mongolia's next prime minister and tensions would be diffused. He was confident of that—he had done it before and he could do it again.

Zorig picked up the phone and called Bulgan, saying that he would be home within 20 minutes. Her calm voice on the other end said that everything was fine at home, but she wanted him back soon—she missed him. Zorig grabbed his leather satchel, put on his overcoat and walked with his chess companion out the back door of the Government House.

It was a chilly autumn evening in Ulaanbaatar and Zorig pulled his scarf tight around his neck. Parting ways with his companion, he was driven home by his chauffer and let out by his Soviet-style apartment-block, just down the street from the Russian Embassy. Zorig banged open the metal door at the entrance to the building. Two men, smoking cigarettes and chatting in the stairwell, nodded when he passed them. When Zorig arrived at his door, he jangled his keys free from his pocket and unlocked the door.

What Zorig did not know was that behind the door were two "burglars" who had entered his home just minutes earlier. They had already tied up his wife Bulgan, who was now incapacitated on the bathroom floor. They had already stolen $300 and a pair of gold earrings. But these were no ordinary burglars. Inexplicably, they had also taken a bottle of soy sauce and a bottle of vinegar from the refrigerator. And instead of stealing more valuables or just leaving, they turned off the lights and hid in a corner of the room. One brandished a knife.

Zorig inserted his house key into the lock, turned it, and opened the door to his home. Before he even had a chance to turn on the light, he was on the ground. One of the intruders pinned him to the floor while the other began attacking Zorig with the knife. The struggle did not last long. Within half a minute, Zorig had been stabbed 16 times, thrice in the heart. Covered in blood, the masked assailants opened the door to the bathroom and flicked on the light. Seeing blood dripping from their hands, Bulgan became hysterical. But her screams were muffled from behind the cloth gag, sealed tightly across her mouth.

"Bat-Uul is next" one of the killers said, referring to Zorig's old Democrat comrade. They closed the bathroom door, stepped gingerly over Zorig's body, and ran down the stairwell. The two smokers Zorig had passed just moments earlier were stunned to see the masked pair run past. They hesitated for a moment and then gave chase, but they weren't quick enough; the killers had already vanished into the night.

There was nothing out of the ordinary when I stepped out of my apartment that Saturday morning, October 3, 1998. An autumn chill hung in the air as I walked to the office; I greeted Baatarjav at the doorway and then scampered up the marble staircase to *The Mongol Messenger* office. Bayarmaa, the only other person in the office, was translating one of Indra's pieces on Mongolia's latest economic profile. She looked up at me but said nothing. Bayarmaa had been skulking of late and I took her silence as a sign to leave her alone. Then Ariunbold, a bit tipsy, stumbled through the door.

"It's very sad," he said. "Zorig is dead."

"Zorigt?" My mind raced. Was he talking about Zorigt, the Montsame editor? "Zorigt is dead?"

"Yes, Zorig is dead. It's very sad."

"How did he die?"

"He was stabbed. It's very sad."

"Zorigt was stabbed!? Jesus! Zorigt, the editor from the third floor!?"

"No, no, not ZORIGT the editor! S. ZORIG, the Infrastructure Minister! He was a good boy."

A picture formed in my mind of the chubby Zorig with his cropped hair and thick, black-rimmed glasses. "He was my favorite

MP," said Ariunbold, talking about him in the same way Americans regale Major League Baseball stars.

"My God. Ariunbold, who would do that? How did this happen?"

Ariunbold lit a cigarette, inhaled deeply and shook his head.

My mind was racing. I needed to confirm the news but the agency was completely empty. I couldn't believe it. The biggest story of the year, and the national news agency had taken the day off.

Since government offices would be closed I started calling some of my diplomat friends and the Members of Parliament that I knew could answer rapid fire questions in English. They had cell phones and would have to answer. But before I could reach anyone our phone rang.

"Hello?"

"Michael Kohn please?"

"This is he."

"Hi Michael, this is Elaine Kurtenbach at the AP office in Beijing."

"Hi Elaine," I said, biting my lip. What would I say?

"Hey, we're hearing from Reuters that the Infrastructure Minister Zorig was found dead in his apartment last night. Can you tell us what's going on?"

"Umm, yeah. I just heard that too. I was just about to call some people." Geez. How does Beijing get the news faster than me? I must be doing something wrong.

"Elaine, can you call me back in about thirty minutes?"

"Sure. Try to get something from police, okay?"

The phone clicked, I hung up the receiver, reached for my phone book and started to make my rounds. The rest of the day was like that. As I tried to make sense of what happened, a constant barrage of phone calls came into our office from editors as far away as London and New York, but I had little more than the basic information to tell them. I myself had many questions about the murder that were simply not getting answered quickly enough.

News of the assassination spread quickly. As the sun set, people gathered in Sükhbaatar Square. The crowd was emotional; they held their heads and shed tears. Old women twisted rosaries and mumbled prayers. Candles were set on a wall in front of the Government House, precisely where Zorig had led his protest movement eight years earlier. Thousands of flickering flames illuminated their faces with an orange glow. Hot wax melted down the candlesticks like the tears from their eyes. They were not here just for Zorig the man; they had come to defend democracy.

The candlelight vigils continued each night. The mourners, even the reclusive politicians, wandered around the Square with their eyes cast downwards. Some sat in large circles around Zorig's name, spelled out with candles. A bus from the radio station parked in the middle of the square and read Zorig's achievements over a loudspeaker. Monks chanted low groaning hymns and Buddhist prayers.

Monday, a huge rally was organized in the square. Politicians ascended a stage to remember Zorig, and some took the opportunity to point fingers. It seemed like the start of a witch-hunt. The president quickly realized this and urged "public restraint."

One of the early suspects was the controversial Member of Parliament O. Dashbalbar, the xenophobic legislator who had earlier organized anti-American protests. Only a few days prior, Dashbalbar had attended the first session of the autumn Parliament dressed like a Nazi. He explained that his military regalia were meant to "symbolize Sükhbaatar," but feeling among the public was that his outfit smacked of the Gestapo. After the Zorig murder, people started sending him death threats.

"Someone called my house and threatened to kill me with a brick," he told the press.

The conspiracy theories soon reached well beyond Zorig's fellow Members of Parliament. Many assumed that this was a contract killing organized by someone who was about to lose a lot of money if Zorig became Prime Minister. Zorig, after all, was the Minister of

Infrastructure, and had managed several big money deals. Maybe the killing was connected to the giant Erdenet copper mine, forty-nine percent Russian-owned. Perhaps it was a petroleum and energy contract gone wrong? Maybe the Macanese mafia was involved; a Macau group had been lobbying Mongolia to let them open a casino. (The fact that a bottle of soy sauce had been stolen seemed to symbolize some Chinese element). If Zorig had been elected Prime Minister the whistle could have been blown on any number of lucrative but illegal business deals.

Even Zorig's wife Bulgan became a suspect. She did have a "black widow" history. Her first husband, well-known in the criminal underworld, had also been murdered. Another husband had died under mysterious circumstances. Now Zorig was gone. Had she somehow been involved?

The case overwhelmed the local police and detective units, none of whom had experience in solving a complex, high-profile murder. When their investigation got off to a slow start, private citizens were asked to make donations to pay for petrol for their squad cars.

Meanwhile, the local media was filled with rumor, innuendo and character assassination. Every newspaper had a different take on the murder, each blaring rampant, uncorroborated rumors. Ulaanbaatar Police Chief Muren found himself at the center of a category 5 media hurricane after being repeatedly misquoted in the press. Some of our journalists wanted to follow suit. Others thought the safest route was to paraphrase government press releases. I knew we had to be careful about our coverage, but as a weekly paper we had an obligation to outperform the dailies. We had to talk about Zorig's life and legacy; the fact that he had been stabbed to death was already four-day old news. The impact of the event was now as important as the event itself.

On Monday, after we had all assembled in the office, tasks were divvied out for a one-day blitzkrieg of coverage. Amarbat and Bayarmaa were assigned to the streets where they would collect interviews from the general public.

"We want a mix of young and old people, doctors and cleaners, anyone who looks interesting," I advised. "Find people with a strong opinion."

An hour later they returned with a notepad full of quotes and photos of the people they queried. They typed up the interviews and laid them out on page eight while I edited stories.

Meanwhile, Indra and Undrakh collected quotes about Zorig from various Members of Parliament. We dropped these onto page two alongside a photo montage of Zorig. It was nearly 6pm. As the minutes ticked by I plunged into the lead article, consulting with Indra and Ariunbold when I needed background on Zorig. Everyone stayed in the office well after closing time until it was just a matter of proof reading and throwing in photo captions, headlines and other details.

I caught a few hours of sleep on the floor of the office, woke at dawn and printed the last page at 8am. Amarbat stuffed the proofs into a reinforced cardboard satchel, dashed out of the office and hopped in a taxi to beat our printing deadline. He returned with a stack of papers several hours later and we all stood in silence for a moment, staring at the shocking front page. "Democratic leader S. Zorig murdered" was displayed in 48-point Helvetica black, over a four column wide file photo of a thin, boyish-looking Zorig that must have been seven or eight years old. Our usual format, with the weather, market information and air quality, was sent to the back page to make room for the oversized mug shot.

"Let's get this paper out," I said, and we all grabbed a stack of Messengers. Closing down the office, we fanned out across the city and delivered the papers to the news stands. Ironically, it took a tragedy to make us a stronger journalistic team. The tragedy had also united Mongolia and renewed its commitment to democracy. The old totalitarian-style disappearances and executions had no place in the new Mongolia.

A steady flow of mourners came to the Square to pay their last respects prior to Zorig's funeral the following Wednesday. On the day of the funeral, Zorig's body lay in state at the Government House and a line of visitors snaked all the way around the building and across the Square. Inside, friends, relatives and peers filed past his coffin with bowed heads. There wasn't enough time for everyone to enter and a near riot broke out as people tried to fight their way though the wooden doors. Police pushed them away and Zorig's coffin was carried outside and loaded onto an army truck. A procession—joined by thousands of stone-faced Mongolians—plodded slowly up the street.

Zorig was taken to Altan-Ölgii Cemetery on the outskirts of town and given a prominent place at the top of the hill. We all looked on—politicians, journalists and family members—hardly believing that the Father of Democracy was dead.

The political crisis leading up to Zorig's death had been reverberating in Ulaanbaatar for several months. It began one dusty, windy spring day the previous April when I got a phone call from a friend named Kieth, a British expatriate who had friends close to the government. Chatting on the phone he idly mentioned that the government was about to resign. Prime Minister Enkhsaikhan, he said, was being bumped out of office by a fellow democrat, Ts. Elbegdorj (one of the leaders during the 1990 Revolution).

When I heard the news I rushed into *The Messenger* office and told Indra straight away.

"Oh Michael, that happens every spring," she said, waving me off and returning to her Russian newspaper.

"Are you kidding me? This has never happened before!"

"Michael," she said, putting down her newspaper and getting flustered, "In 1990 Batmönkh resigned in the springtime. Every spring there is trouble. It's just Mongolia."

I could scarcely believe my ears. She was talking about the resignation of a Prime Minister as though it was a traffic pile up. I expected her and the other journalists to be flying out of their chairs, but instead their initial response was to completely ignore the news. Baffled, I later realized there were several reasons for this nonchalance. First of all, I was a foreigner. They really didn't like foreigners meddling into news that was not about positive economic indicators or the anniversary of one of Chingis Khan's victories. There was still a lot of communism in their journalist ethics. Bad news was a difficult concept for them to grasp or cover. Second, Indra's passive reaction was a reflection of Mongolia's stoicism. Showing outward enthusiasm was considered un-Mongolian behavior. No wonder the Prime Minister's resignation went down in the local press with no more fanfare than the latest livestock census.

At the time, however, none of us knew that Enkhsaikhan's resignation was just the start of a rolling snowball of problems and that Indra's unconcerned reaction would essentially prove correct.

Prime Minister Elbegdorj's troubles started only a few weeks after he had taken office. In one of his first decisions he allowed the merger of the state-owned Reconstruction Bank and the private Golomt Bank, which was owned by Democrats. The merger, illegal and corrupt, made several Democrats and their friends extremely rich.

News of the merger led to public outrage. Seeing their chance to capitalize on the inexperience of the Democrats, the opposition MPRP walked out of Parliament. The Elbegdorj government found itself high and dry. Without any way to convene Parliament they accepted their only option: resignation.

Zorig, a moderate, was a compromise candidate to take the place of Elbegdorj, a safe bet for all the parties involved. Days before his death, closed-door meetings between the parties agreed to have Zorig step in and take control. Zorig's sudden murder following these talks made it clear that somebody with insider information did not want him to become Mongolia's new prime minister.

Following the death of Zorig, the Democrats scrambled to find a suitable person to lead the government. Week after week they submitted names to President Bagabandi for approval; each one was dismissed for one reason or another. One had approved of the bank merger, another was too inexperienced and one other had just been arrested for drunk driving. None would set a good example for the nation, Bagabandi stated.

The crisis reached a new low one night in a downtown bar when a fistfight broke out between two Democrats. One accused the other of being disloyal to the party, both were drunk, and they ended up sending each other to the hospital.

Meanwhile, newspapers were brimming with allegations about the Zorig murder and corruption within the Democrat ranks. Public dismay over the whole crisis sent throngs of protestors to Freedom Square, where they held daily rallies calling for the dissolution of Parliament.

The first snow fell on the city a month after Zorig's death. People wrapped themselves up in fur coats and wool *dels*. Icicles formed on my balcony and the snowdrifts piled up against the buildings. Candle wax, leftover from the vigils held for Zorig, lay frozen on the concrete in Sükhbaatar Square.

The change of seasons forced our Montsame journalists inside, causing a serious epidemic of cabin fever. We got on each other nerves and staffers began bickering over petty issues. Journalists were angry with translators for incorrectly interpreting their stories and translators were angry with journalists for not meeting deadlines. Ariunbold found the best way to deal with these problems was to avoid the office as much as possible. In lieu of any management presence, I ended up bearing the brunt of the flawed end results.

We attempted to resolve our differences in group therapy sessions with the director Mr. Amarsanaa. He'd listen to everyone's gripes, make wide sweeping promises to help resolve our problems, and then shuffle us quickly out of his office. Once I remained in the office after everyone left and admitted to Amarsanaa that I had contemplated quitting. We spoke at length as he tried to convince me otherwise. He remarked that if he and his friends had quit when they were fighting those damn communists in 1990, Mongolia might not be a democratic country now. I should stay he said, and continue to improve the paper.

To get my mind off the onset of winter and tensions at *The Messenger*, I joined my Australian friend Chris, who worked at the radio station, and we started a radio program. At first we just played music but later we were joined by two other friends Dave, who worked at the United Nations, and his wife Jill, the editor of the *UB Post*. We called our program *The Gray, Short, Curly and Glasses Hour* (I was curly) and talked current affairs—the political crisis, the economy and Zorig.

We watched the situation evolve from our broadcast booth. Since Dave (gray) worked for the UN he sat out of the most controversial debates, but Jill (glasses) and I were free to put on our pundit caps and rant, rave, condemn and applaud as we pleased. Chris (short) acted as our moderator. Together we pondered the police as they continued their futile chase of the assassins (everyone assumed that they were already dead). We deliberated how Elbegdorj and his ministers could safely depart the scene without any more bloodshed. We discussed the protestors, who had erected *gers* at Freedom Square to keep warm and stood in front of television cameras to condemn the Democrats to hell.

It was easy to see why the Democrats were so loathed. They lived luxurious lifestyles; driving around in expensive SUVs, chatting on mobile phones (a privilege at the time) and throwing away thousands of dollars at the country's only gaming place, Casinos Mongolia. No one believed they were spending their own salary, which amounted to just $100 per month.

When not in the radio broadcast booth, we took our political debates to Millie's Café, Ulaanbaatar's hippest expat hangout. An overnight success story, the café was launched by an Ethiopian woman named Millie who had spent recent years in Palo Alto before moving to Mongolia with her American husband. Several other foreign-owned restaurants had popped up in recent months, including a Swiss steakhouse, a German brewery and a French bistro, but Millie's was the place to be seen.

Millie hired as her chef a fiery Cuban named Daniel (who had found his way here via Tashkent and Moscow) and together they whipped up a menu of Californian and Cuban dishes. Probably 95 percent of the clientele were expats. For Mongolians, having lunch here was like going on holiday in Europe for an hour. For myself, it resembled the typical neighborhood watering hole because I recognized everyone there. As the main meeting ground for foreigners young and old, Millie's became a rumor mill, thick with intrigue about the latest love affairs, break-ups, scandals and peregrinations of local expats, not to mention the latest grumblings about the failures of Parliament. For $1.50 you got a great cup of coffee and a week's worth of gossip.

Millie's was also the first place any expat took friends and colleagues visiting from abroad. When John flew in from China, Bayarmaa and I whisked him straight from the airport to his hotel and then on to Millie's. John, a journalist from Beijing, had come up to Mongolia a month after Zorig's assassination to file a series of reports for the Associated Press. He ordered a cappuccino, a Cuban sandwich (with a side of fries and salad), and a lemon meringue pie. I ordered a cheeseburger and a strawberry smoothie—decadent fare in UB.

It would have cost me a week's salary, but the bill was on John's news agency. He had been sent here to review the chaos that had paralyzed the government and cost Zorig his life, and as a resident "expert" he'd called on me to fill in some of the blanks. His questions, however, raised more questions, and the higher powers had been very parsimonious with information. Instead of running around in circles, we agreed to hire a translator and comb the halls of Parliament for answers.

Our translator, who I will call Amar, was well connected in the Government House. Everyone knows everyone in a country the size of Mongolia, but Amar's connections were intimate. Rather than setting up interviews, we just wandered the rambling Parliament halls and collared people as they stepped out for coffee.

The first MP we sat down with was Zenee, a pockmarked, brutish old hardline member of the MPRP. He told us that the government was "too young" and that it would be better if they handed power to more seasoned politicians (like himself). "What do these young boys know about Mongolia?" he asked us "They just went to Russia, came back, shouted in the street and took power. They can't ride a horse or milk a cow. They only know how to cause trouble!"

Zenee thought the pace of change had come too fast and wanted to stop the Westernization process dead in its tracks. The changes, he said, had erased the Mongol code of ethics. Children did not respect their parents. Youth culture fed on pornography and thieving. Leaders had been hypnotized by foreign agencies. Herders were being poisoned by imported food. Patriotism was gone. "The Mongolian soul is as clear and fresh as water from the mountains," he told us at last. "But foreigners have tainted us."

Amar, whose best connections were with the Democrats, introduced us that night to Elbegdorj. Like an apprehensive schoolboy, he sat on the edge of his seat with his elbow on his knee and matter-of-factly shouldered blame for the crisis.

"Ok. The bank merger was a bad idea. We should have consulted with the MPRP first. This is a sign of our imperfection," he said.

The young leader seemed ambitious. As his round spectacles reflected the light he spoke dreamily of privatization, major infrastructure development and super economic growth. But he slid back in his chair when he admitted that half his time was spent trying to figure out who will serve as the next Prime Minister.

"What is the fundamental problem?" I asked.

"Because we are young, people say we act too fast and irrationally. But we are brave and have courage! We are not so unnerved by these problems." Then he became despondent again. "Personally, I don't like being the boss. I can't make my own decisions because I must rely on my party. Like a fish, I prefer freedom."

The interview descended into an affair of idle chit-chat, and I easily forgot that this 35-year-old was the prime minister. He said the ball was in the president's court, but Bagabandi had rejected all his best candidates.

"It's out of my hands. If Bagabandi won't accept anyone for prime minister what can I do?"

The next day, Amar took us to meet Dashbalbar, who played a lead role among Mongolia's colorful cast of Parliamentarians. He had grown up in a herder's family in the southeast part of the country and quickly gained fame as a poet—describing with eloquence the beauty of the countryside; its grand mountains, bubbling streams and brilliant blue sky. In the mid-1990s he started the Mongolian Traditional United Party, a movement with fascist elements.

Dashbalbar grew more reactionary by the year. He sent birthday greetings to Sadaam Hussein and the Russian firebrand Zhirinovski. He admired Hitler. He advocated that Mongolia disband its army and hold only a couple of nuclear bombs. The logic was that Mongolia would save money and if anyone should give them trouble they could simply nuke 'em. He also claimed to have a list of 35,000 debtors. In a proposal to the government, he wrote that the proper method of dealing with these people was to drag them out to Sükhbaatar Square and hang them from poles.

Handshakes went round and the ethereal figure of Dashbalbar sat opposite us. He lit incense sticks and lines of smoke twisted and curled before him. His long black hair fell onto his shoulders, and his huge curving eyelids were like those of a Buddhist idol. He spoke in clear calm tones and remained unprovoked by our prodding questions.

"Mongolia went down the wrong path in the 20th century," he began. "These huge concrete cities conflict with our traditional interests as Shamans and Buddhists. The land has been poisoned. It would be much better if we gave up these cities and moved back to the countryside."

Pol Pot immediately sprang to mind.

We asked him why he lived in Ulaanbaatar when he could easily go back to the countryside.

"I have a duty, an ambition to stay here and fight for my people. It is true that I could give up and go home, but that would be too easy."

"So what is wrong with the society?" we asked.

"It is not just Mongolian society that is at fault; the world is crumbling. The earthquake in Kobe, the hurricane in Central America, the tidal wave in Papua New Guinea, volcanic eruptions in the Philippines, floods in China, drought in Africa, the rising of the Earth's oceans..."

"What's all this fire and brimstone!?" John finally burst out in frustration.

"My point is that humanity is being punished by God. Just look at Ulaanbaatar. Pornography is on the television, alcohol is on the streets and garbage is piling up in our rivers. This was once a pristine valley but it has been desecrated. This is the fault of foreign pressure and brain washing. We are being punished for not being true to ourselves."

"Do you want to kick foreigners out of the country?" we asked.

"English teachers offer something constructive, but the missionaries and the political advisors must go. They say they are "offering suggestions," but they are just dictating the American or European way of life. I will chase them away."

"What about TV? That has a lot of influence on youth culture," we noted.

"There are some foreign things I like to watch on television: Michael Jordan flying through the air, beautiful scenes of nature. We can accept these things. But everything else—car crashes, guns and drugs—has no place here. We see more of America on TV than Mongolia. This foreign lifestyle is pushed on us. When people have no money they will accept anything."

We asked him what he remembered about his childhood.

"I remember lying on my back in the grass, next to a river with my animals nearby," he said, leaning back in his chair. "The sound of the fast-flowing stream filled my ears as I stared up at the blue sky. Birds flew by. I would roll over and plant my cheek on the ground and the sweet smell of grass and flowers filled my nostrils. That is what I remember about my childhood. Europeans cannot understand this. They are slaves to cars, four walls and money. It suppresses their soul. Humans are born to be enlightened. We Mongols were once enlightened and can be again."

I left the interview a little bit humbled by the desire of this man. His theories were too radical to be widely accepted but his desire, I am sure, occupied the hearts of many of his countrymen. The crisis, as he saw it, was punishment from *Burkhan*, God. All he really wanted was for his people to be left alone.

John stayed for the rest of the weekend and we continued our rounds with the politicians. We spoke with the House Speaker, other MPs and the president himself. All parties agreed that modern Mongolia was a hothouse flower that had begun to wilt.

No one had a viable turn-around plan for Mongolia; they had all been hoping that Zorig could have figured it out. Only S. Oyun, who was about to become Parliament's newest member, gave us a sense of hope. She was a shoo-in for the upcoming election in Zorig's district; partially because she was clever and honest, but mostly because she was going to fill Zorig's shoes comfortably. She was his sister.

Oyun had spent the past few years working for a mining company in England. She knew little about politics, though when it comes to Mongolia, this was probably a good thing. Her only experience, she admitted, was translating some of Zorig's speeches into English during the pro-democracy protests in 1990. But she seemed a quick learner and, like her brother, had vision. She wanted to attack and weed out every last bit of corruption that blackened the country. It was her obsession. It was an improbable task that she shouldered for herself, her country and her brother.

"Zorig's ideals should continue," she told us over coffee at Churchill's English restaurant. "His work was broad and global. He supported human rights, freedom, pluralism, and transparency in government. Zorig was not easily influenced; he had his own mind. He played a moderating role between the Democrats and the MPRP and had his own code of ethics."

Her inexperience, she said, hardly mattered. What did matter was a united front against the evils of society. Soon after being elected, Oyun pulled behind her the scattered ranks of honest politicians and set up committees and organizations to fight corruption. Meanwhile, the political crisis was showing signs of resolution. Finally in December, all sides agreed upon a candidate to replace the beleaguered Elbegdorj. The President and Parliament agreed to give the job to Ulaanbaatar's apathetic mayor, J. Narantsatsralt.

The selection of Narantsatsralt showed some promise, but the Democrats still faced daily street protests, a growing trade deficit and a recession that had held up teachers' salaries for three months.

Then, in the darkest days of winter, something strange and remarkable happened. Without warning, all the Parliamentarians convened and decided to shut down a multi-million dollar casino operation backed by investors from Macau. It was supposed to be a huge revenue earner and its construction, in the basement of the Chingis Khan Hotel, was nearly complete. I had never seen Parliament act on anything so fast. MPs said they did it because they feared "gangsters, drugs, weapons and prostitution."

"We didn't know anything about casinos a year ago," one politician told me. "Then we learned what casinos were doing in other countries and decided it wasn't right for Mongolia."

Soon rumors started circulating about the casino's sudden death. They were dark, nasty rumors about corruption, bribery and money laundering with official involvement. The tabloids were soon filled with startling, unsubstantiated stories that named names. Jill and I were delighted to explore all the terrifying implications on our radio show.

We made an editorial decision at *The Messenger* to avoid the scandal for as long as possible. Then on April 9, 1998, police announced that three MPs were under arrest for taking bribes from the Mon Macau casino company. (One of them had been a school mate of Ariunbold's back in his Leningrad days). Tens of thousands of dollars and some Nissan SUVs had been exchanged for their services. (Mon Macau had allegedly paid them off to win the casino tender). There was certainly more people and money involved, but the arrests had thunderous ramifications. Members of Parliament, stripped of their immunity, were now behind bars.

The case was a Mongolian Watergate. For the first time the public saw "infallible" politicians tossed in jail. Never again would a seat in Parliament equal a free ride. MPs, now fearing for their own safety, publicly returned expensive gifts. One night a somewhat cynical Democrat named Baabar invited a TV camera crew into his office to film him as he emptied his cabinet of knickknacks—neckties, wall clocks, wristwatches and other spoils—which he had accepted from foreign friends during his business negotiations.

New buzzwords were in the air. "We must be more *transparent*," said Indra one day. Where had she learned that? Bayarmaa, Undrakh and Amarbat joined the discussion as we started talking about ways to end corruption at Montsame. Together we proposed new ideas to Ariunbold and Amarsanaa on how to better monitor advertising money, which had grown significantly since my arrival but was being funneled into the wrong pockets. Soon a profit sharing system was in place and our monthly earnings suddenly jumped by 30 percent. Bayarmaa and Amarbat, for example, saw their monthly incomes go from 30,000 to 40,000 tögrög ($30 to $40). Since both were the sole breadwinners for their families, this money was going far to help those who needed it a lot more than me.

Word spread quickly and soon every office across the city was talking about graft and how to end it. Behind it all was Oyun, and behind her the memory of Zorig. The police could never prove any of the assassination theories and probably never will, but their incompetence made the mystery more profound. Competing theories merely strengthened Zorig's martyrdom.

On April 20, a statue of Zorig was unveiled on the corner of the busiest intersection of town. Naturally, some people hated the design. They said he didn't look heroic like Lenin or Sükhbaatar down the street. He looked ordinary—a satchel stuffed under his arm and a cigarette between his fingers. The artist wanted to portray Zorig as he had looked every day for the last ten years—just strolling to work.

I passed that statue regularly for two years. In the summertime, flowers gathered around its base. In the winter, snow clung to his arms and head. On Zorig's birthday and day of his assassination, candles flickered around his shoes. The statue was personified. People walked up to it and said *"Sain bain uu, Zorig?"* What's new? Others meditated in his presence. Zorig's courage and memory gave him a kind of patrimony over Mongolian democracy that caused people to love him.

The jailed politicians accused of graft and corruption remained in custody throughout the summer. Their punishments, which came in the autumn, saw one sentenced to prison for three and a half years. The other two got five years each.

The *coup de grace,* however, came in July. Word swept though unflappable Montsame that Narantsatsralt, Mongolia's Prime Minister of seven months, had been sacked for mishandling the Erdenet copper mine. He was accused of secretly setting up the mine for a cheap sell off to the Russians (in exchange for a suspected bribe). But after all the country had gone through since Enkhsaikhan, Elbegdorj, the Zorig murder and the Mon Macau scandal, the incident was about as shocking as static electricity.

"Every spring," said Indra.

I nodded. This time I couldn't help but agree.

8

THUNDERING HOOVES

The Mongol cannot be dissociated from his steed. Indeed, they resemble each other; they were born of the same steppe, formed by the same soil and the same climate, broken in by the same exercises. The Mongol is short, stocky, big-boned, heavy framed, and of prodigious stamina. His horse too is small stocky and without grace.

—Rene Grousset
Empire of the Steppes

"Did you bring the vodka?"

Choijil spoke softly, shifting his eyes back and forth as if we were in a speakeasy. We happened to be in his summer tent, along with his grandchildren, but he wasn't about to let his wife in on our secret. Out of my backpack I pulled a brown paper bag that contained a liter of clear spirits, just what Choijil had asked for when I met him a day earlier. "Chingis Khan: Premium Vodka" was stamped on the label, along with a drawing of the 12th century cat-eyed warlord. Accepting it with craggy hands the old nomad uncapped the bottle and filled a small shot glass produced from the folds of

113

his del, making sure that his wife wasn't peeking in. Choijil flicked some ceremonial drops into the air and then threw the vodka to the back of his throat.

"So, you want to know the secret do you?"

"Of course."

Choijil leaned closer, lifting his rheumy eyes to mine.

"*Khöls,*" he said.

"Sweat?"

"Yes, you've gotta make 'em sweat. Come, let me show you."

Choijil put down his vodka, lifted up his five foot frame, and stumbled out of his tent. His wife looked on suspiciously as we ducked behind the tent to a row of 25 beautiful horses, standing proud with firm bodies and heads high. Several were wrapped in thick blankets, causing them to sweat profusely.

"The more they sweat the faster they will run," said Choijil. "That is the secret to training horses. We wrap them in a blanket and walk them up and down the hills; then they sweat. When their pores open up their muscles breathe and they grow strong."

"Can they ever sweat too much?"

"Of course, you have to be careful, they could collapse from exhaustion. Keeping them well-watered is a key part of the training."

Choijil pulled a wooden palette from his silk belt and started scraping the sweat off a fine looking black horse, sending droplets of perspiration flying into the blue sky.

"These two have the best chance of winning," Choijil continued, without a breath. There were two horses standing side by side, the black gelding that Choijil expertly scraped, and a reddish stallion. They were chosen for special training when they were colts, he said, because they showed promising signs: long ears, long legs and a wide flank. He called them Black and Red—Mongolians name their horses as often as Americans name their automobiles, but there is rarely any confusion since there are around 300 different ways to describe a horse's coat.

"Look at his tummy," said Choijil, nearly climbing under the gelding for a better look. "Very narrow, this is a good sign. He is standing evenly on all four legs, his sweat is clear and his eyes are large and black."

Choijil then pressed on the gelding's back as though he were testing the shocks of a Russian Lada. "Yes, yes. Very straight. Straight and balanced."

"And look at this horse shit," he said, picking up some manure that had dropped behind the Black horse. "It's very dry. Yes indeed, he's ready to run."

Choijil was clearly an experienced *uyach* (trainer); I had come to the right place. My reason for coming here was to learn something of the Mongolian pastime, and Choijil said he would impart some of his knowledge. The bottle of vodka was a fair exchange. The more he drunk the deeper the train of his intellect, and he was soon waxing lyrical on distance training, weight loss and sweat consistency.

"You've really gotta punish these animals," he said after another shot. "After we've walked them up the hills with the blanket we start racing. First the *tar* race, which is roughly one mile. At this time the sweat will be frothy. Then we gradually increase the distance to the *sungaa*, about eight miles. The key is to stabilize the breathing and wait for the sweat to become watery; but I'm no expert, it's just a hobby."

A hobby it may be, but Choijil was the most dedicated in his class. Still, I wondered why he was the only one training horses on this massive field. The national horse races were only a week away, but where were the other trainers? Choijil said he had arrived ahead of schedule to allow his horses time to get used to the "new grass and new air." This would give him an advantage when it came to race time.

"I've come to the national Naadam every year since 1970," said Choijil. "I've got my technique down now; younger trainers aren't so experienced."

In his younger years Choijil had come with his horses all the way from Zavkhan aimag—700 miles away. Competition had always been tough. Indeed, with 600 horses competing in each race it was hard to train a winner. Although none of Choijil's horses had ever won a national race, they had finished in the top five on several occasions. Small prizes were awarded during Communism—Choijil said he had won some medals and a couple of saddles—but the stakes were higher in these heady days of capitalism. Big prizes were now given to the top five finishers; usually a Russian jeep for first place, a motorcycle for second place and cash prizes for third, fourth and fifth.

For all the hardships of training his horses, it's been years since he had actually crossed the Tuul River and entered Ulaanbaatar proper. Naadam was Mongolia's biggest festival of the year, complete with archery and wrestling at the central stadium, and I wondered why Choijil had stopped going into town.

"No time for such things," he explained. "We have to take care of the horses. We must stay up all night to make sure they eat at the right times. Eating too much or eating at the wrong times will cause them to run slower. My grandchildren and I take turns sleeping to make sure they eat properly."

I posed the same question to his assorted grandchildren who had gathered around. Wouldn't they want to go check out the big city, the bright lights and the video arcades? What about the brand new Sky Shopping Mall? It was a first in Mongolia and everyone had been there—not to shop but to go for joy rides on the escalator. They shook their heads.

"Boring," the oldest one said. "We went to the city today. There is nothing to do, it's much more exciting to stay out here, watch the horses, wrestle."

It was this sort of dedication to their horses that made trainers and their families a unique part of Mongolia's famed equestrian lifestyle. Horse training was a religion in Mongolia; the best trainers have the aura of spiritual advisors and the horses and jockeys are treated like national heroes. No one expected them to venture out of the Yarmag fields to the tawdry carnival-like atmosphere around the stadium. Recognizing this, Naadam organizers had set up a no-frills "mini Naadam" at Yarmag featuring elite wrestlers and archers.

In Mongolia, jockeys are not the small adults that Westerners are accustomed to seeing at the track. The jockeys are children, aged five to twelve, usually the offspring of the trainers. I asked Choijil's young jockeys if they were nervous about battling 599 other horses over 20 miles of rough terrain. They'd have to hang on tight, maybe have their feet tied to the stirrups or ride bareback. They would need enough stamina for a race that could take more than an hour to finish. They all giggled and shyly shook their heads.

"What have they got to be afraid of?" Choijil burst out. "They are not afraid of anything!"

The Naadam races were a celebration of Mongolia's national symbol; the beast that won them an empire. Without the horse, the Mongol hordes would never have gotten past the Gobi Desert, much less to Krakow, Baghdad, Moscow, Kabul and Burma. Horses not only transported the Mongol troops across the Eurasian landmass, they also provided an effective method of communication; afforded by a vast pony express system set up by Chingis and his generals. Horses even provided sustenance—when food was scarce the soldiers would pierce their mount with a blade and suck the blood: medieval fast food. And for all this, the horses have proven to be very low maintenance. Feed costs are a pittance because the horses are basically left alone to forage for themselves. Even in winter the hardy Mongol horse is able to claw through snow to get at bits of grass, while enduring temperatures that would kill a European horse.

Despite this benevolent neglect, the Mongol horse is tremendously loyal. During the Vietnam War a team of horses sent to North Vietnam to help carry supplies along the Ho Chi Minh trail. The gift horses were eventually let go and years later they were discovered in Mongolia, having instinctively walked north, back to their home, 3000 miles away.

The horse is Mongolia's national symbol, seen on money, in poetry, in artwork, on stamps, even on the tail of Mongol Airlines airplanes. When dignitaries visit Mongolia they are usually presented with a horse, which they name and pose with for pictures. During my time in Mongolia, I saw horses presented to Madeleine Albright, Jiang Zemin and Keizo Obuchi. Donald Rumsfeld was also given a horse, which he promptly named Montana after his wife's home state. The horses, of course, were spared the trouble of being airlifted abroad; they stayed on their home turf and have never been ridden by anyone.

I should note, however, that there are two distinct breeds of horse in Mongolia. The domesticated horse favored by nomads, and the takhi horse, a wild breed that sports two extra chromosomes. Takhi are better known in the West as Przewalski's horse, named after the Polish explorer who "discovered" them during an expedition in 1878. An oddly shaped beast, sand-colored takhis are noted for their thick necks, bulging heads and short, Mohawk-like manes. Rather than trying to tame these ornery creatures, ancient Mongols hunted them; so much so that they became extinct by the 1960s. Fortunately, the species had been preserved in zoos in Europe and Australia, and a recent re-introduction and breeding program brought some back to Mongolia where they now roam free again.

A couple of days after learning the secrets of Choijil's success, I returned to the race grounds to find several families having joined Choijil, their *gers* scattered across the field like fresh mushrooms after rain. Dust floated in the summer breeze as I admired the steeds and chatted with their attentive *uyach*.

The Mongol Messenger had never paid much attention to sports, we didn't even have a sports section, so I thought I'd ramp up our coverage of the Naadam and focus particularly on the horse races. I began by interviewing the uyach, asking the various training methods.

"*Khoils*," they all said. "Keep 'em sweating."

At last I came upon a collection of three *gers*, one with the red and blue Mongolian flag poking out of the skylight. The doors of each *ger* were made of finely crafted wood with intricate native designs, and I wondered what sort of outback wrangler could afford such opulence.

Stepping inside the central *ger*, I found the same ambiance that might have graced the tent of a 19th century Mongol prince. Intricately designed carpets lined the floor and leather couches nudged against each wall. The chests, tables, chairs, and *ger* poles were all hand-crafted in matching detail.

A pudgy man with dark skin sat at the far end of the *ger*. He wore a brown cowboy hat and a spotless gray *del* cinched with a large leather belt that was fastened with a mighty silver buckle. He introduced himself as Ganbold and said the *gers* were his, used especially for Naadam just three days each year. He was the Director of the Mon-Ted construction company and, with his brother Gansukh, had come to Yarmag every year to watch the races.

"We're just city boys, me and my brother," Ganbold admitted. "But we've hired one of the best *uyach* in the country to raise our horses."

This was the new Mongolia. A few years before the playing field had been equal and your average Joe Blow *uyach* (like Choijil) would have had a good chance of winning. But the past couple of Naadams had brought the sport of horse racing up market with a touch of celebrity status. Now top trainers were put on salary and hired by wealthy businessmen. Horses were now officially registered as company-owned. Although corporate horses didn't seem traditional, I started to see it as a throwback to earlier times. Looking around the grandness of Ganbold's *ger*, and seeing his specially-bred horses outside being tended to by hired hands, it really did feel as if the *noyons* (princes) of old had returned, after the long hiatus of communism.

"Drink!" Ganbold ordered me, holding out a glass of vodka. "This is our tradition."

I accepted the shot of vodka and took a ceremonial sip, getting into the spirit of Mongolia's second national pastime. Ganbold cajoled me into drinking more but eventually I had to decline, explaining that, like most Americans, I simply wasn't used to shots of straight vodka at 9.45 in the morning.

"You're right," he slurred. "We Mongolians drink too much vodka. We should drink more *airag* (koumiss)."

He blamed the Russians for his vodka addiction.

"In the old days, before the Russians introduced vodka, there were *airag* drinking competitions. A group of men would sit around a table and drink; if you got up to go to the bathroom, or if any airag spilled in the *ger*, you lost."

"There is a story about one man who drank 40 liters in one sitting. Then he pushed in his stomach and spewed a stream of *airag* through the door of the *ger*. Because none of the airag touched the ground inside, he won! So you see, in the old days, we Mongols could drink more *airag* than now."

He glanced in my direction, laughed aloud, and tossed back another shot of vodka.

The holiday had emptied the news agency but I still had to pop in the next morning to layout some pages for the next week's paper. Having no one to interrogate, Baatarjav appeared anxious and jumped out of his chair when I opened the front door. Wrestling my way past him, I went upstairs, flicked on my Mac and found... nothing. Three days had passed since the last paper had come out, but still no stories had been prepared for this week's paper, save for a few briefs taken from the dailies. The translator's desk was likewise empty; our three journalists were either on strike or had taken an ill-planned joint vacation. I called Indra, who promised to submit two stories, and suggested that I take a couple days off. It was a holiday. Didn't I know?

Indra was right. If no Mongolians were working, what was I doing here? Although I didn't realize at the time, working on Naadam must have been the equivalent of sitting in the office on Christmas Eve.

Rather than getting bogged down in work, I dashed out the office, flagged down a cab, and asked the driver to take me to Yarmag. I was soon lined up amid the other spectators, looking into the distance for the first sign of the riders.

The minutes dragged on and we all cowered from the summer sun. At last we saw a cloud of dust moving closer. It appeared like a dark ominous warning that centuries ago would have meant one thing: run and hide, the Mongols are coming.

Luckily for us, these weren't the club wielding warriors, nor skilled archers of Chingis Khan lore. They were the child-jockeys, and soon the first rider came within sight. Two more appeared, then a fourth. And, suddenly, a full cavalry of horses rumbled behind them, the dust cloud forming a menacing backdrop.

This was the two-year-old race *(daaga);* the American equivalent to watching a high school basketball game. The horses are young, full of vigor, and bounding along anxiously in their first big race.

There are several other classes, each grouped by age. The older the horse the longer the distance, with some races going up to 20 miles. The two-year-old race is the shortest but is still the most popular.

As I held my camera at the ready, the noise from the crowd and the thundering of hooves sounded like a gathering storm until a patchy brown horse with a tiny boy bouncing up and down on its bare back galloped across the finish line, two body lengths ahead of its pursuer. Then came a small girl dressed in a pink silk outfit, a yellow crown perched over two pigtails. After the top five finishers raced past, the crowds—men, women and children—mounted their horses and chased after them.

Police watched helplessly as the stampede of fans bowled over horseless spectators. A boy, whose ankle was caught in the stirrup of a runaway horse, thumped across the ground at dangerous speeds. Children emerged bloody and disorientated. A horse reared from the tumult, threw its rider into the air and landed belly-up.

Dodging the chaos, I dashed in the direction of the crowds and caught up with them at the winners' corral. Trainers in bright wool *dels* and huge leather belts were busy glazing the sweat from their steeds. The child jockeys sat on their horses, exhausted but proud.

The spectators grabbed horse sweat off the palettes. Then, they wiped the sweat *on their faces*. I learned afterwards that this was a good luck custom. The only thing stranger than this occurred down at the stadium where fans collected the sweat off successful wrestlers. (A cultural tidbit usually left off tourist brochures).

Following the sweat collecting ritual, the crowds migrated back to the finish line in time to greet the last place finisher, an exhausted horse with trembling knees. Special recompense is given to the loser of the two-year old race, and together the crowds sang to it, chanting "This Year's Big Fat Stomach, Next Year's Great Leader."

After the race, spectators retired to a happy-hour area of *ger* restaurants and snack sellers. I found Choijil's grandson Sambuu devouring a bowl of mutton. As part of his training, he had eaten lightly on his race day, and was famished. The race had covered him with dirt, though he seemed satisfied with his finish "somewhere in the hundreds."

Together we walked back to his tent where we found Choijil cinching up the tails of his horses with pieces of blue silk. I asked about the results of the first day. He said that several of the top finishers were company sponsored horses, including one owned by Ganbold, my friend in the nearby *ger*. I asked Choijil what he thought of this, expecting resentment, but in typical Mongolian fashion he merely shrugged it off as uncontrollable fate.

"Rich people don't make good herders, so they have to hire someone to train their horses. They specially breed them and give them good medical treatment. They are better looked after than I am!" he chuckled. "But it is good competition for us, it makes everyone work harder."

A crowd of people had amassed at Ganbold's camp. Friends, relatives and neighbors were on hand to inspect their third place finisher, an exhausted looking brown horse with silk scarf tied around its neck. Ganbold and his friends toasted their achievements, and, as a sign of the times, a shiny new medal was stuck to Ganbold's *del*. Meanwhile, Ganbold's pool of trainers busily completed their chores—tending to the horses' wounds, scraping their sweat and feeding them specially prepared milk.

Later I found a young, bleary-eyed *uyach* pissing on the leg of one of Ganbold's horses. I thought he was just drunk but then he called me over to show me his business, pointing at a sore on the horse's ankle.

"We are trying to heal it quickly before the race tomorrow," he said, as if that explained all. I assumed urine was the Mongolian version of disinfectant. Since the grass was poor around the *ger* camp, the trainers were getting ready to take their horses to the mountain where they would be properly fed. There they would stay the night, sleeping on the ground by their horse's hooves.

The races continued for the rest of the day and the next. I tried my best to keep up with the action and monitor the results, but as a spectator sport, it's pretty well disorganized. The main problem was that there was no set track. The horses raced over the plains for about 10 miles to an *ovoo* (sacred pile of stones), circled around it, and came back. This allowed plenty of scope for cheating and many of the jockeys would simply turn around and join the pack before getting to the *ovoo*. The only crowds along the way were some lone horsemen peering across the steppe through their Russian spyglasses.

Each race was guaranteed to offer some drama and tragedy. The crowds cheered the winning horses and clamored for their sweat. Meanwhile, the losers limped quietly away. In the 5-year-old race the fans dashed madly between the horses as they crossed the finish line—believing that running through the dust kicked up by a five year old horse would bring them good luck. Deaths occurred too. Horses collapsed from exhaustion in almost every race. Twelve horses alone died in the five-year old race. I found one of these poor beasts just beyond the finish line. A sobbing young jockey and her father knelt over the horse and held its head. Gawking ranks of foreign tourists were shooed away by police. It was a sad but common sight.

I headed back toward the horse trainers' tent city that was beginning to break down. Naadam was coming to an end and the weary crowds were going home. Ganbold was packing up too. While he chatted on his cell phone, two big trucks were being piled high with his *gers*, his horses and his relatives. In the midst of packing, a TV crew from World Sport came to interview Ganbold's uyach. The jockeys were a bit young to provide more than a two word testimonial, but the trainers were happy to relive the glory moments of the race. Standing up, the *uyach* struck a gallant pose for the camera as he described the finer points of training, the varieties of tack and saddle, and fearlessness of the fluorescent-clad jockeys. The TV crew packed up and left, followed quickly by Ganbold and his clan.

As I followed them toward the road I found old Choijil, his wife and his grandchildren. Choijil was busy repairing his horse cart while the others were packing up the tent. The bottle of vodka I had given him now lay empty amid other discarded items.

"Our autumn pastures are four days away," said Choijil. "We've got a lot of ground to cover before dark."

There was no medal for Choijil this year. He had been beaten by a younger and wealthier class of horse breeders and trainers. He had come from far away to race his best horses, but failure to finish among the top class did not diminish his spirits. No sweat, there was always next year.

I helped him mend his cart while the others loaded up the tent, pots, pans and the rest of their belongings. The last thing they did was to remove from the ground the poles that held the horse tether. The holes left in the earth were filled with dung—a symbolic gesture that would ensure their safe return following year. Then Choijil and his clan boarded their overloaded horse cart and trundled away, pots and pans clanging against each other as they rode toward the horizon. Eventually, all that remained of Yarmag was neat little piles of horse dung, and a layer of dust that was left to settle for another year.

~ 9 ~

THE WILD WEST

"ALL THE PROVINCIAL GOVERNORS ARE VISITING MONTSAME," Indra said. "Do you want to interview any of them?"

"Can we get the Uvs Governor?"

I had heard a lot about Uvs lately. The Montsame correspondent in the provincial capital Ulaangom was sending us continual reports of attacks by cattle rustlers from neighboring Tuva. It was one of the few breaking news stories coming out of the countryside.

Moments later, a rail-thin man in a suit, identifying himself simply as Baatar (Hero), Governor of Uvs Aimag, was led into our office. His hair was matted across his forehead in long spikes and he gave a timid handshake; not exactly cutting the Wyatt Earp image I had expected for a man running a territory infamous for its gun slinging cowboys.

"We hear you are having a problem with cattle theft," I said.

"It's getting worse," he lamented. "We have not found a solution. As long as there is money to be made off it, it will just continue."

From the reports we had gathered, Tuvans living in Russia were roaming across the mountainous border by night, rounding up

126

livestock from *gers* and homesteads, and returning safely to their home territory before dawn. (The Mongolians, of course, were doing the same thing, but this fact received *far* less media attention). The problem had recently dissolved into chaos as civilians defending their cattle had been accidentally shot by trigger happy border guards.

"It is unfortunate that our border guards have shot these people," the governor lamented. "But we're doing our best to stop this thieving."

I thought perhaps implementing some laws might solve the problem—Chingis Khan had decreed that cattle theft was punishable by death.

"Would you like to visit Uvs? Maybe you need to see this crisis first hand."

"*Tiim,*" I answered. ("Hell, yes!").

Baatar tipped his head with an accepting smile. At the time it seemed like quite a serious offer, though looking back I am guessing he never thought I'd take him up on it.

When Baatar left the room I yanked an atlas off our bookshelf to try to determine the size, and possible military strength, of Tuva. Bayarmaa and Amarbat joined me and our eyes scanned the map until we were finally able to pinpoint the tiny wedge of Russian territory. The capital of the province was named Kyzyl, and there seemed to be no other towns whatsoever. Mongolia looked like a superpower in comparison.

"Ah, that's a little country. We can take 'em!"

"Do you want to get shot too!?" squeaked Bayarmaa.

"Oh, I am sure it's not as bad as they make it out to be. Tell her Amarbat."

Eerie silence filled the air.

"Don't worry," I promised. "I'll send a long story; all the less for you to translate."

Shaking her head she disappeared behind her monitor while I

returned to the map. The distance to Uvs from Ulaanbaatar was 800 miles. The only way to get there would be by plane. I started making plans straight away.

Tuva was once known as the Uriankhai Frontier Region—the outermost limits of the Chinese empire during Manchu rule. The inhabitants speak a Turkic language quite unlike Mongolian and more closely related to Uighur, although their cultural habits, including dance, costume and religion are nearly indistinguishable from the Mongols'.

Following the collapse of the Manchu dynasty, remote Tuva, with a population of just 30,000 people, followed in Mongolia's footsteps and declared independence. There wasn't much of a country to speak of however, as Tuva was virtually ruled from the inside by Soviet NKVD (fore-runner to the KGB) agents. Gradually, the Soviets convinced Tuva's leader Salchak Toka that it would be much easier to run his country if it were a part of the Soviet Union. Toka followed the order and gave up his independence. This decision infuriated Mongolia's proud leadership, and the next time they met, Choibalsan smacked Toka across the face.

Cultural similarities, however, kept the two republics close during Soviet times. After 1990, however, hard times increased crime, particularly cattle rustling. I had been following the situation for months from my desk at *The Mongol Messenger*. And then, one May afternoon, I found myself in the cramped confines of an Antonov airplane, soaring across an empty landscape toward Ulaangom, the capital of Uvs. White knuckles to the armrest, Jill Lawless, my partner at the radio station, sat nervously in a nearby seat. A Toronto theater critic in a previous life, Jill was also intrigued by the idea of masked bandits and sensitive border regions, and we had decided to travel together. Surrounding us were large crates of personal effects, sacks of flour and *del*-clad Mongols with children on their laps.

It was going to be my first extended summer journey in Mongolia. Ulaanbaatar's political intrigue had waned of late, and I thought I'd take this period of relative quiet to explore some of the western provinces. Until this point in my life I had always felt more like a traveler than a writer. I had backpacked across more than 35 countries over the past four years and still felt that rush of adrenaline seeing the horizon over the next hill. My new career in journalism, however, was changing my perspective. Rather than looking for more mountains to climb, I thought it might be more interesting to meet local people and write about them. Ariunbold agreed and we worked out a plan to publish a series of my dispatches sent in from the countryside. I didn't go far as to print up business cards, though I rather enjoyed my new status as *The Mongol Messenger* roving reporter.

Both Jill and I were also preparing our field reports for the radio. Mongol Radio lent us tape recorders, which I hoped we could use to capture the shouts of bandits and perhaps a gun shot or two. Jill had procured a new Sony tape player, while I was stuck with something that resembled a 747's "black box," a monstrosity that dated from the 1970s and bore a large "Made in East Germany" emblem on its backside. It was powered by six D batteries and doubled my luggage weight.

Ulaangom was a concrete version of Dodge City. The cattle rustlers were there somewhere, amid slabs of cement, bunches of cable, and piles of car parts. A massive salt lake located nearby was the reported home of deadly serpents. The local legend sounded vaguely like a story originally reported by Roy Chapman Andrews who promised Mongolia's prime minister that he would capture the dangerous "allergorhai-horhai."

"It is shaped like a sausage, about two feet long, has no head nor legs and is so poisonous that merely touching it means instant death," the Mongol premier told Andrews. Never one to back down from a challenge, Andrews promised he would seize the beast with long steel collecting forceps and wear dark glasses "so that the disastrous effects of even looking at so poisonous a creature would be neutralized."

Before tracking down dangerous serpents and cattle thieves, Jill and I deposited our luggage at the local hotel, a brick-fronted affair with rambling halls and wheezing faucets. We met another guest that had taken up residency there—a French ornithologist named Anna, who was stuck in Uvs with a broken down motorcycle and her brutish Mongol driver. For Anna, Mongolia was *the* ultimate destination, not just for watching birds, but for thrilling adventures.

The standard tour of Mongolia involves hiring a jeep and driver to visit the Gobi, Karakorum or Khövsgöl Lake. Breakdowns were an inevitable part of the experience, but most tourists got back to the capital relatively unscathed.

And then there were folks, like Anna, for whom only the most arduous, self-made expedition would satisfy their wanderlust. They would usually turn up in the summer with half-baked plans to ride a horse across the plains, or hitchhike on the back of sheep trucks—living out their Wild West fantasies in the Far East.

These wayfarers were typically young, impoverished backpackers, fresh out of the university and looking for the cheapest, most painful method of transport. Each year, the travelers came to one-up the last group with ever increasing outlandishness. Andre topped them all.

Andre, a 35 year old native of New Hampshire, decided the best way to conquer the steppes was to golf across them. His 18-hole, par 11,800 course had a total fairway distance of 1200 miles. Each "hole" was actually a small town, and there were conveniently 18 of them. He lost more than 600 golf balls during his round, which took two summers to complete. When it was over, Andre enjoyed a little more than 15 minutes of fame, appearing on a number of talk shows, including a sit down with Jay Leno.

Europeans failed to see the humor in golfing across Mongolia. A Scandanavian woman working in Ulaanbaatar frowned at the thought of Andre's tomfoolery. "I don't think he's serious!" she declared through pursed lips. This is because Europeans never left home without a goal in mind. The French in particular were ruthless in their approach toward tourism. They were there to map, document and explore. Anna the ornithologist didn't know what she would do with her data on bird sightings, but collected it nonetheless to provide some purpose to her journey. Riding around in a sheep truck or smacking golf balls down marmot holes struck the French as mindless tourism. (Granted, it was. But that didn't make it any less fun).

Other tourists came because Mongolia was, well Mongolia, a synonym for "remote," an attraction in itself. This notion emerged in *Lost*, one of America's short-lived reality TV shows. In the first episode, three teams were blindfolded and flown from America to the Gobi Desert, given $100, and told to make their way back to New York as quickly as possible. Two of the teams quickly figured out where they were, and the third—two guys from New Jersey—wandered aimlessly for days. Every few hours a person with Asiatic features would pass by on a motorcycle, yet they remained convinced they were somewhere in the Czech Republic.

Like me, Jill also had a taste for adventure. Our goal, we decided, was to reach the Mongolian-Russian border and keep an eye out for bandits, hoping to take photographs and collect sound clips on the way. First we paid a visit to the Government office for a meeting with Governor Baatar. He was less congenial than I expected—the first thing he asked was how much money we had. Jill and I shot each other looks of distress.

"There is no time for an interview," Baatar continued, waving us away. "But you can go to the border office with my translator tomorrow."

This was an inauspicious beginning. I had sent a fax a week before detailing our intentions, a gesture that seemed to have gone ignored. I felt a touch of anxiety about the trip, but for the rest of the day, Jill and I had little else to do except wander the dusty avenues of Ulaangom.

From the near-empty market and boarded up monastery to the stray dogs and numerous raptors circling overhead, death seemed to wait around every corner. At the end of town was a cracked Soviet-Mongolia friendship monument surrounded by broken glass and swirling rubbish. Jill and I stood in the shadow of the monument as the sun set to the west. Russia was somewhere in the distance; and along its borders the cattle thieves were lining up for their evening raids.

Bathishig, the portly assistant to the governor, met us the following morning and said the first order of business would be to procure travel permits from the army. Together we walked to the barracks, but I immediately started to doubt a favorable welcome when we saw through a locked gate two blindfolded Caucasian men (we assumed Russians), being led between buildings with their hands tied behind their back. All that seemed to be missing was a cigarette between their lips and a firing squad at 10 paces. I suddenly realized the locals might not take kindly to strangers in this time of "war."

Since we were not allowed inside the compound Bathishig headed into one of the buildings alone, only to return with disappointing news: the border and all towns near it were heavily patrolled, she said, and therefore off-limits to both locals and foreigners.

"How can we tell the world about your plight if we can't see it?" I asked, pleading my case. Bathishig gave us a puzzled look, perhaps wondering if anyone really did care. She shrugged her shoulders and wandered off to her apartment, leaving Jill and I alone.

As the hours passed, our hopes of attaining newsworthy information dwindled. I called Mr. Amarsanaa in Ulaanbaatar and he promised to get in touch with "his friends" at the army. Nothing came of it. Loitering around the Government House didn't help either. Pencil-tapping bureaucrats gave us unconcerned looks when we asked about the border situation. Only Norov seemed interested in our plight, and for good reason: Norov was the local Montsame correspondent, and therefore a co-worker. When we met he greeted me like a long-lost cousin and we vigorously shook hands and clapped each other's shoulder. Finally, we had someone on our side.

"We read your reports about the cattle rustlers," I said. "So we came to see for ourselves." Norov, who had reported news from this lonely outpost for 35 years, described the sordid details.

"The problems began ten years ago," he said as we dined to-gether at the hotel restaurant. "Before that, the border was open and we knew our neighbors. Tuvans and Mongolians grazed their livestock on both sides of the border. There was no chance to steal from each other.

"After 1990 the situation changed," he said with despondency. "The economy worsened and the border was closed. People became poor and desperate; they saw their chance to go across the border and steal livestock."

He explained that letters written by the affected nomads had been sent to Ulaanbaatar, urging lawmakers to open up the border again. "There is one part of Tuva where they speak Mongolian and some Mongolians can speak Tuvan; if they open the border they will be friends again."

Norov suggested that we visit a place called Davst, where most of the action had occurred. The town fascinated me, for both its name (*Davst* means "Salt") and its location between Uvs Lake and Russia—a sliver of land that might well be the end of the earth. This time we asked Norov to help us with the permits, but even his influ-ence was of no use. We were forbidden to visit Davst. The officials, however, did give us permission to visit Turgen, a nearby village that was home to herders who had their livestock stolen.

Jill and I were delighted—we'd finally made some headway.

Bathishig, keenly aware of our underlying desire to sneak away to the Russian border, acted as our guide, translator and monitor. She made a hurried phone call and a jeep materialized from the dust, ready to take us to Turgen. We squeezed inside the olive green vehicle and Bathishig provided curt instructions to the driver.

"Turgen," she demanded.

"Oros, *zugeer?*" I said to the driver ("And Russia, if it's convenient").

"Turgen!" said Batkhishig, folding her arms tightly across her bosom. "Oros, *nyet!*"

Staring blankly ahead, the mustachioed driver adjusted his golf cap, cranked the gears, and stepped on the gas. Turgen it was.

Our trip to Turgen didn't last long. We bounced along a potholed road for about 20 minutes; then swung south toward a quiet village sitting timidly under a wall of mountains. The mayor of Turgen was roused from his midday nap and instructed by Batkhishig to take us to a herder who had lost his livestock to the rustlers. The mayor obediently climbed into our jeep and pointed the way up the side of the mountain.

"*Tishee,*" he said, indicating the way to go. "Sambuugiin *ger.*"

The jeep sputtered its way uphill until finally pulling to a stop in front of a bow-legged figure holding a Russian spyglass. He had spotted us coming from a mile away, as had his wife, who was busy brewing the customary welcome tea.

Sambuu had lost all 26 of his horses to rustlers, forcing him to tend to his sheep on foot. Jill and I had thought all along that these people would be lusting Tuvan blood and we expected stories about how they dreamed of going to war. But Sambuu, like everyone else, was simply resigned to his fate.

"The horse thieves make me curse, but it is both the Mongolians and the Tuvans who steal livestock; none is worse than the other," Sambuu said, calmly slurping his tea as he listened to our probing questions. We asked if the cattle thieves would make him move.

"I can't," he said simply. "This is my homeland."

Sambuu was faced with the classic Catch 22. Moving was not an option, for better or worse this would always be his home. But he was not a thief or a fighter and had no intention of taking up the bandit lifestyle. There was nothing else to do but ride out the border battle. If the frontier guards could stop the movement of the rustlers, he hoped, his troubles would be over.

Jill and I were carefully escorted out of Turgen, given a token tour of a locally famous lake with sweeping mountain views, and then given a police escort straight back to Ulaangom. Batkhishig breathed a deep sigh of relief when we arrived back in front of the Government House. It had all been quite flustering for her, this break from her normal routine of bureaucracy and computer solitaire, but fulfilled her final duty by granting us permission to visit the local prison.

The Ulaangom jailhouse was a small mud-brick affair similar to the old Nebraska stockades. Security measures appeared meager. Indeed, the warden explained that in the past eight years, 130 people had escaped. Despite this, all had been found—there simply aren't enough good hiding places in Mongolia.

Of the 105 people being held in jail, 80 were being held for livestock theft. The warden allowed us to speak to a few. One Tuvan hunter had been arrested and sentenced to eight months in jail for straying over the border while tracking a wolf. Another was serving three years for his part in the heist of 37 horses.

"I don't know who stole those horses," he said bitterly. "Some people have stolen my livestock and *they* were never arrested!"

While Jill and I scribbled down notes, the others squinted at the convict, clearly not buying his story. But the next prisoner seemed to garner a hint of sympathy; he was a 22-year-old Tuvan who looked so much like a Mongol that we were taken aback by his thick Russian accent. Nachin was not a thief. He was arrested with his father and brother for trespassing in Mongolia while looking for their lost livestock. He received six months while his brother got a year and his father, 18 months. Barefoot, dirty and ragged, he was also frighteningly underweight and had the look of a war refugee—fatigued, sad, and powerless.

Jill and I were prepared to go through our normal round of questions, when he asked for permission to sing a song about the rivers of his lost homeland. With our microphones poised and my giant East German machine set to record, Nachin emitted a low hum and then a growl. Eerie tones flowed from his throat, then rose and fell unpredictably like the howl of a strong sea breeze. The sun-baked prison walls echoed the haunting sounds. Then he coughed and wheezed until the warden passed him a bowl of water.

"I used to be a great throat singer, a concert master, and I earned many awards," Nachin told us. "But when I was put in jail I had to sleep on a damp cement floor. I became sick, so I lost my voice; now I don't sing so well."

"How did you end up here?" we asked.

"Twelve cows were stolen from us," he began. "My mother was very sad when this happened and she cried. So my father, brother and I went looking for them and suddenly soldiers appeared and arrested us, they said we entered Mongolia illegally."

"While we were in court an old Mongolian man appeared and said he knew what had happened to the cows. He said he wanted to help us because he and my grandfather used to be friends when they were children—that was when there was no border. The people lived peacefully and there was no stealing. He told the court we were innocent but they charged us anyway. I never thought this would happen to my family," Nachin said solemnly.

He took another gulp of water, stood up and wandered off to join the other convicts, disappearing behind a cloud of swirling dust.

Nachin had been victimized by Mongolia's border fiasco as badly as any of the herders who had lost their horses. Enraged officials, both the army and the court system, were taking the matter personally, but it was innocent folk like Nachin and his family who were suffering. The only thing left to do for a great many locals was to get out. Unlike old Sambuu, hundreds of younger, less conservative herders were leaving Uvs for other provinces, trading their ancestral homelands for their personal safety.

Jill was leaving too. She was booked on a flight out the next day. We took a taxi the half mile to the airport and wandered out to the tarmac. As we waited a low drone could be heard in the distance, and after it the plane from Ulaanbaatar. The little aircraft skidded to a halt and out popped families and their cargo. As soon as the way was clear, Ulaanbaatar-bound passengers scrambled up the gangway and into the plane. Jill following fast on their heels, dragging her own luggage, plus extra bags belonging to Anna the ornithologist, who thought lightening her load might get her motorcycle moving faster. I watched as the little plane wheeled around on the dirt airstrip and buzzed away into the blue sky.

I wasn't quite ready to call it quits, and planned on traveling south into the mountains before heading back to Ulaanbaatar. But before leaving town, I'd need to write up a story for *The Messenger*. Batkhishig graciously lent me her computer for an hour.

I called the office, got Indra on the line, and asked her to leave some space on page seven for my story. She asked how my reports were coming along. I lied and told her everything was great, I'd send something in soon. The truth was that I had a bad case of writer's block. I didn't feel like all the material was there for a thriller. Not even a token shoot out. Perhaps I had just set my sights to high.

An hour later I was down at the jeep stand, looking for a ride out of town. I thought I'd head south, into Kazakh territory, where I hoped to do some hiking in the mountains. But while chewing the fat with the locals, I bumped into a driver named Tuvsanaa who said he was looking for passengers to take to Davst, the border post Norov had mentioned. He still had an empty seat and said I could come along. Knowing I really shouldn't be doing this, and feeling kind of good about it, I accepted.

With a touch of nervous adrenaline I slipped into the car and we rolled out of Ulaangom. Myancott, one of the passengers, asked why I was traveling in his direction. I told him about my assignment and he immediately warmed to me, lamenting that his animals were stolen too and that I ought to write about the bastards who had done it.

"Does the government do anything to help?" I asked as our jeep jangled north over dry prairie, toward Russia.

"The border patrol does nothing; they only sleep," he said, feigning a snooze. "They are like the Mafia, but the army has been here this summer and they are doing a good job." Between the army roadblocks and the Mafioso border guards, I was beginning to fear the potential cost of this mission. Still, Russia inched closer.

Tuvsanaa let out his passengers at their *gers* and we pressed forward along the winding road to an army roadblock. In the distance I could make out jeeps, soldiers and canvas tents. Realizing that I had trod into no-man's land, I attempted to hide my face under the bill of my baseball cap as we rolled past. The young conscript manning the gate was not fooled. He ordered us to pull over.

We stopped near a green mess tent where a second soldier sauntered out to examine our documents. I presented a letter from Montsame intended for just such a situation. The soldier looked at us, scrutinized the paper and mumbled something to Tuvsanaa who in turn shot me a look of suspicion.

"How we doin'?" I asked after the soldier disappeared into his tent.

"Bad," was all Tuvsanaa said, with a lowered head and gritted teeth.

An hour passed, really not much time in these parts, but long enough to make me ponder the fate of the two Russians that Jill and I had seen back in Ulaangom. A soldier finally returned, looked at me and showed no emotion as he spoke with the driver. He shook Tuvsanaa's hand, gave a little wave and stepped back. This was looking promising.

Then, much to my relief, Tuvsanaa started his jeep and headed back to the road. It looked like I was out of the woods and we'd be heading safely back to Ulaangom. But instead of turning south, Tuvsanaa turned north. I could scarcely believe my luck—they were letting me go to the border!

We had entered no-mans land; a broad sweep of tall grass that was devoid of *gers*. The entire area had been evacuated by the army as a way to create a buffer between the warring Tuvan and Mongol nomads. Over the rolling hills we went, until a wide valley opened before us. Tuvsanaa pointed directly ahead toward a long range and mountains.

"*Oros!*" (Russia!)

At last a gate on the border ended our journey. Tuvsanaa skidded to a halt near a collection of buildings under a guard tower. I got out of the jeep and surveyed the land; the sun was plunging into the western sky, igniting Tuva's wild mountains with a deep purple light. Here on the border between Mongolia and Tuva, under a huge domed sky, with Kazakhstan a mere mountain range away, I was literally in the heart of Asia.

A uniformed man with thick glasses and a peppery moustache strode briskly toward us. He did not look pleased. After formalities and some smooth talking from Tuvsanaa, we were reluctantly welcomed into the frontier post.

"The cattle rustlers," I asked. "When was the last time you've seen them?"

The guard looked at me with suspicion. He still could not fathom how I'd managed to get through the last check post. He looked at Tuvsanaa who nodded in approval, indicating that I was harmless.

"They come by night," the guard said, "from this side and that side."

He was pointing to the mountain passes on the far end of the valley.

"Sometimes we see them coming. Other times they slip by unnoticed. But the army is here now so it is harder for them to get through. It's more of a risk. They don't want to get shot at so they go to other places. We hear from other border posts that they are moving further south."

"Who are those two?" I asked, pointing to a pair of men on horseback, floating through the tall distant grass.

"Russian border guards. They are patrolling the area tonight."

The Russians moved slowly across the landscape, trotting toward their own guard house in the distance. I could see how easy it was for the rustlers to get across; it was a huge steppe landscape without roads, towns or fences. Four or five men would have no trouble moving a herd of stolen horses or cattle to the other side of the valley.

Ten years before this place would have been inhabited by Mongolian and Tuvan herders, peacefully grazing their animals together. They may have been cousins or friends or just acquaintances but they would not have been shooting each other. But the times have changed; with Mongolia asserting its independence from Moscow, a line had to be drawn in the dirt. They needed border posts with Mongolian flags and checkpoints to search for contraband. The territorial integrity of this born-again nation depended on it.

"It's getting late," the border guard announced, watching the sun set behind Russia. "You'd better go."

I agreed. Enough laws had been broken for one day, and I had no intention of returning to the Ulaangom jail. I nodded, got back in the jeep and Tuvsanaa took us home.

In the weeks ahead there were more moves to strengthen the border, but even this was not enough to stem the tide of stealthy cattle rustlers. The border troubles continued—one tragic incident saw the shooting death of a local man and his wife by five Tuvans who made off with their 68 horses. Jill and I had always referred to Uvs as Mongolia's "Wild West"—it's a title that neither the Tuvans nor the Mongolians appear willing to back down from anytime soon.

~ 10 ~

THE FALCON SCOOP

MONGOLIA IS THE SORT OF COUNTRY that breeds curiosity and invites eccentrics. It's as though only the bravest or most foolhardy could reach Outer Mongolia. Such adventurers appeared on my office threshold on a regular basis, eager to tell their story to the world. *The Mongol Messenger* seemed as good a place to start as any.

These uninvited guests found a home here because of the Mongolian people; their friendliness, naïveté and willing acceptance of others welcomed the outcasts of the outside world. Of course, the Mongol patience was not boundless and one man managed to strain it as far as he possibly could.

It all began during the summer of 1999, just a few days after I had returned from my western Mongolia mishaps. I was enjoying an espresso at Millie's Café when I spotted a man dressed in white from head to toe: white robes, white turban and white shoes. His whole attire was spotless—pure as fresh Mongolian snow. Behind his round spectacles peered limpid blue eyes above hollow cheeks. His frame was tall, lanky and slightly crooked. A stringy brown beard flowed down his face and chest, all the way to his trim waistline. He bore a striking resemblance to John Lennon, but I knew better: this could only be Alan Parrot.

He introduced himself to one and all as Alan "Parroh" but everyone called him Alan "Parrot." It was fitting: Parrot was an ornithologist, or rather a falcon trainer, and, as he enjoyed telling folks, one of the world's best. At the age of 18 he left the comfort of the United States to train falcons for the Shah of Iran. He loved to spin yarns about his days in sun-drenched white marble desert palaces of the Middle East and claimed to be on a first-name basis with every Islamic leader from Cairo to Tehran. Of course, in that neck of the world, he is known by his Sikh name, Hari Singh Khalsa.

I had never seen Parrot before in person, but I knew of him through his controversial run-in with the government in late 1997, just before my own arrival. The scandal had been widely reported in the papers. From what I gathered, Parrot, an American citizen, had been in Mongolia since 1995 pitching to the government his "plan to save the Mongolian falcon." The scheme, he had said, was a win-win situation for Mongolia, a sure-fire deal that could not fail, and if it did, he promised it would not cost the government a cent.

Parrot's plan was rather simple: take rare Saker falcons from the wild, train them to hunt, pack them off to the oil-rich leaders of the Gulf states on a six-month "rental agreement," then return the birds to Mongolia and release them into the wild.

He promised that each six-month term could earn $20,000 per falcon and the whole contract would net $8 million per year—the money to be split by the government and Parrot's company, the grandly titled Crème de la Crème.

Parrot's figures sounded absurd. Who, I wondered, would pay $20,000 to rent a falcon for six months, and why? Arab Sultans, Parrot explained, needed them for their hunting expeditions. He later showed me pictures of their hunting parties, which rode around the desert in all-terrain custom made Mercedes vehicles complete with automatic seat elevators that lifted the hunter out of his car.

During the expeditions, princes stayed in luxurious movable palaces: three-story Winnebagos for the super rich. Some princes took their falcons to Pakistan where they hunted the Lesser MacQueen's Bustard, whose cooked meat is considered an aphrodisiac. Apparently the best falcons had sold for up to a million dollars in the 1980s, when the market was at its peak.

The Crème de la Crème business plan included building a "falcon hospital" in Ulaanbaatar, where the falcons would receive top medical treatment upon their return from the ravages of hunting on the Arabian deserts. Parrot also wanted to train a whole team of Mongolian specialists in the art of falconry and falcon care.

As it turned out, the government of the time rejected Parrot's plan and created its own. The Saudis sent a jumbo jet to Mongolia in September 1997 and made off with a planeload of falcons at a fire-sale price. Parrot, now completely out of the loop, smelled a rat. He organized press conferences and decried to local journalists what he called "a massive smuggling operation organized by government officials." He went public saying that the Minister of Nature was in cahoots with the Arabs to send illegal numbers of falcons, while scooping up thousands of dollars in kickbacks.

The Minister of Nature launched a $100,000 anti-defamation suit. Parrot hired a Mongolian lawyer and was prepared to fight it out in court, backed up by a mountain of evidence. In the end, after Enkhsaikhan's government resigned, the Minister dropped the case, claiming it was no longer relevant since he had left office.

Since animal rights had never been a major issue for Mongolia, the scandal became a mere footnote to Mongolia's political corruption. I had thought it to be over, until I saw Mr. Parrot at Millie's Café.

A few hours later I found myself at the cushy penthouse of a yellow apartment block down by the train station. Parrot's home was large and comfortable. A brief tour, first of the kitchen, displayed all sorts of tasty imported nibbles stacked neatly in the cupboard. The nightstand in his dimly-lit bedroom was filled with mystical little tokens of the Sikh and Arab world, including a drawing of an elevated guru with crossed legs and a thick white beard. Shown into the living room, I found a workbench with a mound of *dels* next to a sewing machine.

I placed a hand on the *dels,* rubbing the soft felt between my fingers. "I have a girl make them," Parrot said, "I sell them to American Sikhs; just a pet project."

"Ahh haaa."

"And this," he said, drawing my attention away from the dels and toward a skinny Indian fellow on the couch, "is Jagdeesh; one of my business partners. We are going to start a chain of kebab restaurants together."

I recognized Jagdeesh as the former manager of Hazara restaurant. He placed an agitated hand into mine and gave a feeble shake and a wobble of the head.

Shish kebabs, *dels* and falcons. One could not doubt Parrot's entrepreneurial spirit. I indicated my positive impression with a nod and raised my eyebrows.

"Seems like you run a tight ship. Nice place too," I said, craning my neck around the room.

"I have a maid clean it. Last week she used my imported shampoo to scrub the floor," said Parrot, visibly irritated at losing one of a Sikh's most prized possessions.

I flipped on my recorder and Parrot spent the next two hours talking with hardly a breath taken. He showed me the evidence he had collected over the years—evidence, he said, that would land half the government in jail. Dangerous stuff, I thought. One was an actual videotape of the Saudi jet landing in Ulaanbaatar for its falcons. He also showed me a rather suspicious statement from the Trade and Development Bank. It proved that on August 1, 1998 over $650,000 had been wire-transferred to one Abdulatif Al-Manea. By December

3 of that year, only $48 remained in the account. Al-Manea had come to pay the Ministry of Nature $90,000 as part of an official contract to buy falcons, but ended up spending six times that. Half a million dollars could have bought Al-Manea a heck of a lot of cashmere sweaters for his friends back home, or as Parrot suspected, the money went straight to the minister and his cronies.

"Oh, by the way," Parrot added, "last January, twenty thugs entered my apartment, stole my passport and smashed a kitchen sink over my chest. I was knocked unconscious and woke up the next day in my own excrement."

He had been a victim of the "falcon mafia," as he called them. He remained paralyzed for nearly three weeks and lost two inches in height due to the crushing of two vertebrae. The incident, he noted, had caused his slightly hunched-over shape.

By the end of it all, I was left exhausted and with more questions than answers. The interview covered international crime racketeers, underground falcon Mafiosos, heavy Russian-built sinks, official corruption directed by the highest of authorities and, or course, Alan Parrot. I found it a bit difficult to digest in one sitting. What was most curious was the way he was handling it all. He was on his own—self-financing the whole investigation with his personal fortune earned through a family oil business. He was convinced that if he were to win this war it would be with the help of the media. Indeed he had become somewhat of a darling—appearing in several international newspapers, most recently the *Wall Street Journal*. PR work though it was, Parrot's determination had forced the government to cancel the earlier contract with the Saudis but now he claimed the exports were going further underground. A new and nasty chapter was about to unfold and, he assured me, it was the scoop of the century.

I didn't write anything about Parrot at first; his accusations and controversial reputation were intimidating. Instead, I spoke with people on both sides. I contacted the local wildlife conservationists, the US Embassy, the Ministry of Nature, and the boundless worldwide contacts that Parrot had provided for me. I was warned by several people not to go near the story. "Don't give him your phone number," advised Jill, who had covered the Parrot story for the *UB Post* a year earlier. More often than not, their misgivings had less to do with the plight of the falcons, than about Parrot himself, whose "mercurial personality," as one put it, had strained past relationships.

It was Mongolia's tightly knit band of Western biologists who had the strongest opinions on the matter, but none wanted to be mentioned by name. The falcon issue had become taboo and the biologists distanced themselves from Parrot, not wanting to be dragged into a quandary that might ostracize themselves from the Ministry of Nature. Some of his ideas, however, did carry merit, they said; and everyone wanted to improve the falcon situation.

The Ministry of Nature said the problem, as usual, boiled down to money. One official there had told me the difficulties of maintaining environmental sustainability. "People need money so they steal the resources. They cut down trees, dig mines and shoot animals and we can't afford to hire rangers who can stop it," the official said. For the Ministry, the answer was simple: sell the wildlife before the poachers do.

"We must sell the resource. Foreigners will pay a lot to hunt animals or buy falcons. Every country needs money. If we make money we can put it back into protection."

A good idea in theory, though in practice, the biologists admitted, none of the profits made it to their intended destination. Accountability was unfamiliar terminology in Mongolia.

One reason why Parrot and the other biologists had such a hard time implementing their methodology was that they wrongly assumed that the media, the politicians, or average Mongolians actually cared about what they said. It would take years, if not a whole generation, for the public at large to rally for an obscure cause like falcon preservation. The Mongolian mindset is more geared to shooting wild animals than saving them. Parrot's second mistake was assuming that blowing the whistle would bring him admiration and adulation. Perhaps it would have if he had been vague in his accusations, but pointing a finger directly at those involved was one of the great no-nos in Mongolia. Ulaanbaatar is a small town where family ties run far and deep. By picking a fight with the Minister of Environment, rather than with the system as a whole, he probably alienated a third of the city.

While Parrot was unable to grasp these localized concepts, he encountered obstacles in international circles, specifically in one Nick Fox, an English falcon breeder who had scooped Parrot's earlier attempts to set up a falcon management plan in Kazakhstan. Now he was behind Mongolia's current falcon research program. According to the project, Fox's team would survey and monitor wild Sakers and then do biological studies on habitat use, pesticides and migration.

According to Parrot, Fox was also behind the new falcon sales and had a theory about "secret" falcon breeding farms near Ulaanbaatar where falcon fledglings were kept before being sent out by road to Russia. He was constantly searching for these farms—tracking suspicious cars around town (sometimes attaching radio devices to their rear bumper a la James Bond), scouring the nearby hills and abandoned buildings. One day, I went along with him into the hills in a hired taxi as he attempted to track down the smugglers.

"This will be the biggest bust ever," Parrot said, recalling his role in a 1984 sting called Operation Falcon, when 300 falcon smugglers were arrested simultaneously worldwide. Parrot alleged that what he was doing in Mongolia was bigger than Operation Falcon. "It's going to make that look like child's play," he said, and added one of his many quotable lines: "These birds are feathered cocaine."

I went across Sükhbaatar Square one day to visit Parrot's opponents at the Ministry of Nature. The spokesman I met described the falcon exports planned for October. At the moment, he said, a team was working in the desert to catch the birds at an undisclosed location that was off limits to reporters.

The official explained that under the new deal with Kuwait, each falcon was being "given for free." There was however a "tax" of $2,760. This overly technical 'tax' was going directly to the state fund (but not to falcon conservation). After the fiasco of two years ago, no private business was being allowed to sell the birds. It wasn't exactly clear why they were being given away for free. But in the coming months we saw Kuwait start funding various "road projects" in Mongolia, as well as an overpriced $33 million hydro-electric dam in the Gobi Desert. When I heard about such projects, I was reminded of the fleet of $40,000 off-road vehicles parked outside the offices of the Democratic Party headquarters, where employees made $1200 per year.

The spokesman became irritated when I brought up Parrot's charges of corruption, dismissing them outright. He was annoyed further when I asked about the price of the falcons, stammering that foreigners—journalist or otherwise—had no right to question a decision made by the Mongolian government.

Even more irksome was the mention of David Ellis, the US researcher who had worked with Parrot. "I know Dr. David Ellis," said the female translator before the spokesman could answer. "I answered all his stupid letters!" I carefully scribbled this into my notepad. "David Ellis came here without any permission. He just came here as a tourist. He did all his work illegally!" she said in fits and starts. (I was later given copies of Ellis' letters, which revealed spine-tingling details of corruption, mismanagement and negligence). The translator went on. "We don't need David Ellis' project because we work with Dr. Nick Fox. His agency says we have plenty of falcons in Mongolia. They live peacefully." Peacefully, that is, until some Syrian stuffs them into his suitcase and smuggles them out of the country.

The spokesman was on full defensive mode and tension in the

air was thick. I tried cooling things down by changing gears; asking about his job duties and such. But by now the situation was hopeless and through gritted teeth he declared the interview over.

My research finished, I shuffled back to Montsame and typed up my article. Appreciating the sensitive nature of the matter, I took an academic approach, doling out facts and figures, dropping in the odd quote and paraphrasing a letter written by David Ellis. The letter really said it all—a veritable shopping list of alleged crimes and other wrongdoings committed by the Ministry that portrayed the officials as modern day pirates. Accusations of corruption, theft and negligence were probably inevitable for a ministry managing grants from wealthy donors in the Middle East.

The article won me no friends at the Ministry of Nature. It also made them conclude I was in cahoots with Parrot. One official, speaking to me in his office, insisted on knowing how much bribe money I had taken from him to publish such an article.

While Parrot was hardly treated well in the story either, he felt that the front page exposure had bolstered his cause, and started calling at all hours, always with "fresh developments" about the scandal. "They are moving shipments of falcons. I am going to the airport," he would say over the phone, often in the wee hours of the morning. Or "They are after me, they want me dead." Parrot called them the "The falcon mafia"; shadowy men sneaking about town, moving their feathered cargo and deposing rivals by sinister means. "I can't say everything; my phone is bugged. We should meet."

Parrot liked to rendezvous in different parts of town. He had a hired driver who ferried him to our designated meeting locations; at cafés, behind buildings, and underneath lampposts in the dead of night. It was always in secret. Passing documents, moving about, making plans. "I am going to win," he promised. "It's my mantra; I am going to have it tattooed on my body."

Our relationship stood on shaky legs. I was fascinated by his stories and undercover activities, but we had our periodic differences, particularly when I brought up sensitive issues. When I asked Parrot about a rumor that he had once smuggled falcons himself he went ballistic:

"Adyasuren started that lie! That fucking yak herder!" he screamed over the phone, referring to the Minister who had tried to sue him. I later learned that my question caused the destruction of Parrot's telephone—smashed to little plastic bits against his kitchen wall. In his defense, he warned me that I might become a target since I had joined him on some of his periodic missions around town.

"They know who you are, they are going to kick me out of the country and you are next," he would threaten. "You had better report everything you know now."

Such thoughts instilled a sense of paranoia in me and when I went home at night I'd look over my shoulder in fear of the "falcon mafia." Double locking the door, I made sure that all copies of my falcon-related notes and "evidence" were carefully stashed in a hidden place lest they be wrested from me. Shortly thereafter, and without prompting, two foreign friends separately offered their apartments as a safe house.

Not long after the article was published, Parrot got himself into a bit of a quagmire. He went to the Ministry of Nature seeking a license to capture 40 falcons at the quoted price of $2760. He said he would take the flock to the Middle East and sell each bird for $20,000, just to prove that Mongolia was being "ripped off." The minister, however, was not going to play the game. He told Parrot that he would sell him the falcons at a cost of $20,000 each, if that's what he thought they were worth. The offer was not appreciated and Parrot went back a few days later to request another meeting. The secretary, however, said the minister was "too busy to talk" and refused to let Parrot inside the minister's office. Parrot's feathers were ruffled. In a moment of rage he barged in, spat on the minister's beige carpet and called him the leader of the "falcon mafia," combined other colorful obscenities.

This seemed an unlikely path to signing a contract. Five days later Parrot was arrested and spent a day in jail on charges of "showing disrespect to a government official." He was released within a day, but getting tossed in prison only fired Parrot's imagination and he ranted about human rights abuses and other illegalities. He said North Carolina's right-wing senator Jesse Helms was writing letters on his behalf. A Sikh falcon trainer in Mongolia and an ultraconservative Southern xenophobe made strange bedfellows. Helms, however, was perhaps just trying to score political capital by criticizing the resident US ambassador, a Democratic appointee, who had not thrown much support behind Parrot's crusade. But Helms' mere involvement indicated how far Parrot was taking his case. Indeed, Parrot also had enlisted the aid of an attorney and a retired US congressman. He could maintain a certain show of confidence with this support and his refusal to apologize made him appear even more valiant, or intimidating if you happened to be an official at the Ministry of Nature.

"Why should I apologize? They are the ones who are smuggling the falcons, hiding the export numbers, robbing Mongolia!" he ranted. Jail time only gave him another angle against the government. "I've got Jesse Helms on my side! The US State Department has tagged Mongolia for human rights abuses! The whole purpose of this exercise is to kick me out of the country!"

Meanwhile, my article continued to capture attention, and most of the grumbling was in my own news agency. Mr. Amarsanaa called me into his office and ordered me to "never write about falcons again." He had apparently gotten a call from the Ministry of Nature dictating just that. Indra, Ariunbold, Undrakh and the others were ashamed that we had to print letters of objection from the ministry, and regretted that I had been anything less than ecstatic about the performance of their elected officials.

Other media outlets around town continued to ignore Parrot, but a few found him newsworthy. *Huumus (People)* newspaper featured him on their front page. The lead photo showed him on a mountaintop at dusk, his white robes floating in the breeze like those of a Greek god. One of the journalists from Eagle TV pigeonholed Parrot and patiently examined his piles of evidence. The interview ended in failure, however, when the journalist offered to sell him a contraband falcon after the cameras had been turned off. This was rather common, Parrot said. After five years in the country and dozens of press conferences, nobody understood that his entire mission was to *stop* the sale of falcons. A major part of the problem, I learned, was that because he wore a turban and robe, most people just assumed he was an Arab looking for a cut-rate deal.

"Sometimes I feel like a little boy trapped at the bottom of a well, yelling for help that won't come," he told me. Even so, Parrot did quite a job of ostracizing anyone who could have been of use to him, including environmentalists, politicians and journalists. Anna the ornithologist, the girl Jill and I had met in Uvs, was the most recent casualty. We had met up again in Ulaanbaatar and I had suggested to Anna that a meeting with Parrot might help her research. Anna reappeared at my office a couple of hours later looking completely frazzled, in a state of shock. "That man is the devil," she whispered with glazed eyes. "Really, I think he is Satan."

By early October the falcon exports were in full swing, as was the smuggling. We only found out that the exports had started through Parrot's airport informant. Unlike the frenzy in 1997, the media was not invited to see the birds fly away this year. A plane owned by Turkmenistan's President Niyazov left with 21 falcons on October 6. On the same day the police arrested two Syrians trying to smuggle eight contraband falcons on a Mongolian Airlines flight. There was speculation that another Arab managed to get away on the same flight with 15 falcons.

"The Syrians didn't pay the right people," said Parrot's Iraqi friend, a diplomat living in Ulaanbaatar and on the run from

Sadaam Hussein. The diplomat, who had himself been caught with falcons in his home, said Arabs were making off with hundreds of the birds that autumn. "It's common that falcons are smuggled out of the country, under everybody's nose," he said.

Frankly, you couldn't blame the smugglers for trying. The fine for getting caught with a falcon was only $25; absolutely nothing compared to the profit they could realize. Even if they were caught, there was no jail time. The smuggler could simply return to the desert to gather more falcons.

One weekend in October I mounted a small expedition to the desert to look for the smugglers at work. The plan was to find the Arabs, photograph and videotape them taking the birds. If they had more than the allotted numbers as Parrot alleged, or were mistreating the animals in any way, it would be the smoking gun needed to prove wrongdoing. Parrot thought this a good idea, and sent his translator Ochka and his burly Kazakh bodyguard Baka along for the ride.

We were a motley crew: an American, a Mongolian and a Kazakh, driving round the Gobi Desert in search of Arab falcon smugglers. The idea was thrilling, yet our mission foundered when each leg of our journey failed to reveal significant evidence. After speaking with local officials we eventually found the remains of the Arab camp; a nearby nomad told us we had missed them by just a few days. The site was a jumble of garbage and dead pigeons (falcon bait). Rather irresponsible of them to leave these behind, I thought, particularly since an official from the ministry was with them. What we were really looking for was piles of dead male falcons; Parrot said these are sometimes used to lure the prized females into traps. But we had no luck in finding any proof of wrongdoing, and all I managed to catch was a cold.

A similar stroke of bad timing occurred a couple of weeks later. Parrot's informant at the Ulaanbaatar Hotel (he had various informants about town on his payroll) called to say that he had seen suspicious boxes being carried up to a room occupied by Arab businessmen. The boxes had holes in them and rustling noises emanated from inside. Suspicious indeed. It was 6am when Parrot came banging on my door to give me this breaking news summary. I hauled myself out of my apartment and we soon had in our company a Member of Parliament and a policeman. Forcing our way into the room an hour later, we found a sleepy Arab and his translator, a young bearded Mongol, but no falcons. Flapping his arms and whistling, the grizzled old Arab mocked Parrot for his tardiness. "Fly away, already fly away," he said with a toothless chuckle.

Parrot refused to give up. At the end of November he traveled to Mörön in Khövsgöl Aimag with his bodyguard and translator to meet with local officials, trying to convince them to jump on board the good ship Crème de la Crème. He typed up a press release upon his return home, though I found much of it too biased and opinionated to be published in *The Messenger*. A couple of quotes: "At the airport I expected to see a welcome sign reading, 'Proud to be a Moron!' commemorating the ethnic identity Mongolians are so keen to establish." And his observations of Buddhism: "We heard rhythmic drumming close by. Inspecting the origin of the sound we learned there is a Buddhist Monastery engaged in ceremonies that are genuine. We filmed the stuff going on inside. There were no farm animals involved."

Parrot claimed victory because he was able to rally the officials (Morons he called them) behind his project. Unfortunately they never made good on their promise: when he arrived at the airport in Ulaanbaatar, an official from the ministry apparently offered to sell him a contraband falcon. "I wonder what new torturous chapter would unfold in my life that I now consider as distinctly abnormal," Parrot wrote in an e-mail.

Following Parrot's return I interviewed him for a radio report. A short, stocky fellow with boyish looks and a Russian accent an-

A ger with a view: Bayan Olgii Aimag

Kazakh children, Bayan Olgii aimag

An elderly Kazakh woman fries bread in her home

*A pair of Buriat youngsters dressed in their finest
on the opening day of the Altargana Naadam*

The Altargana Buriat Festival, Dashbalbar Soum, Choibalsan Aimag

Two Buriats greet each other enthusiastically
at the Altargana Buriat festival.

Buriat elder, Altargana Buriat festival

Hundreds of horsemen approach the starting line for the big race.

Young jockeys pose for a photo before the Naadam horse race.

Two horse riders greet me in eastern Mongolia.

A group of kids ride the range in eastern Mongolia.

The first public appearance in Mongolia of the Ninth Bogd Lama

A trio of monks of different sizes congregates outside their monastery in Choisbalsan.

Eric and the Candy Man

Nomad family transporting their goods on camel back

Camels are often used by nomads to move their homes.

A rainbow hangs over Sukhbaatar Square.

A lone ranger on Sukhbaatar Square

*Democrats rallly for political reform
outside the Lenin Museum, Ulaanbaatar.*

Left: Turkic-era anthropomorphic figure, probably erected in honor of a chief. Sukhbaatar Aimag.

Below: Statue of Chingis Khan at Chingis Khan "Mausoleum," Ejim Horo, Inner Mongolia, China

Right: This statue of Stalin once stood in front of the national library until it was removed in 1990 and discarded in a field. An entrepreneur recently rescued it and placed it in his bar.

Below: Culture clash: Lenin peers over the roof of a Mongol ger.

Montsame Christmas party. Left to right:
Indra, Amarbat, Undrakh, Michael Kohn, Bayarmaa, Narantuya

Below:
Ariunbold
(Editor-in-Chief)

Above: Indra (reporter) and
Amarbat (administration)

swered the door; this was Taleep, Parrot's second bodyguard. He led me inside and I found Parrot lolling on his couch. He pointed up above the window and led my eyes to the edge of the curtain rod, upon which rested a tiny bird, a fledgling Saker falcon. At last, after so much talk of falcons, I had finally found one. The bird, he said, had been injured, and he was nursing it back to health.

As I marveled at its grace, and the fact that it was living in Parrot's apartment, a knock came at the door. One of the bodyguards answered it and led inside three young Russian women; their good looks sadly buried under layers of heavy make-up. Taleep and Baka invited them into the kitchen for beers. One of the girls, differentiated from the others by an eyebrow ring, said they were dancers from Ulan Ude, a city in Siberia. They said they had come to Ulaanbaatar for work. As I tossed the empty Tiger beer can in the trash, one of the bodyguards called me out to the hallway and ushered me toward the door. With a thrust of his hips he informed me that the dancers had found an alternative source of income, for which they had been hired that evening. Our manly banter died down quickly and the door was soon shut behind me.

* * *

Parrot continued his fight as the autumn turned to winter, but his days were numbered. His visa would expire soon and it seemed like his adversaries were simply stalling until he had to leave the country. Parrot knew this and told me that he was barred from receiving a visa extension. Meanwhile, the Chinese Embassy was not going to give him a visa either. He was trapped in Mongolia, he told me, there was no way out.

"This is the final showdown," Parrot announced, and he organized a press conference.

This time he brought all his evidence. Piles of papers and a stack of mini-CDs littered the table. He played one of the disks for the press pool—it was a secret recording of a ministry official trying to sell him contraband falcons. A dozen microphones swirled around him as the journalists leaned close to the disk player. They gasped when the official made his illegal offer.

"How many falcons do you want?" the official asked on the recording; he then proceeded to explain the prices ranging from $12,000 to $15,000. The official recounted the sale of 50 falcons for a total of $550,000, or $11,000 each. As the journalists listened, Parrot just leaned back and basked in the glow of the media attention.

The journalists reported Parrot's recent revelations, but still the falconer was no further along. Any public interest in the matter had long since evaporated. In an interview with the media afterwards, the official caught offering a bribe cynically denied the charge, which somehow absolved him of the crime, and no investigation into the matter was conducted.

The snow on the dark streets of Ulaanbaatar had always imparted a sense of peace. This winter, however, Parrot's late-night phone calls put me on edge. One night he called me from his cell phone. He said he couldn't go home because the police were searching for him. There was a palpable sense of anticipation in his voice. "I am being deported," he said. "I'll go to the ministry tomorrow for my final chance. Our supporters in Parliament and elsewhere are coming on strong, while our adversaries are trying to outwit us by kicking me out of the country. This is a wonderful contest of wits and vigor—better than any chess game!"

This was not without precedent. In 1925 Roy Chapman Andrews learned that his expedition had been banned from operating in Mongolia. The government accused him of mapping military installations, carrying illegal weapons, digging in prohibited zones and "threatening to kill anyone who hindered his research." Although the accusations were later proven false, the political climate prevented Andrews from continuing his work in Mongolia. Parrot was heading for the same fate.

I was in Millie's Café the next day and met an American lawyer living in Ulaanbaatar who had recently lunched with Parrot. "He was bragging about how his bodyguards cost him $20,000; to me they looked like B-movie thugs," the lawyer said. "I am skeptical of his stories but I wonder why the ministry would care so much about some expat freak. There must be something behind it."

Parrot frequented Millie's, which he called "the Mexican restaurant" because its Latin influenced menu. Daniel, the Cuban chef, admitted his fear that one day someone might come in and shoot Parrot, and perhaps shoot him too for being a witness to the crime. Parrot went to the café to chat with other expats about his relationship with the US Embassy, which he loathed passionately. The falconer had been removed from the embassy on different occasions after erupting into shouting matches with the personnel there. Likewise, the ambassador and his staff had elected not to answer his incessant phone calls.

That night Parrot called to say his phone line was getting cut off and one of his Yahoo! e-mail accounts had been mysteriously deleted. We examined how he had been cheated by the World Wide Web and later discussed a recent report given by the working group investigating the falcon issue. It stated that Parrot's assistance was no longer needed; one MP suggested he be deported immediately. Parrot was disheartened that the report appeared in *The Messenger* and suggested that I balance the story with one about his evidence of wrongdoing and allegations against the ministry. A siege of accusatory remarks ensued from his end, largely regarding my inability to spin the ball in his direction. The tirade was not unusual, though it would be his last. Parrot's time had all but run out.

His fight for a visa failed for the final time and he could do nothing else but leave the country. There was an article summarizing the falcon controversy in the Mongolian Airlines in-flight magazine. "The Mongolian people neither support Alan Parrot nor do they abuse him," observed the author.

As for the falcons, they still soar in the breeze and are occasionally found atop telephone poles strung across the steppes. Every autumn, when the falcons are most abundant in Mongolia, the smuggling begins in earnest. They usually leave in carry-on luggage aboard MIAT flights. I can only assume that airport security and immigration officials have become very wealthy.

In the summer of 2004, while driving around eastern Mongolia, I finally did discover a camp of Arab falcon hunters. They said they were having trouble finding enough falcons to meet their quota, and cold weather was approaching.

"Next year," they said, looking at each other. "Next year there will be more."

Postscript: In 2005, the New York-based Wildlife Conservation Society (WCS), announced that populations of endangered animals—marmots, argali sheep, antelope, red deer, bears, Asiatic wild asses and wolves—have plummeted by 50 to 90 percent over the past 15 years. WCS says that nearly all of Mongolia's annual $100 million revenue earned from wildlife trade is illegal. In the words of one noted biologist, Mongolia's wildlife is facing an "extraordinary and unnoticed extinction crisis."

Meanwhile, Alan Parrot never returned to Mongolia. Despite being on good terms with Prime Minister Enkhbayar; the ban on his re-entering the country stood firm. (This good relationship quickly soured when Enkhbayar dropped contact with Parrot; he is now featured on Parrot's website as one of the most wanted criminals in the world of falcon smuggling). There was the occasional mysterious rumor of Parrot's whereabouts, one being that he had died or been killed. But the occasional e-mail that he still sends me suggests otherwise.

A GOD KING RETURNS

I WAS SIPPING WINE AT A FRIEND'S APARTMENT one evening when a young, French anthropologist named Laetitia came bursting in with a news flash.

"The Bogd Khan has come to Mongolia!" she blurted out like a giddy school girl. It was a disorienting statement, but coming from Laetitia, not entirely surprising. She was doing her dissertation on Shamanism in Mongolia and part of her research meant hanging around with Ulaanbaatar's clan of Buddhist monks. If anyone would know about pending visits by Buddhist God-Kings, it would be Laetitia. Still, I couldn't help but be skeptical.

"Bogd Khan? Hasn't he been dead for most of this century?"

"C'mon man. Open your mind a little! I am not talking about the *Eighth* Bogd. This is the *Ninth* Bogd Khan! He was found in Tibet years ago and now lives in India with the Dalai Lama."

Laetitia beamed as she revealed that this ninth Bogd Khan was going to appear at Gandan Monastery the next day. I couldn't quite believe my ears, particularly since we had seen off the President of China just a few hours before. Jiang Zemin had spent the past two days touring factories, delivering speeches and attending a mini Naadam festival. Buddhist God-Kings and Chinese Presidents have never been a great mix and I started to wonder about the ramifications of such a magnificent bureaucratic blunder.

I was skeptical from the start, but who knew? Maybe there really was a reincarnated Bogd Khan, plucked out of a Tibetan village and secretly trained in the darkened recesses of an old monastery in far away Lhasa. Certainly he would never have been brought to Mongolia during the Great Purge of the 1930s. Perhaps as Laetitia had suggested this ninth Bogd survived the red tide of communism and disappeared to India. There were plenty of questions, but I was sure that any answers, no matter how dubious, would be front page news.

Gandan was bursting with Buddhists the next morning, each of them held in great anticipation at seeing the mystery God-King. We waited, and wilted, under the hot summer sun until the crimson gates of the main temple finally swung open, allowing a retinue of silk-robed monks to part the crowd. The faithful jostled for a better look as trumpeters heralded the appearance of a cloaked figure. Craning our necks for a better look, we finally saw him. Sixty-eight years of age, the ninth Bogd Khan had finally made it to Mongolia.

He had a hard, square face, smooth brown skin, turned-down lips and engaging eyes, just like the portrait of the eighth Bogd I had seen many times before. The resemblance was uncanny.

The sudden appearance of this new Bogd, whose hairless pate glowed as brightly as his yellow silk robes, was enough to drive the crowd into the kind of frenzy usually reserved for rock stars. Desperately trying to touch the Bogd, the onlookers scrambled forward, only to be driven back by an army of whip-wielding monks. The God-King had a little trouble handling his sudden fame, but with the help of the police he managed to duck into another barricaded temple.

What an unreal and bizarre sight, I thought. A few political rallies aside, I had never seen Mongolians so stirred up. But here they were trampling each other to touch the robes of a monk they had never seen before. It was as if the 75-year absence of the Bogd Khan had built up a powder keg reaction.

While snapping photos of the monks and interviewing the onlookers, I ran into an old friend of mine, Batbold. A journalist at *The Mongol Messenger* before my time, Batbold was a hard core Buddhist working for the resurrection of the faith in Mongolia. An interesting personality, he exuded a constant *joie de vivre,* taking nothing seriously and bursting out in laughter at his own jokes. Yet I managed to catch Batbold in a rare moment of seriousness, the Bogd's sudden appearance having a stunning effect.

Batbold, who spoke flawless English, explained how for the past decade the Bogd Khan had been living in Dharamsala, a British colonial town in northern India that is now home to the Tibetan Government-in-exile. He had never been to Mongolia before, although he had submitted many requests to visit the country since the fall of communism.

"Where did he live before Dharamsala? When did he escape from Tibet?" I asked.

"I have no idea," said Batbold, letting off a grin. "Really, I don't. Maybe Tibet. Maybe India. Nobody seems to know a thing."

Batbold always knew about the latest scandals, cover-ups and information leaks coming out of the monasteries. How was he in the dark about this episode?

"All I know is that the Dalai Lama found him in 1990 and that's it."

"Okay, then why all the secrecy? I only heard about this last night from a friend."

"Well, the Chinese President was here yesterday. You know how it is. The Chinese would have gone crazy if the Bogd Khan was waltzing around town in front of Jiang Zemin," said Batbold, returning to his old self and now giggling uncontrollably at the thought.

But Mongolia's foreign policy with China was not all that was at stake. Actually, Batbold explained, the Bogd Khan had never been welcomed by the government of Mongolia and had never received an invitation to visit the country. The Bogd Khan, it seemed, had forgone protocol and slipped in the country on an ordinary tourist visa, a fact that would have dimmed any prospects for red carpet treatment at the airport.

As Batbold and I discussed the ramifications of these events, the crowd of Buddhists burst into a frenzy at the sight of a black Lincoln limousine. There were rumblings through the crowd that this must be the "God's Chariot." In their excitement, they descended upon the car, believing that touching it would bring them good luck. This was not the case. The driver had no intention of pausing before he reached the temple. This resulted in a few minor casualties as the Buddhists were bowled over to the pavement. When the car did stop, red-robed security monks surrounded it and escorted the Bogd Khan up the steps of a temple to a specially built platform and throne.

Then, as if on cue, a storm cloud suddenly came from no where, wafted over the temple and burst open. The heat had been oppressive over the past week—and Mongolians do not function well in the heat—so the rain was a magnificent relief. Naturally, everyone believed that the Bogd himself had brought the thunderstorm to cool them off.

"It's a gift from the Gods!" wailed one lady as sighs of relief fell over the crowd.

I must admit, the storm cloud made for one hell of an entrance. The Bogd took the moment of hushed silence to begin his sermon.

"I have wanted to come to Mongolia since 1990 and today my dream came true," he said, allowing time for a monk to translate his words from Tibetan to Mongolian. "I'm glad to see so many believers and I will meet you again but when that time comes, please do not kick and beat each other to see me."

"Now I would like to lead you in prayer," the Bogd continued.

"This is a prayer of peace so everyone deep in your heart should dream of attaining enlightenment and doing saintly things. Be pure in your heart and you will bring happiness to yourself and others," he said in such a hoarse voice that he sounded out of breath.

The audience was hanging on his every word and it was amazing to see religious fervor in Mongolia. Until now, most people I had met claimed atheism as their true belief, or were a recently converted Christian. Some people, particularly the elderly, were fond of Buddhism but little was known about the religion; the result of a long hiatus caused by communism. I wondered what this visit by the Bogd meant for Mongolia. Would it spark a religious revival? I envisioned hordes of Buddhist revivalists descending on Gandan once word got out. But then again, why had the government been preventing his arrival for so long? Were the young ministers afraid of a new monarchy or was it a fear of incurring the wrath of China?

The Bogd Khan had some big boots to fill. Fondness for the line of Bogd Lamas (Jebtzun Damba in Tibetan) was a sentiment that ran back several centuries.

The first incarnation, Zanabazar (1635-1723), was a revolutionary figure who built monasteries and invented the Soyombo script (an alphabet used to translate Tibetan textbooks into Mongolian). More than anything else he was a master craftsman—his artwork is still preserved inside the Ulaanbaatar museum named after him.

When the Manchu Empire collapsed in 1911, it was the eighth Bogd Khan who declared Mongolia an independent country. He was installed as the head of the government and proclaimed "the champion of religion, the harbinger of happiness to the masses, the ruler of Mongolia elevated by the Multitudes, the Theocrat, Sun blessed, long-living Bogd Khan."

Foreign explorers who traveled in Mongolia in the early 20th century chronicled the life of the eccentric Eighth Bogd. Andrews, for one, described how he enjoyed playing practical jokes on his ministers and subjects. One of his favorite gags was to shock them with a wire attached to the battery of his Ford motorcar. Andrews also described how the commoners received his benediction.

"A great crowd of Mongols had gathered near the palace and at last a long rope was let out from one of the buildings. Kneeling, the Mongols reverently touched the rope, which was gently waggled from the other end, supposedly by the Hutukhtu (Bogd Khan). A barbaric monotone of chanted prayers arose from the kneeling supplicants . . . The Mongols rode away, silent with awe at having been blessed by the Living God."

Dr. Ferdinand Ossendowski, another visitor to old Urga, described the Eighth Bogd in his book *Beasts, Men and Gods* as "a stout old man with a heavy shaven face resembling those of the Cardinals of Rome. He was dressed in a yellow silken Mongolian coat with a black binding. The eyes of the blind man stood widely open. Fear and amazement were pictured in them."

Ossendowski, himself a Polish refugee fleeing the Bolsheviks, met the Eighth Bogd several times, calling him "clever, penetrating and energetic." Because of the Bogd's blindness, explains Ossendowski, the great temple at Gandan Monastery was built in hopes that its dedication would restore his sight.

"The deepest esteem and religious faithfulness surround the blind Pontiff. Before him all fall on their faces... Everything about him is dark, full of Oriental antiquity. The drunken blind man, listening to the banal arias of the gramophone or shaking his servants with an electric current from his dynamo, the ferocious old fellow poisoning his political enemies, the Lama keeping his people in darkness and deceiving them with his prophecies and fortune telling—he is, however, not an entirely ordinary man."

During the last years of his life, Mongolian independence groups sprang up and met secretly with the Bogd, seeking advice on how to liberate the country from China. Under his guidance, they enlisted Soviet aid and were near an uprising when in 1920 a hell bent white Russian General, Baron Roman von Ungern-Sternberg unexpectedly invaded the country in the midst of the Russian Civil War.

The "Mad Baron," as he was nicknamed, had been fighting communist troops in Siberia when he fled south into Mongolia. Proclaiming himself the God of War, the Baron liberated Urga from China and freed the Bogd Khan, who had been held prisoner in his own palace.

Urga's citizenry, however, found the new army to be no better than the vanquished Chinese. During a three day killing spree the band of drunken "liberators" rode through the streets slaughtering anyone they took to be an enemy. Jews and Bolsheviks were rounded up and shot, women were raped, banks and shops were looted. Those who resisted were strung up in trees and skinned alive or set on fire. Despite this, the Bogd Khan, happy to be set free, crowned the Mad Baron "Emperor of Mongolia."

The Mad Baron's reign was one of the briefest in Mongolian history. A few months later, after being shot by his own troops, he fled on horseback and was captured by the Red Army. Put on trial in Novosibirsk, the Baron was found guilty of treason and executed by firing squad. With the White Russians out of the way, the young Mongolian hero Sükhbaatar, who wisely befriended the Reds, marched uncontested into the capital and declared Mongolia's independence.

The Bogd remained a figurehead leader, but upon his death three years later, a republic was established and the new Communist government forbade the selection of a ninth Bogd Khan. But what the government of Mongolia did not know was that the Buddhist clergy in Tibet went ahead and selected their own Jebtzun Damba in 1932. It was not until he turned up at Gandan Monastery that hot summer day that anyone in the country knew he actually existed.

* * *

When the ceremony ended, I dashed back to *The Mongol Messenger* office to type up the story. In the doorway I bumped into Ariunbold and Baatarbeel, both chatting idly and smoking cigarettes.

"You guys aren't going to believe this!" I said, almost out of breath. "The Bogd Khan has come to Mongolia. I just saw him at Gandan!"

"Bogd Khan?"

"Yeah, the ninth Bogd. He is here!"

"What's his name?"

"Name? I dunno. Actually, no one knew much about him. He led the audience in prayer and left as quickly as he had come."

"*Ninth* Bogd?" Ariunbold repeated, totally mystified. "But we only had *eight* Bogd Khans."

"Well, that's what I thought. But this one is new. I think the Dalai Lama chose him a few years ago."

"Where is he?"

"He was at Gandan, but he's probably gone now. They said there would be more ceremonies this week. "This is big news, front page!"

He looked indifferent. I knew Ariunbold wasn't the religious type, being more of a business and politics kind of guy. Baatarbeel appeared equally lost.

Still, I knew our readers would love the story; this was just the type of thing that my colleagues were always loath to report. We were coming from different worlds. They preferred to speak of great achievements and the future of the country while foreigners wanted to peek into their past. Somehow, all these elements were colliding in one week. Mongolia's past, the Bogd Khan; and its future, the President of China. The excitement of the moment blinded me from this danger and I went upstairs to happily type up the lead story.

Two days later Amarbat banged through the office door carrying a stack of 2000 hot-off-the-press *Mongol Messengers*. A sort of weekly tradition, the rest of us (well, most of us anyway), had been waiting around in anticipation of his return. Usually we'd each pull a paper off the top of the pile and beam with delight at our collective accomplishment. This week was different. While I happily read through my scoop story on page 1, "Bogd Khan Returns: Worshippers cheer as Mongolia's ninth 'living Buddha' makes a surprise visit," Indra, Ariunbold, Narantuya, Undrakh and Baatarbeel rifled through the pages with wide-eyed shock.

"What? What's wrong?"

"Who is this lama!?" Indra bellowed. "What is he doing on the FRONT PAGE!"

"Whaddya talking about? This is a HUGE story. This is the Bogd Khan!"

"Michael," she said in a tone of voice that approached motherly reprimand. "The Chinese President is on page three!"

"Oh my God," muttered Undrakh from behind.

"Hey, C'mon. Since when did you guys care so much about China? Besides, we gave him a full page and four photos."

Ariunbold shook his head but said nothing. Amarbat and Bayarmaa sat by in confused silence.

"You've insulted the Chinese!" said Indra. "Their embassy is going to call the President's office and the President's office is going to call us!"

"I don't believe I'm hearing this. So what if they don't like our news? We don't work for the Chinese Embassy. We can print whatever we want!"

"Michael, you should have showed us this first," Undrakh said.

I didn't know how to respond. They hadn't bothered to look at the pages before press time, so who was to blame? It was a stalemate.

Ten years ago, a visit to Mongolia by the President of China would have blanketed the front pages of every newspaper in town for a week. By the same token, stories about Buddhism would have been relegated to a tiny sidebar on the back page, if included at all. In many ways, my colleagues had not left that era. I suppose that the existence of *The Mongol Messenger* was to serve as a promotional tool for the government, and from a political standpoint, China was a lot more important than Buddhism. I had ignored state affairs—a no-no where you're a state employee.

Yet from another perspective, Mongolia was a democratic country with a vigorous free press. Didn't independence from China and Russia give the right to make their own decisions? Thousands of Mongolians had come to see the Bogd Khan on Sunday. How many had gone to see Jiang Zemin? None. If nothing else I could pin my layout decision on economics. Which lead story would sell more copies?

But it was a hard sell. I felt outnumbered and clearly they felt at risk. I decided to let it lie. Scooping up a bundle of papers, I grabbed my backpack and headed out the door to make my deliveries.

The first fall out from the story came from the Mongolian government. I visited the Foreign Ministry the next day on an unrelated assignment, and ended up with an earful from one of the top brass in the department.

"This 'so-called Ninth Bogd Khan' was never invited to the country. It's dangerous to give so much press coverage to an unannounced intruder," the official said in a measured response.

There was a genuine fear by the secular government that the Buddhists, suppressed for so many years, would gain strength and try to vie for political power. Having the Bogd Khan in their camp gave the Buddhists one more card to play. Who knew the intentions of the 68-year-old Bogd Khan? Did he harbor political aspirations? This was unlikely, but the prospect had the government on pins and needles. Surely, heads would roll in the Moscow embassy where the Bogd Khan had received his tourist visa.

Amar, the same translator who had earlier helped me during the political crisis, was also working with me on this story. Although trained as a monk in his youth, Amar was now a closet Christian. He had given up on Buddhism, calling it an archaic and backward religion.

"Are you nuts? How could you put this charlatan on the front page?!" he bawled as we walked to an interview with an official from the ministry.

"Charlatan? What are you talking about? He was appointed by the *Dalai Lama!*"

"Rubbish! He is a thief. He has only come here to rob our pockets!"

Amar reflected a common suspicion about Mongolian monks, who were believed to horde donations given by their devotees.

Journalists and politicians disapproved and now I even had a lama on my case. Baasan Lama, one of the 13 original democrats and a friend of the Montsame boss Amarsanaa, dropped by the *Mongol Messenger* office to chat with me. When I showed him the most recent edition his eyes turned downcast. "He is the Bogd *Lama*, not the Bogd *Khan*," said Baasan, reviewing the headline. "We have no king. It is very dangerous to write such things." I saw it in his eyes: *The government will be angry, the Chinese will be angry.*

I realized that fear of China was not the only issue at stake here. There was also a fear of the Bogd Khan, excuse me, Bogd Lama. He was an unknown. The Dalai Lama, who had made several trips to Mongolia as early as 1979, was adored here and probably would have played well on the front page. The Bogd Lama, on the other hand, would take some getting used to. Time would be needed before secular Mongolia could trust him.

Meanwhile, back at the monastery, the monks were going to do their best to make sure the Bogd was appreciated and cared for. They escorted him around the city in their Lincoln limousine while he enjoyed sermonizing at Buddhist temples. He met with top Mongolian clergymen and blessed his believers. Monastery donation boxes overflowed.

He also took a tour of the Eighth Bogd Khan's winter palace, located on the southern edge of the city. Though slightly alarmed at the crumbling state of affairs, the Bogd said he felt at home there and that he recognized the palace as his residence in a former lifetime. He was taken to the countryside, all the way to Kharkhorin—Mongolia's first capital city and the location of the great monastery Erdene Zuu. A remarkable thing happened here as his hosts named him their new national leader, giving the Bogd Lama authority even higher than that of the Khamba Lama of Gandan Monastery.

The monks made it clear that the Bogd Lama was to remain under their protection, but new information dashed their hopes of keeping him as their high lama. The local press reported that back in 1995 the government had made a decision to forbid any new Bogd Lamas. Labeling the nation's highest spiritual leader as persona non grata was seen as an affront, and the monks launched a petition to cancel this resolution.

The appeal met with no response and we wondered what the monks would try next. Hoping to answer this question, I set up an interview with the Bogd Lama himself. Amar arranged the meeting and we went to visit the Bogd Lama at his suite in the Chinggis Khaan Hotel.

A knock on the Bogd's door was answered by a young Tibetan who introduced himself as a Choefel. With a strong build, unshaven face and menacing look, we guessed he was the Bogd's bodyguard. When introductions went round we learned that Choefel was the Bogd Lama's son. We were baffled. Either the son was the product of an illicit relationship outside the monastery or the Bogd had at some point abandoned the life of a monk. It was just another question to add to our long list.

Choefel described the proper etiquette for meeting his father, showing us how to present our ritual silk scarves and where to position ourselves in the room. Until now I had only seen the Bogd in various temples, sitting cross-legged upon his throne, swathed in silk and blessing his followers. But when the door swung open, we entered the room to find the Bogd looking a little less regal. Having just woken from sleep, he smiled from inside his rumpled bed, half covered with sheets and blankets. His thin yellow shirt was unbuttoned, expose a pale, hairless chest. We presented the silk scarves and he draped them around our necks, touching our heads gently.

Easing into our chairs, we began asking questions about his life. Where was he born? Where did he study? What had happened to him after China invaded Tibet? Choefel translated.

"I was recognized at the age of four by the Regent in Lhasa," the Bogd said in his familiar husky voice. "Other lamas and oracles confirmed that I was the incarnation of the Jebtzun Damba Khutagt. I was supposed to go to Ulaanbaatar but the Mongolian lamas were being persecuted so I stayed in Tibet.

"One day a lama named Hureltsorj came from Mongolia looking for me. But I couldn't go with him and he never returned to Mongolia, he died in Tibet," said the Bogd somberly. "When I was 21, I left the monastery and started practicing yoga in the mountains. I went to different holy sites and meditated."

Straightening his back, he spoke with fondness of his youth but became dour as he remembered China's invasion of Tibet in 1950. At that time he gave up his monastic vows but the reason for this wasn't fully clear to me. Perhaps he feared imprisonment. Or maybe it was because he fell in love. The Bogd told us that he was married shortly after giving up his vows.

"I took my family to India and we wandered for many years," he said, speaking of his life after fleeing Chinese occupied Tibet. "First we lived in Mysore and Darjeeling, then in 1981 we moved to Madhya Pradesh. But I continued to study Buddhism. People knew who I was and they would come to me for my blessing. Sometimes I gave teachings at the Tibetan refugee settlements."

When Buddhism returned to Mongolia after the Democratic Revolution, a group of monks from Ulaanbaatar met the Dalai Lama to ask if there was any trace of the ninth Bogd Lama. The Dalai Lama himself did not have an answer to their question but was determined to find out. Messages requesting that the ninth Bogd appear in Dharamsala were spread across the Tibetan communities of India.

After months of interviews with other monks vying for the Bogd Lama title, the man before us arrived in Dharamsala. The Dalai Lama may have remembered studying with him when they lived in Lhasa because after their meeting he determined that this man, until then known as Jamphal Namdrol, was the true Bogd Lama.

"Mongolian high lamas began meeting me in 1992 and made plans to bring me to their country. I wanted to go, but I couldn't receive a visa. The government refused to invite me," he explained.

Month after month, year after year went by and no visa ever arrived. Meanwhile, the suspicious Amar was still trying to dig up a scandal and prove the Bogd's illegitimacy. He asked him why he had remained in hiding for so long and why he had failed to join the Dalai Lama in Dharamsala. Surely if he was the real Bogd Lama he would have been close to the Tibetan leadership.

"The problem was that Mongolia was a communist country," he said. "So I decided not to advertise myself. Most people knew I was the ninth Bogd but nothing became official until 1991. I just led a simple life."

We asked how welcoming the government had been since his arrival. Relations seemed sour.

"Perhaps there are a few people in the government who don't want me here. I tried many times to visit but the government would not receive me. You see I still live here in this hotel."

Entrapped in the hotel, under surveillance, the Bogd Lama remained an enigma for his Mongolian followers, but he was also willing to honestly answer disturbing questions posed by Amar about his predecessors.

"You're right," said the Bogd when Amar chronicled the eighth incarnate's life of debauchery. "My previous incarnation drank and smoked in excess. This was unfortunate. But many elderly Mongolians tell me that he was one of the most important figures in modern Mongolia. He helped free Mongolia from China."

"Do you think Buddhism can be rebuilt?" I asked. "There seem to be very few people truly interested in it."

"I think this is possible," he said, "because even though the knowledge is not there, they have faith. I don't know if it can be as it was before, but maybe if the people study, then it will slowly return." He paused and sighed, "But I don't know if I can stay here. I will leave this up to the Mongolians. If they want the Jebtzun Damba then I would like to stay. If they don't then I will leave."

I told him that many Mongolians had suggested that (someday, many years from now) the tenth incarnate could be reborn in Mongolia. No Bogd Lama had been born in this country for centuries; they had all come from Tibet, a legacy of the old Manchu policies. (The Manchus feared that a Mongolian Bogd Lama would stir up nationalism and dissent). My words hung in the air for a moment before being addressed.

"Maybe," he mused. "If the people of Mongolia want this then it could happen."

There were solemn nods all around.

"It's all a hoax!" Amar grumbled as we walked away from the hotel. "He is not a real incarnation. And did you see his son? He looks like a truck driver! He is just using his father to get money from us."

Amar groused about the many failures of Mongolia, blaming them on Buddhism. No longer, he insisted, was it a legitimate religion shaping the nation's destiny. When I countered that Buddhism was a peaceful faith and a centerpiece of Mongol culture, he began shouting.

"*Yagshte!*" ("Bullshit") "Westerners like Buddhism because it makes us Mongolians look backwards. They only want to imagine us living as nomads and riding horses. They don't want the Internet or other modern things to come here."

Amar's position represented the modern Mongolian conundrum—how to catch up with the world without sacrificing centuries of cultural identity and a belief system that rang true. For him, Buddhism was the biggest hurdle. He had come to the conclusion that Christianity was the force driving Western advances and without it Mongolia would remain hopelessly trapped in an obsolete world and shuttered in the past.

I pointed out that there are impoverished Christian countries the world over, not to mention a number of wealthy countries that adhered to Islam, Buddhism, Judaism and other faiths. Technology, furthermore, was nothing new to the world when Christianity started to flourish.

Amar countered that mixing Marxism and Buddhism gave Mongolia an ideology that mired the country in a spiritual and economic crisis. Like my co-workers, he was so keen to advance Mongolia into the 21st century that he was willing to sacrifice all the Bogd Lama's handiwork. It was a big risk, but one that many Mongolians were willing to take.

The Bogd's visa expired after 30 days, but he remained in the country as an illegal alien. I called Choefel on a daily basis and received updates. The problem was that top Buddhist leaders had confiscated the Bogd's ID card. He would remain in Mongolia and serve as their leader while negotiations continued with the government.

In the middle of August, officials came to the Chinggis Khaan Hotel and asked the Bogd Lama to leave the country at once. He might have obliged them if he still had his Tibetan/Indian ID card. Unfortunately, he had become a tool caught between two systems vying for power. It was an unexpected and dangerous showdown between the traditional Buddhists, with their long legacy, and the politicians, young men bred on Marxist-Leninist doctrine but now adhering to Western values.

Finally, with the media catching onto the story about the "outlaw monk," the Bogd did what any clearly thinking lama would do, he called a press conference. Surrounded by Mongolia's heavy-set cast of leading monks, the Buddhist leader told his story to a throng of journalists, describing his troubled past as a hidden boy, a refugee, and a peasant farmer.

"I see back to my life and I think it gives a lesson to others. My life as a peasant and a trader was difficult. I endured many obstacles."

He described how the Dalai Lama had found and trained him in 1991—trying to shake off recent allegations that he was an imposter.

"I wrote my biography and sent it to the Dalai Lama. He confirmed me and there was a large ceremony at the Burmong Datsum Monastery. None of this was forced. It was an organic development based on the fact that the Jebtzun Damba is an important religious figure in Mongolia. Whenever the Jebtzun Damba is supporting religion in this country, it will contribute a great deal to the enlightenment and well-being of the Mongolian people."

Then, pressing toward the microphone, he apologized for keeping his identity hidden from the Mongolian Embassy in Moscow. The journalists began scribbling in their notebooks.

"When I came to Moscow, some Mongolians proposed that I visit their country. When I applied for a visa I did not call myself Jebtzun Damba. They didn't ask. They didn't know and they couldn't have known I am the Jebtzun Damba. Maybe the fact that I didn't tell who I am was a mistake and I am ready to apologize. I went to Kalmykia (a Russian province with ethnic Mongols), and one night while having dinner with my hosts, they asked, 'Why is this lama, who is so respected in that country, unable to go there?' The next day, the Mongolian Consul in Kalmykia assured me the visa would arrive. He also provided an invitation. I didn't feel inside like it was going to happen, but it did."

Perhaps this confession was his way of ending his visit. A few days later the ID card was returned. After sixty days in Mongolia the Bogd was driven across the Russian border, and that was the last that Mongolia saw of him.

A couple of months later, Enkhbayar, the leader of the Mongolian People's Revolutionary Party, had an audience with the Dalai Lama on a trip to India. The Dalai Lama expressed "disappointment" over the Bogd's behavior and apologized on his behalf. He said he was not aware that the Bogd had intended to go to Mongolia, and said the Tibetan government-in-exile had no intention of meddling in Mongolian internal affairs. The Dalai Lama said he would provide consultation to the Bogd Lama and added that he would not be permitted to return to Mongolia.

I wrote a piece on the Dalai Lama's statement and put it on the front page. This time, when the newspaper was published, Indra, Undrakh, Ariunbold and the rest of the staff breathed a sigh of relief. Now that the Dalai Lama had condemned the incident, my co-workers considered it okay to do the same.

From my perspective, the entire episode had diminished my romantic view of the Democratic Revolution. If the Bogd Lama and his ideas were banned from Mongolia, then much of what the Democrats had worked for in 1990 was rendered meaningless. Did they understand that they were guilty of the same crimes that they fought so hard to expose ten years earlier?

Religion in Mongolia was now open to debate. What would happen if the Bogd's followers demanded his return? Would their numbers swell? Lenin had been Mongolia's spiritual leader for 70 years, spreading atheism to remote corners of the country. But his departure had left a spiritual vacuum and Mongolians seeking spirituality were now prepared to return to their Buddhist roots. The gap, however, was wide open and there was plenty of room for competition in the spiritual supermarket. Christian missionaries, arriving in droves from the US and Korea, had found a suitable new breeding ground for their faith. Their evangelism, I would soon find, was soon to test the plucky clique of Buddhist believers.

Postscript: Several years later, I traveled to India where I met the Bogd Lama at his meditation center in Dharamsala. He and his son had not heard from their contacts in Mongolia. They said they had left $20,000 with the monks as Gandan Monastery to build a Children's Center. I knew that no such center had been built. The whereabouts of their donation remains unknown today.

~ 12 ~

ON A MISSION

"ALL THESE RELIGIONS ARE MAKING LIFE UNBEARABLE," said Darsuren, the monk I was interviewing in his small monastery on the outskirts of Ulaanbaatar. "When many religions come to one place there are fights and terrorist acts like blowing up airplanes, cars and buildings. I am for one religion in my country and many people agree with this."

When Darsuren advocated amending the constitution to forbid other religions, particularly Christianity, I was not particularly surprised. I had heard similar resentment in the voices of those defending Buddhism.

"But our government would never do this," he lamented. "They need money for themselves and their campaigns, so they allow other religions to come to Mongolia. We've seen how these missionaries come and give away food and money. They prey on the weak and say that their God has helped them. It's not real religion. They are just taking advantage of these people. Buddhism and Mongolia have coexisted for many centuries and that tradition should live on."

Reality is sometimes hard to deal with, but what Darsuren really failed to recognize was that these missionaries were here to stay. They had already been around for ten years and in that time they had built churches and translated the bible into Mongolian. They had given out clothes, food and medicine. Jehovah's Witnesses, Presbyterians, Seventh-Day Adventists, Southern Baptists, the Roman Catholics and Lutherans: they had all come marching into Ulaanbaatar, eager to preach to a nation they saw sleeping under a blanket of atheism.

New laws prevented them from preaching in public places, but these were ignored. The main source of converts was the schools. The missionaries were doubling as English teachers, which gave them unlimited access to young, eager students, hungry for a new language, new ideas and a change of pace. A copy of the bible was always on hand for anyone willing to take the good book home. "Mongolians," one missionary told me, "will read anything."

A wary government sent in undercover detectives to pose as students in their classes. This worked to a degree. In one raid, a group of missionaries was caught distributing illegal Christian video cassettes that contained thinly disguised anti-Buddhist messages in a made-for-children cartoon.

Some missionaries were more passive in their approach; delivering aid without promoting faith. But the fact that they could afford charity work at all was a major advantage over the religious efforts of the Buddhist monks, who like all other Mongolians, found it a struggle simply to survive.

One missionary group even set up a TV station—they called it Eagle TV. A group of Democrats (including ex-Prime Minister Elbegdorj and his finance minister Baabar) invited the Christians into Mongolia in exchange for a set amount of CNN coverage and other American TV programming. The Christians agreed and brought CNN, along with *The Beverly Hillbillies, The Flintstones,* Shirley Temple films and the odd NBA game. It seemed like a reasonable deal for Mongolia until the airwaves were suddenly awash with religious propaganda: Christian rock videos, biblical passages and testimonies by recent Mongolian converts. A show called *Bible Muscle Hour* had Oklahoma beefcakes proclaim their devotion to Jesus before destroying blocks of ice with their heads.

Some missionaries turned up in Mongolia as uninvited guests, echoing the 19th-century preachers who arrived in China, bible in hand, with mass conversions in mind. I had a bizarre run-in with one such missionary at the office. A tall, portly American man entered the room and asked to speak with me. He wore a checkered shirt and blue jeans, held up with red suspenders. Jowls shook mightily and a gray moustache bristled as he crossed the room. Faded sailor's tattoos were branded onto his thick forearms.

"What religion are you?" he demanded, his eyes focusing on mine like an animal staring out from a cave.

"Ummm. Jewish," I said with noticeable hesitation.

"So you don't believe that Christ is the savior?" he asked, tightening up his lips and narrowing his eyes. "You don't believe that He came down from almighty heaven to pay for the sins of man?!"

Behind him stood a large Mongolian man with a ponytail and black hat that had the word "CAT" on it. My mind started racing back through my recent work, thinking that I must have written something in the paper to earn this man's ire. I was coming up empty.

"I'm Jewish," I reiterated, feeling my heart pounding inside my chest. I glanced back at Indra, who had taken a break from her work to see what was going on.

"I believe that Christ came down to Earth to save mankind," he said with a raised finger. "Almighty Jesus died on the cross to pay for our sins, yours and mine." Spittle was forming in the corners of his mouth. "And you know something? I know where Satan is. He lives in Ohio."

"Good lord."

"I know where he is, I know who he is, and I been tellin' all them bastards for years about it, but none of 'em'll listen. I told all them radio stations about it, but they didn't care none."

"And now you want to tell Mongolians that Lucifer lives in Ohio?"

"Damn right."

"And you're from Ohio too?"

His eyes narrowed slightly but he said nothing.

"Well, why Mongolia?" I asked.

He then pulled out of his pocket a folded photocopy of a page from a *National Geographic* magazine that showed the descendants of Chingis Khan.

"You see," he said, pointing to a family tree.

"This Mongol king was named Berke, spelled just like my name is. Maybe I am related to this Berke."

"Maybe," I said, agreeing mostly out of fear. "So you think Mongolians will listen because you are a descendant of Berke Khan?"

He nodded and asked if I would publish a story about his Ohio-dwelling Satan, passing me a disheveled stack of papers that attempted to prove his theory. I explained that our newspaper only ran stories about Mongolia but I would consider it. Silence stung the air while he thought about this. Then, perhaps realizing he had been rejected for the umpteenth time, he snatched the papers away and left the room in a huff. His pony-tailed thug smiled meekly before closing the door.

I saw the Ohio missionary a few days later at the International Shaman Conference, announcing his mission to the Mongolian anthropologists. He wanted them to join Christ in a battle to defeat Satan and tried to explain his whereabouts and identity.

Columbus? Cleveland? Toledo?

I couldn't quite make it out. The anthropologists smiled politely before slipping away for coffee.

There was no doubting that America's Bible Belt was securely cinched around Ulaanbaatar. The Buddhists, however, were doing what they could to unbuckle it. The Bogd Lama's visit was followed by the opening of a new monastery financed by Bakula Rimpoche, the Indian ambassador to Mongolia. It was an important development in Buddhist religious circles and I felt that it would make a great story for *The Messenger*. Here was an ambassador from India promoting Buddhism in Mongolia, it was too obvious a headline to ignore and Ariunbold agreed to let me run a full page story.

When you saw the Indian ambassador you knew immediately why he was financing a monastery. The ambassador was also a monk. But Bakula was no ordinary monk. He was a living Buddha, a Ladakhi prince and the 20th incarnation of Arkhad Bakula (one of the 16 apostles of Shakyamuni Buddha). In the early 1990s he spent his spare time traveling about the countryside, holding revival sessions in remote provinces. By the time I arrived, old age had forced him to remain ensconced inside the Embassy.

I called up the Indian embassy and arranged to have an interview. When I arrived the next day, Bakula's personal assistant Sonam met me in the Embassy atrium and led me up a spiral marble staircase. At the top he pushed open a set of heavy wood doors that led to the Ambassador's office. I found Bakula sitting behind a mammoth desk that dwarfed his shriveled frame. Gold and crimson attire clung stiffly to his withered body. A bony, stick-like arm poked from his wrap. His ashen head featured droopy eyelids over intelligent rheumy eyes, thin brown lips and large ears—the mark of brilliance according to Buddhists. He nodded delicately at my presence and when I leaned over to deliver a special silk scarf in his honor, he grasped my head with his skeletal hands.

Bakula mumbled a short mantra and released me from his clutches. Then he leaned back to describe how his new monastery was to be the most puritanical in all of Mongolia, a beacon of hope among the lamaseries of Ulaanbaatar, abiding by strict laws of celibacy and sobriety. This was no easy task in Mongolia where promiscuity and drunkenness within the lamasery ranks had become commonplace. But Bakula had confidence in this mission and invited me to see the opening ceremony of his temple.

The monastery opening was held a few days later. All the usual diplomats and Members of Parliament came to the first ceremony and kneeled before Bakula Rimpoche, who sat on a throne, wrapped up in red blankets.

During a performance of Tsam mask dancing, I noticed something different—Caucasian monks, their glossy bodies standing out under crimson habiliments. They turned out to be a delegation of American Buddhists on hand for the ceremony. Their guide, my old friend Batbold, introduced me to the visitors, who said they represented the "Foundation for the Preservation of the Mahayana Tradition" (FPMT), an organization with a strong following in the US and Europe.

Batbold gave his guests a briefing on the state of Buddhism in Mongolia. He did not paint a rosy picture: the missionaries, he said, were taking over. And the Buddhists were helpless because they didn't understand their own faith.

The Americans were shocked. Buddhism must be revived, they declared. One told me how Mongolia had the opportunity to become a Buddhist cultural center, now that Tibet had fallen into the hands of Communist China. They had just the answer to Batbold's problem. They would send one of their own to bring the faith back.

A couple of months later we began seeing him on the streets. He was hard to miss; standing six foot two in his black sandals and wearing a flowing set of monks' robes. His shorn scalp reflected the autumn sunshine. If you walked up to him, you were greeted with calm blue eyes and an easy smile. His name was Thubten Gyatso, or Gyatso for short, and his assignment was daunting: he was to teach Mongolians to be Buddhists again. By now, only the elderly attended religious ceremonies and even they had little knowledge about their nation's traditional religion. Buddhist philosophy, scriptures and meditation were unknown, and there was a general apathy toward the faith. Often, the best way to reverse such a trend is to bring in someone from the outside; someone who could bring a worldly perspective and not be constricted by petty local debate. Tibetans had long ago played this role when they converted Mongolia from Shamanism in the 16th century. In a bizarre case of *déjà vu,* an Australian would try the same thing at the end of the 20th century.

His given name was Adrian Feldman. He had grown up in the suburbs of Melbourne, the son of a Jewish father, and like any other middle class Australian kid he played cricket and surfed the south coast beaches. Adrian graduated from medical school in 1968, but his curiosity for the world couldn't be held back. One day a friend sent him a letter from Afghanistan and suggested that he go there for a visit. Kabul at the time was a Mecca for hippies and soul searchers.

The letters were too enticing and he made the journey to Afghanistan, as well as a side trip to India. An introduction to Taoism and a float down the Indus River on a boat sealed his fate—he knew he would live his life in the East. His wanderings eventually landed him in Nepal where he took a course on Buddhist meditation. He was skeptical at first and doubted the ideas of karma and reincarnation. "If they were true," he told me, "then I would have to become a monk, and that was the last thing I wanted to do."

Gyatso continued to argue with his teachers but failed to prove them wrong. Thus he made the fateful decision to put aside his medical career and dedicate his life to Buddhism. He came under the wing of the philanthropist and living Buddha, Lama Zopa Rimpoche, the founder of the FPMT. It was Lama Zopa who sent Gyatso on the mission to Mongolia.

Gyatso settled in quickly and started giving lectures in the sweltering basement of Bakula Rimpoche's Monastery. Just like the Bogd Lama's audience, those who attended were mostly elderly folk. They sat cross-legged, hanging on every word and taking notes. They asked endless questions about superstitions associated with Buddhism, and each time he dismissed one of their myths as false, a sigh of relief would overcome the congregation. When it was over, he would bless them one by one. Those with bad vision would ask him to blow on their eyes, believing he had mystical curative powers, and Gyatso would oblige. The Scottish missionary James Gilmour had received similar requests when he arrived in Mongolia:

"A foreigner is often asked to perform absurd, laughable, or impossible cures. One man wants to be made clever, another to be made fat, another to be cured of insanity, another of tobacco, another of whiskey, another of hunger, another of tea... Most men want medicine to make their beards grow, while almost every man, woman and child wants to have his or her skin made as white as that of the foreigner."

Gyatso also gave a talk on Thursdays to the expatriates of Ulaanbaatar. His pupils—mostly New Age-type Americans and British—sat on cushions in a yellow room at his FPMT center, itself located between the Mormon tabernacle and Millie's Cafe. His lectures were thought provoking and I enjoyed his whimsical approach to the eastern faith. "The meditative experience is the best wave to catch," he once said to me, appealing to my California sensibilities. "But we always want more; we are always searching for that perfect wave. And when we experience it we want to go back. Buddhists meditate to conquer this desire." It was this personal, Western touch that brought him local fame. He was so popular, in fact, that I persuaded him to write a weekly guest column in The Mongol Messenger. It became apparent however, that most of his readers were actually Christian missionaries, seeking tips on how to fuse their gospel with Asian philosophy. Although neither side would admit it, the battle for Mongolia's soul had begun.

Of all the mission groups, the Mormons were easily the most noticeable. They came in the greatest numbers and were frequently seen matched pairs. None ever walked alone. They were clone-like—all blonde 18-year old boys with short cropped hair and perfect teeth. They wore matching black suits, pressed shirts, ties and badges. Their names all began with Elder. Eyes followed them as they ambled about town and soon everyone had heard of a place called Utah, which, rumor had it, had streets paved in gold brick.

The Mormon Tabernacle was located halfway between my apartment and Montsame. I passed its cream-colored stucco façade on my way to and from work each day, and noticed as the months went by that increasing numbers of young Mongolian girls in long skirts gathered outside its front door.

One Sunday I dropped by for a service. In the polished foyer I found a sharply dressed group of students seated on a couch, giggling softly among themselves. I was introduced to a young woman named Sister Ankhtuya, who told me she had been a Buddhist nun but converted three years ago after seeing a movie on Jesus' life. When I asked her why she had left the nunnery, she explained that it was impossible to learn anything because there was no money to buy books.

"Why did you become a Mormon?" I asked. There was more giggling between her friends before she could continue.

"The movie changed me. I saw all the love that Christ offered and I didn't feel that kind of love at the monastery. I learned that God is just like a person. I wanted to learn more, but my parents were against it. I had to go to church in secret." She said some of the American Mormon leaders fasted on her behalf and finally her parents allowed her to go to church.

I was skeptical, but Sister Ankhtuya said she was grateful that the Americans had shown so much concern for her well-being. Leading me into the main hall, she directed me to a pew where I found a place amid pimply American and Mongolian teenagers, dressed in their Sunday best, listening attentively to the preacher. One thing that struck me was the spotless nature of the hall, right down to the preacher's shiny black loafers; a marked contrast to the colorful and dust-caked Buddhist temples with their darkened corners and jumbled mass of religious icons.

"We can be like Christ in our calls to serve. Never lie, cheat or steal," said the elderly preacher. "Be like Christ and tell your family and friends about the church. Christ will come again and there is much to do before he comes, and much to do in Mongolia."

The preacher concluded by suggesting that the congregation pay ten percent of their earnings back to the church. "Suggested" was the key word here. It would have been silly to have used stronger language to a congregation that was largely unemployed and impoverished. I sat for a moment while the pews emptied around me and then made my way to the front of the church to greet the preacher. Dressed as if he were on his way to a funeral, Elder Thomas sported a dark suit, crisp white shirt, tie and spectacles. He walked sprightly for a 79-year-old, holding himself tall and looking intently with clear blue eyes.

We started talking and he told me how he lived much like other expatriates in Ulaanbaatar. He had a small apartment, rode around town in taxis, ate lunch at Millie's (Elder Thomas recommended the quiche) and in winter he stayed inside to beat the cold. He loved the countryside, he said, and enjoyed visiting with Mongolians in their *gers.*

"When did you arrive in Mongolia?"

"Last year," he said, fiddling with his glasses. "My wife and I, well we're from Utah you see, we came together. I was hired to teach English to the employees at the National Archives."

"National Archives?"

"Yeah, ya know, where they keep the historical records."

"Oh. They needed English lessons over there?"

"Sure, every Mongolian agency needs English. They are modernizing, they need to use the Internet and make contacts abroad. Well, the lord sent us to Mongolia to do good deeds. Teaching English is one way that we can help people."

"Do you also teach the bible in class?"

"Heavens no," he said, disturbed by the suggestion. "We're not allowed to do that. According to the law we can't teach religion in the workplace. Of course, because of the way we dress everyone knows that we're Mormon, and they are free to talk to us outside of work, here on Sundays or in their homes."

Interesting, I thought. They used their clothes to advertise themselves. It made good marketing sense.

"Tell me," I asked, interested myself in knowing his strategy. "What do you say to make them come back? Is preaching here different compared to Utah?"

"It's very different. Here it's a learning experience. We learn about them and they learn about us. Some stay and some leave. The message that I have tried to deliver today is that we are the sons and daughters of an actual God in heaven. It is something that is very attractive to young people—this direct relationship with a heavenly being. The space between our God and the individual person is one thing that draws the younger people."

"And what do the older Mongolians think of this?"

"The older people I meet have strong feelings about the teachings of the Buddha," he explained. "But the younger generation is not holding onto their religious teachings. Young people are unlimited in their acceptance of other people and other things."

It made sense. After years without religious training, any spiritual person was ripe for conversion. But Elder Thomas said he had visited three monasteries and was impressed with what he saw. "The lamas we met are very learned individuals. I think they try to live good lives, and that is what my church teaches too—to live a good life."

"So why not encourage them to study Buddhism?" I asked.

The possibility must have been too abstract.

"Son," he said. "If a missionary is giving the teachings of Christ, regardless of what country he is in, then the country will be better and the people will be better. If the teachings of Christ make bad men good, it will make good men better."

Elder Thomas had taken Mongolia's spiritual well-being upon his shoulders with aplomb. At nearly 80 years old, long since retired, he had packed his bags and went on the adventure of a lifetime in Mongolia. Not only did it say something about his fortitude, but also his faith in God. One had to congratulate him for his determination, although this did little to placate the native faith holders about the prospects of their own future.

If Gyatso were to succeed in diverting attention away from the popular Christians, the first step would have to involve cleaning up the monasteries. The picture perfect, white picket fence image that the Mormons portrayed conflicted sharply with the rowdy atmosphere at the monasteries. Mongolian monks drank; they fraternized with the opposite sex; and they got into fistfights. Some took money for bogus prayers and healing potions. Others were serving time in jail for stealing priceless relics from their own temples.

They were, in fact, much like their 19th century counterparts, who drew similar criticism from Western travelers. "(The monks) lead a lazy, worthless existence, supported by the lay population and by the money they extract by preying upon the superstitions of their child-like brothers," Roy Chapman Andrews wrote. The Russian explorer Nicolas Przevalski described Buddhism as the "most frightful curse of the country."

Mongolians are a proud people. Especially among the young, they realized that they could go farther in life with the religion that took itself seriously. Clearly, the Mormons meant business, and appeared to be rather progressive (despite their conservative values).

A year after Gyatso's arrival, the missionaries were still gaining strength. No one knew for sure how many Mongolians had been converted, but the 65 Christian religious centers were getting awfully crowded. The Christians also seemed more confident. One day, a Mongolian pastor explained to me that Buddhism was a "scourge."

"It bred laziness and homosexuality," he added. "If the Russians had not crushed it, the Mongols would certainly be extinct now."

Meanwhile, the Buddhists were making little progress. Historically a nation of mystics, wanderers and warriors, Mongolia had nurtured a philosophy that embraced Shamanism, which was perhaps the most appropriate religion for the Mongols given that it is tied much closer to nature than any other religion.

In Ulaanbaatar, Christianity was fast becoming a trendy, preppy religion, while in the countryside it was a faith in service of the poor. There was considerable worry that this would only exacerbate class distinctions and incite violence. This concern reached the upper echelons of the Government House. Enkhbayar, the minority leader in Parliament as well as a faithful Buddhist, was the strongest advocate of one religion policy. I spoke with him often on matters of politics, usually over the phone before, during and after the collapse of another government, but we sometimes met in his office and it was here that he revealed his belief that a single religion would stabilize the country.

"When I think about Kosovo, India and Pakistan, when we see violence in the Philippines based on religious hatred, it is a very sensitive issue, especially in a society which is poor, one which is in transition, one where there is no stable middle class," he told me, leaning over folded hands. "When the government does not know what to do about regulating all the economic and social issues, people will try to find easy solutions for their problems.

"Someone can come here and say that because of a certain religion we are poor or having all these problems. So I think that in order to avoid all these problems and contradictions I would prefer to have a society based on its traditional religion, which is Buddhism."

Then he added tactfully, "But it doesn't mean that I or the MPRP would repress the other religions. It is up to the people to choose their belief. What we are saying is that people should be sure their choice will not be a seed that will grow into an apple of discord."

Enkhbayar's "apple of discord" theory seemed unlikely. Besides the religious purge of the 1930s (which, it could be argued, was a Soviet creation) Mongolians have historically promoted religious tolerance. Dating back to the days of the great empire, every Mongolian khan had enjoyed religious fierce debate in his court. Some Mongol queens even converted to Nestorian Christianity, including the mother of Khubilai Khan and the wife of Ögödei Khan.

Thus, like other controversial movements in Mongolia, the religious debate waned over time, which is why the Bogd Lama controversy, in hindsight, seemed less about religion and more about politics.

The Buddhists continued to flounder and the Christians continued to baptize their followers. Gyatso gave his lessons but the crowds remained small. Batbold, who had defiantly opposed the missionary cause, became resigned to it. Others followed. And, although there is no clear indication of how big it will become in the years ahead, it appeared that Christianity was winning Mongolia's hearts, minds and souls.

Personally I felt even less spiritual than when I had first arrived. I was disillusioned with all the hidden agendas behind Mongolia's religious groups. I was content to be an observer, although I did have a growing interest in Shamanism. It held natural, basic, and respectable beliefs, and I thought it was well-suited for a nomadic country. Most significantly, Chingis Khan was a strong believer in the Shamanic cult. Since he was the national icon, it only made sense that his religious beliefs would be a cornerstone of this society. At the time, however, there was little mention made about this curious faith, and I wondered if it would ever spread again to the masses. Slowly but surely, the answer to this question would reveal itself to me.

~ 13 ~

BURIATS UNITE!

The scene was intoxicating in its barbaric splendor. The women in their fantastic headdresses and brilliant gowns; the blazing yellow robes of the kneeling lamas; and the chorus of prayers which rose and fell in a meaningless half-wild chant broken by the clash of cymbals and the boom of drums—all this set the blood leaping in my veins.

—Roy Chapman Andrews

ULAANBAATAR WAS AN EXCELLENT PLACE to pass a summer. I loved the quiet evenings in Sükhbaatar Square; the alpine meadows overlooking the city on Bogd Khan Mountain; the simplicity of it all. But even so, my mind was constantly drifting to the countryside. To those *del*-clad nomads over the mountains, charging after their half-wild horses with lasso poles.

Another winter had passed. The hoopla surrounding the Bogd Lama and Alan Parrot had died down and I longed for a return trip to the countryside. As the weather improved I looked more often at the map of Mongolia tacked up on our office wall, plotting out my

192

next destination. My eyes kept drifting to the right side of the map: the east—a vast steppe region with seemingly endless grasslands. Pictures of it evoked images of Kansas circa 1850.

I had heard about a Buriat festival to be held in remote Dornod Aimag, Mongolia's easternmost province. The festival, called Altargana after a local flower, was a bi-annual event that brought together Buriats from Mongolia, Russia and China. Buriats make up the third largest minority group in Mongolia, numbering around 48,000. There are thousands more in Russia and China, but when the borders were sealed during Communism the groups were divided, splitting up clans and relatives. Historically, Buriats are considered Mongolia's intelligencia, the result of living in close proximity to Russia's Siberian settlements, which gave them nominal access to a European education and trade with Russia.

It therefore came as no surprise to learn that Indra had Buriat blood. Our senior correspondent had been educated at the Russian school, enjoyed Russian food, preferred to write her newspaper articles in Russian and moved in Russian social circles. Yet when I asked, she said she knew little of the "real" Buriat culture, as it was before contact with the Russians. She was a city girl and genuine Buriat heritage was out on the eastern steppes, she said. The only heritage she could reveal was her family history, and when I prodded, she started to describe the feats of various ancestors—one had been a Buriat lama that had walked from Russia to Tibet, while another had defended Stalingrad against the Nazis in World War II.

Her parents had divorced at young age, she explained, and she had been raised by her father in Ulaanbaatar. She explained her upbringing in the big city and a later love interest with a school classmate that resulted in her only son, Sambuu. She never married the boyfriend however, and now mourned him—about ten years earlier he had been killed in a traffic accident while living in Moscow. She blamed the KGB.

"Badrakh (the boyfriend) had worked for the Central Committee of the MPRP and was an advisor to the Politburo member Namsurai," she explained. "Namsurai worked closely with President Batmönkh and he knew many secrets about the Russian-Mongolian relationship. Badrakh also knew many of these secrets."

"So you think the KGB assassinated him to try and keep their secrets safe?" I asked.

"It's possible," she said. "I believe this because Namsurai is also dead. He died just a few months before Badrakh. They say it was an infection but who knows? I think their deaths were connected."

Indra, like other Buriats who had suffered so greatly during the years of repression, was now trying to come to grips with her misfortune. Communism had shuttered the Buriats away from society but the past ten years had allowed them the opportunity to come forward, release their emotions and have closure by revealing the tragedies that had afflicted them. By discussing her story openly, Indra could also attain some measure of closure. This new found openness is what had paved the way for the Altargana Festival. Indra suggested that I go and learn something about her people. It would be impossible, she said, to understand the Buriats in a city like Ulaanbaatar, I would have to travel to their homeland.

Öndörkhaan was the jumping-off point for the Buriat festival in Dashbalbar. I had just been dumped there after an eight-hour bus ride from Ulaanbaatar, and it would take a couple of more days to reach my destination. I went to the market to pick up some food for the trip: Russian pop, Czech soup mix, Bulgarian crackers, Chinese dried apricots, American peanut butter, Kuwaiti candy bars and German salami; a veritable United Nations snack pack to keep me going until I reached the festival.

Appropriately provisioned, I wandered over to the post office and telecommunications center; always the hub of Mongolian social activities, and also the place to ask about a lift. The spring-loaded turquoise door slammed behind me as I stumbled inside, finding there a half-dozen locals hovering over a 1-month-old copy of the *Daily News*. Behind them, and through a glass window I spotted three operators sitting at a big iron panel, shouting into their headsets, trying to establish a connection with the capital. Their efforts gave new meaning to the term "futility" as they were never able to hold a connection for more than four and half seconds—just long enough to explain where the hell they were calling from.

I tried calling the office to check up on things, but the connection was so bad that I could only hear Bayarmaa's dim voice repeatedly asking "Are you there? Are you there?" She sounded a million miles away. But then, in a small adjacent room, I found something that would soon end this black hole of communication—it was called the Internet Kafe. It was a remarkable thing: a few weeks before, Öndörkhaan had been one of the world's most remote cities. Now with a few clicks of the computer mouse, it was part of the global village.

Outside the Telecommunications center, I bumped into Gana, an old friend and the mayor of Dadal, a Buriat village up north. As luck would have it, he was going to the Altargana Festival and offered me a lift. Gana typified the young, westward-looking Mongol that I usually met on my travels. He was ambitious, full of hopes and dreamed about studying abroad and traveling. Like his peers he had mastered Russian as a youth and was still fascinated by Russian history and literature. But over the past couple of years he had bought into globalization—studying English and business-economics at the university. He was only 30 but had already risen to the top of Dadal's political food chain. All across the country, young people like Gana were pushing out the communist-era bureaucrats, quickly putting the past to bed.

Gana and I waited patiently—there is no other way to wait in Mongolia—for his friends to finish their shopping. This gave Gana time to catch me up on the 1917 Russian Revolution; but being a Buriat from the homeland, he was also partial to his own history and told me something of the Buriat origins. They had a glorious beginning, he said, and he recounted the legend that brought them into the world.

"One day," Gana began. "A hunter was walking near Lake Baikal when a beautiful swan flew down from the sky and landed by the shore. Suddenly the swan took off its cloak and out came a beautiful woman. The hunter was so captivated that he kidnapped the swan-lady, hid her feathery cloak and married her."

They had eleven children, Gana explained, and the hunter was very happy, but secretly his wife longed for her fellow swans. Many years later the woman asked to try on her swan cloak, just once. The hunter reluctantly agreed. She put it on and then flew up through the smoke hole of her *ger*, returned to her swan-people, and the hunter never saw her again. Gana finished the tale, explaining that her eleven children became the founders of the eleven Buriat tribes. That was how the Buriats came into this world.

Unfortunately the fairy tale did not continue. The Buriats have endured a dark history since those illustrious beginnings. During the 18th and 19th centuries they were forced off their lands by Russian pioneers seeking farmland in Siberia. And during the Communist-era they became a favorite target of Stalin, who saw their "intelligencia" as threat to his power. Show trials were held to "prove" their allegiance to Japan, and after enough paranoia had built up, he purged them, sending in death squads to round them up and take them off to the gulag, never to be seen again. It was all done in secret and even today the extent of the genocide remains unknown. This tragic past has been somewhat rectified since the Democratic Revolution of 1990. A rehabilitation commission had cleared many Buriats of the 'spy charges' against them, but on some levels, a stigma remained. Altargana was just one of many ways that the Buriats were trying to regain confidence in themselves and their past.

At last, with petrol and passengers in the car and the shopping complete, Gana, his friends and I set off for Dadal. Somehow, 12 of us managed to squeeze into the five-seat Russian jeep. Ganhuyag sped north, humming a folksong, and soon others joined in. I was always asked to chip in an American tune, a difficult request, as folk songs are not part of my usual repertoire. While Mongolians know dozens of songs, the best I could manage were Christmas carols (although "Over the river and through the woods" was often quite apropos). Finally, I forced myself to learn a Mongolian song. Several hours passed on the agonizingly rough ride toward the Russian border. I was fortunate to share the front seat with a child, but the nine people in the back fared far worse. Still, no one complained. Mongols don't complain. They munched on wild berries and pine nuts, sedated themselves with vodka, and fell in and out of sleep.

Long after dark we stopped to rest at a hunters' *ger*. Gana led the way in. When I entered, Gana's head was down in a plate of marmot leftovers. Marmots, or groundhogs as they are more commonly known in the US, have a distinct taste and are generally regarded as a delicacy rather that an everyday meal. This is largely because they are hunted and only available for a few months during summer after their long hibernation.

The manner of capture, unique in itself, requires the hunter to dress in white with a little fox hat on his head, and creep toward the marmot hole, swinging a tether. The marmot, a curious animal if there ever was one, stands on his hind legs for a better look. When he is close enough, the hunter shoots. Preparation for eating requires the hunter to gut the marmot, stuff it full of scalding hot rocks and singe off the fur with a blow torch. Simmering from the inside, the carcass vaguely resembles a balloon with paws.

Like the puffer fish in Japan, there is also an element of danger when eating marmot, as they are carriers of the Bubonic Plague, or Black Death (which killed off a third of Medieval Europe).

The look on Gana's face was one of ecstasy as he plunged slice after greasy slice of rodent meat down his throat. "Beautiful, beautiful marmot," he crowed with glazed eyes. He had been craving marmot all day. A friend joined in and they sat on the floor smacking their lips. Reaching through bones, I fished out a fatty piece and slipped it into my mouth. It had the texture and consistency of a wet tire but a high oil content that allowed it to slide easily past the palate. I could hardly compare it to lobster, the sort of delicacy I crave when away from civilization, but the taste buds of a Mongol know no better treat.

We continued east after a night in Dadal, carrying new passengers, Gana's staff at the county Government House. We stopped every so often to repair the jeep or relax our aching bones. At the Onon River, everyone stripped down to their skivvies and jumped into the freezing waters.

"This was where Chingis first met Jamuha. Exactly here," Gana assured us as we dried off in the warm sun.

Jamuha was a childhood friend of Chingis and his sworn blood brother. But as Chingis gained power Jamuha refused to submit to him and launched a 25 year civil war to gain supremacy of the Mongol clans. Chingis eventually emerged victorious and the rest is history.

"They were just eleven years old when they met and this is where it all started," Gana said, proudly surveying the surrounding mountains and forests. "Chingis Khan was a Buriat you know," he said, making sure I accurately took note. (Chingis' mother Hoelun was from the Olkhunut tribe, possible ancestors of modern Buriats).

We continued onto the grassy plains of Dornod, joining the parade of Buriats traveling to the Altargana Fair by car, truck, motorcycle and horse. The heavenly grass waved green and gold in the afternoon breeze as far as the eye could see.

Upon reaching Dashbalbar, the car skidded to a halt and we all got out to tidy ourselves. Gana pulled on his heavy Russian army boots and slipped into a gray *del* with a Dadal medal pinned onto his chest. The women sat in the grass and opened up their compacts to powder their faces, touch up their eyebrows and color their lips.

There were throngs of fair goers doing the same, all done up in their traditional Buriat *dels* and peaked caps. They buzzed with the excitement of seeing old friends and the general spirit of a cultural revival.

Dashbalbar was a typical Mongolian soum center. Soums are basically counties, invented by the Soviets when they attempted to collectivize rural areas. During this bureaucratic process, every soum was given a soum a center, a small administrative town designed to house the elements that Russians deemed necessary for settled life: a school, a government house, a theater, a post office, a hospital, a bank, a dry goods store and a market. Soum streets were never paved and no paved roads led to them. Most were ghost towns—nomad families preferred to live out on the steppes where there was better grass for their animals, and only came into town for the occasional shopping spree. Dashbalbar was surrounded by poor *ger* suburbs, each property surrounded by a wood fence. Its center contained five or six concrete buildings, each in a similar state of neglect. The most remarkable thing about the place was that Zorig had once represented Dashbalbar in Parliament, and following his assassination a Zorig Museum had opened in the town center. Zorig, whose father was Buriat, had achieved legendary status in these parts.

Gana and I moseyed to a tiny whitewashed theater where a variety show was in progress, complete with Buriat song-and-dance routines and slapstick comedy skits. The closing performance was a stunning play about the years of Stalinist repression, which described—in graphic detail—how men, women and children were taken from their homes in midnight raids, the women raped and their husbands sent to their deaths. The audience wept. Dashbalbar was one of the hardest hit towns during the purge, and its people were still coming to terms with it.

Just as I was getting into the festivities, Gana ordered me back into the jeep and we left town, apparently headed for our campsite. After a while we veered off the main road and up a dirt track to a collection of A-frame huts. It was an old Soviet holiday camp on the edge of a huge, abandoned uranium mine. This was once a place for Communist party members and Russian brass from the mine to meet and relax. But the camp was now a ghostly place; poorly kept and lacking electricity. There was no water either, which was just as well given our proximity to the uranium deposit. Our Dadal delegation was soon joined by a group of bureaucrats from the Buriat part of Russia, including the General Consular in Ulan Ude. Genadii Nicolovich was a former champion wrestler and proudly showed off his cauliflower ear. He gave me his business card, which included his resume. Among his titles were:

- Head of Representation of the Republic of Buriatia to Mongolia.
- Vice President of the Association of International Mongols.
- Honored Cultural Worker of the Republic of Buriatia and Russian Federation.
- Honored Wrestler of the Russian Federation.

A generator was fired up, the lights came on and dinner was served: potato salad, cold cuts and pickles for appetizers, and then mutton chunks with mashed potato for the main course. Toast after toast was made as the officials thanked each other for promoting the Buriat nation.

It was the first time in Mongolia that I had witnessed "ethnic pride." The Buriats were finally emerging from their anonymity. At the end of the meal, a gallant-looking man with a thick beard (Gana whispered that he was a KGB agent), stood and sang an operatic ballad about the proud Buriats.

The KGB agent gave me a ride back to Dashbalbar in his Toyota 4x4 and we arrived in time to see the opening festival ceremonies. Each Buriat village had elaborately dressed representatives who marched around the stadium. Some delegations included a dressed-up shaman, the traditional healer of the Buriats.

Horsemen in mock-up Chingis warrior garb then charged onto the pitch and planted the eleven Buriat flags in the middle of the arena, representing the eleven original Buriat clans. Dignitaries addressed the crowd in thunderous verse while groups of pig-tailed girls sang traditional songs.

Above the stage flew the Russian and Mongolian flags, but the Chinese flag was missing. The Chinese Buriats were not able to come because of "visa complications." No one knew what had become of them since international borders split the Buriat clans years ago. Their fate remained a mystery.

The wrestling and horse racing tournaments began amidst clouds of dust and cheering fans, but as for the Altargana Festival, the games were merely a side show to the celebration of the Buriat heritage.

Like a secret society, the Buriats had found a place to unleash their pride, with nothing holding them back. In Ulaanbaatar my interviews were always in the form of question and answer; never much in the way of lively elaboration. But these people seemed anxious to spread the word about their Buriat customs and traditions. Perhaps to let the world know they still existed. Even their costumes, which featured a gaudy rainbow-colored patch on the chest, seemed to shout "Hey! We're still alive!"

I went around interviewing people. One man said he wanted to write a new book on Buriat history. Another said he wanted to start a Buriat independence movement. Yet while the Mongol Buriats were hyper-positive, the Russian Buriats chose to be diplomatic. One of the Russians, Dash he called himself, wanted to get one thing straight. There was nothing political about this festival; it only served as a way to promote cultural identity.

"This is an ethnic minority, *not* a nation," Dash repeated as I interviewed him in a special tent erected for the Russian delegates.

But wasn't he relieved that the dark days of communism were over? That the pogroms had ended? Fingers could be pointed at Stalin and the whole evil regime. Compensation might be theirs.

"There is repression everywhere," he snapped. "In your country, in Yugoslavia. What happened to the Buriats happened to people all over the world! These are not unusual events."

Perhaps Dash was merely trying to legitimize living in Russia all these years. Maybe his family had been Japanese agents and deserved Stalin's wrath. Or maybe they had been part of the interrogation squads. It was similar to the defense Khalkh Mongols give to their own blood-stained leader, Choibalsan. They had an amazing ability to forgive the evil done before them. Was this a trait of their Buddhist heritage, or did it run even deeper to their Shamanic core?

I suspect that this spiritual background may be the reason for Dash's defense of Russia, although at the time, I felt it was because he was still living in Russia, and that he still lived in fear of the old Soviet machine. At the end of the Altargana Festival, the Russian Buriat delegation was given the Buriat flag to symbolize the offer for Aginsk (a city in Russia) to host the next festival. The Russians respectfully returned the flag. "First we must receive permission from our government," they said regretfully. It seemed that the question of true freedom and ethnic independence was still a thorny issue north of the border.

The Mongol Buriats were joyful and the Russian Buriats were skeptical. But the fact that the Russians had come at all was a remarkable achievement. What had happened to the Chinese Buriats? What had happened to their culture?

Doguur, the only Chinese Buriat to reach Altargana, had the answers. He was small but sturdy, had beady eyes, and he spoke with uncommon clarity and detail. Where had he come from? What was life like for those Chinese Buriats? My Mongolian really wasn't up to the task for such an interrogation, but fortunately, I found someone to help out. Chris, a Peace Corps volunteer from Chicago, had been living in Dashbalbar for a year. Having spent the past nine lonely months living in a town without any other foreigners had improved his language skills dramatically—he had even picked up the Buriat dialect of the Mongol language. Chris was equally intrigued with Doguur and invited him for a chat inside his log cabin.

We entered the cabin and Doguur and I sat at the kitchen table while Chris prepared hot tea. Rain began to fall lightly as Chris translated my questions about the Chinese Buriats. First of all, where had they all gone?

"One hundred years ago, my family was living in Russia," Doguur began, "They had money and plenty of animals. But after the Russian Revolution, life worsened for the Buriats. They were arrested and some were killed. They were being driven from their homes and villages so in desperation the Buriats asked a high lama what could be done. He told them to emigrate to Tibet. There they would find freedom."

"Over 7,000 Buriats took the lamas' counsel and began the long trek from Siberia to Lhasa. They went south into Mongolia, but they had to change directions. It was 1919 and Chinese troops were invading Urga. To avoid the chaos in central Mongolia, they marched east into Barga."

Doguur's grandfather, a bodyguard for the expedition leader, had made the journey. When the Buriats pushed into Inner Mongolia, they had to stop their advance because of conflict in Manchuria; the Japanese had invaded following their 1918 landing in Vladivostok, and the Chinese had disarmed Russia's railway troops in Manchuria. The dream of creating a Buriat enclave in Tibet stalled in its tracks. Instead they settled in Hailar, an area already occupied by a native ethnic group called the Evenki.

"At first the Buriats got along well with the Evenki. But then there was growing resentment as they competed for pastureland and business," said Doguur. "Then in 1940 a Buriat was killed by a gang of young Evenkis. A Buriat mob retaliated by killing 200 people inside a military office. Each soldier was beheaded and mutilated. Then the Evenkis swore revenge."

He claimed Soviet tanks came to stop the violence. An uneasy truce ensued since then, although the Evenkis and Buriats were never able to fully resolve their differences.

For a while his gaze turned to the storm outside the cabin. Sheets of rain poured down and thunder rolled across the grasslands. A strong wind raked across the village and howled against the walls of the cabin. Doguur took a sip of his tea and described life growing up in Red China.

Being raised on a farm had been a benefit, he said, since the isolated lifestyle kept China at arm's length. "But life was not easy. The Chinese owned all the stores and ran all the factories in the nearest town. All the laws were written in Chinese without Buriat translation, which got some of us in trouble."

His face suddenly ignited with pleasure. "But we did manage to hang onto our customs. In our homes we kept making our Buriat boots and *dels,* and we preserved our language. But the problem was that, officially, all of it was ignored. We were never credited as being a separate ethnic group, but instead the Chinese just lumped us together with the Evenki."

He leaned closer. "When I was young I had to sing Evenki songs at the school cultural show, even though I knew all the Buriat songs. And the school textbooks never made any mention of our existence. They wanted us to forget who we were."

For all of Doguur's indignation, the Evenki have fared no better under Chinese control. Forced assimilation has severed this disappearing Siberian tribes' ties with its nomadic past; their participation in society today is marginal and alcoholism is rampant. Both the Evenki language and reindeer herding are fading quickly under government pressure.

Talking at length on this matter was depressing Doguur so I changed the subject, asking how he had come to Mongolia. Doguur noted that although he had been living as a farmer, his real love was cars. So he devised a plan to travel to Ulaanbaatar, where he heard Mercedes Benz cars were selling cheap. He planned to buy a car and drive it to China where he could sell it for twice the price. He set off for his trip and made it to Ulaanbaatar, but after shelling out $1000 for a Benz he learned that he couldn't afford to export the car because the tax was too high. So he ended up selling it at a $200 loss.

Destitute, Doguur moved to the Gobi Desert to live with a distant relative. He took a job as a gold miner before moving back to Ulaanbaatar, where he found work as a translator and cook. He had an impressive resume for a 26-year-old, but there was still the prickly issue of being an illegal alien—his visa had expired long ago. Doguur said he was working on a solution. He had already sent a letter to the President asking for Mongolian citizenship and although a reply had not yet arrived, he held out high hopes that he would soon became a full-fledged member of Mongolian society.

That night, Chris and I got into the festival spirit and put on the Buriat *del* and peaked cap. We went out with Doguur to a bar (carved out of a disused shop storeroom) and ordered a round of Ochikov, a Russian beer that came in one-liter plastic bottles.

We sat at a makeshift plastic table adjusting our eyes to the dim light. A doleful girl behind the bar distributed Ochikov to her patrons. Young Buriats were shuffling in and out of the pub. Others hovered over their lager, swaying in their drunkenness. A Backstreet Boys tape played on the clunky stereo and every so often a group got up to dance for half a song.

"We should drink because we are friends," said Doguur, the brim of his cap barely revealing his deep-set eyes. "But we should not drink to get drunk." We toasted again and his eyes grew red and blurry.

"I come from a long line of marksman and bodyguards. Shooting is in my blood," Doguur continued, the beer egging on his pride.

"My great-grandfather was a bodyguard for the leader of the Chinese Buriats. And my grandfather was the most famous sharpshooter in Hailar. He was also a bodyguard for the Buriat leaders and protected their cattle. The Evenki always tried stealing Buriat livestock, so he was hired to patrol the grasslands."

I asked him if his grandfather had ever shot an Evenki.

"Of course he did, but he never would say that. A Buriat soldier never brags about killing enemies. Do American soldiers count the people they kill?"

I assured him they didn't. (Although recent reports from Iraq indicate otherwise).

Doguur gulped down more of his beer, Chris ordered another round, and the story continued. "The Chinese government," he said, "learned that my grandpa was a great shooter and they drafted him into the People's Liberation Army. In 1950 he was sent to North Korea to fight against the South. He died there during a bombing raid but he is still considered to be a hero." The tale went on but was becoming incomprehensible. Doguur planted his head on the table, slid off his chair and finally knocked a beer mug to the ground. No one seemed to notice as the shattered glass spun across the dance floor.

We paid our bar tab and left. Doguur staggered beside us and hooked his thumb into my *buus* (silk belt). A large crowd was loitering outside the concert hall where an awards ceremony and fireworks display had started. A man with a flare-gun was supplying the fireworks.

Doguur was sure he could recognize his house, so we tried taking him home. As we wandered aimlessly in the blackness, a huge man with a wrestler's physique appeared from the shadows and latched onto the three of us for support. He was drunk too. It was a Python-esque scene as the four of us staggered aimlessly in the dark, slipping in the muddy streets.

Doguur led us into the wrong house. The occupants were roused, but were not in the least alarmed to find four strangers lurching around their living room, knocking over furniture in the dark.

We meandered back into the warm summer night, thumbs locked into belts. Again we stumbled along, quietly humming tunes and babbling to each other a mixture of English, Russian, Mongolian, Chinese and Buriat. Eventually Chris and I realized that finding our companion's home was impossible. We collected ourselves, said goodnight and passed Doguur and the wrestler off to another assemblage of intoxicated Buriats. Singing loudly, they tripped off into the darkened alleys of Dashbalbar.

That was the last I saw of Doguur. I do hope that he got his Mercedes-Benz and has been burning up the pavement. However, Altargana was not the last I would see of the Buriats. There was still one piece missing to the great Buriat puzzle that I had not discovered. And although I didn't know it at the time, it seemed that the fates were directing me back to the Buriat homeland to find what lay at the core of this society. Shamanism—overlooked until now—was about to meet me at center stage.

~ 14 ~

SPIRITUAL RUN

ALTHOUGH BATBOLD NO LONGER WORKED at *The Mongol Messenger,*
he frequently visited our office to write articles about Buddhism. I
loved his work and published it regularly. One day he rolled in with
a religious piece that had nothing to do with Buddhism. It focused
on an old shaman named Baazar who lived out in Nailakh, the coal
mining town west of Ulaanbaatar. Batbold handed me a great photo
of Baazar to go with the story. Dressed in a rainbow-stripped Buriat
del and peaked cap, the bearded Baazar sat in wide-eyed wonder,
starring into the camera.

Until then I knew little about Shamanism. Batbold's interview
would be my first peek into the Shaman's world.

"When I was just a young man," Baazar began, "I became very
ill, almost to the point of death. I spent month after month bedrid-
den and waiting for the end. The lamas could do nothing for me.
The old holy men of Nalaikh secretly came to my bedside and whispered prayers. But nothing came of it.

"One day, after much prodding, a shaman came to my home and
determined that a spirit was fighting inside of me. If I would not be-

come a shaman I would die, the man said. We Buriats call this spirit *utha*, which is like an extra soul. When the *utha* releases its energy it causes extreme sickness, then the *utha* will come in a vision.

"My mother confided that both my father and grandfather had been shamans. But I was not convinced that my fate lay as a shaman. It was too dangerous and I couldn't accept the responsibilities or the consequences. The year was 1950, and anyone suspected of practicing religion, particularly Shamanism, was thrown in jail. Instead I traveled to Dornod to find my Buriat cousins. I hoped that they could cure me.

"I stayed with relatives in one of the northern villages. One day, while walking through the pine groves, I found strange people running about in the woods. They told me I should go to the mountain with sheep and goats. Maybe it was just a dream, but it felt real. Through the woods I walked, drifting in and out of reverie, until I came upon a small tent encampment. A man approached and said that in order to survive I would need to become a shaman. "The spirits are pounding on your soul," he told me.

"I was directed to the tent of an old woman who said she could help. I sat silently in her presence as she put on the shaman's robe and began reading beautiful poetry. Suddenly I had a moment of clarity. I had never experienced a feeling like that before; a complete letting go. As I sat in this state, my clothes were ripped from my body by an unknown force. The old lady leaned over and with her eyes wide open she blew on me—as if the spirits were being expelled from her body.

"She looked up at me with her bleary eyes and said a spirit had entered my body. It had been searching for me for 20 years by following the footprints of insects. The old woman had acted as a superconductor between the spirit world and me. While in her trance the woman recounted every detail of my life as told by the spirit, a guard named Ogmon Tenger. The spirit said my sickness would soon end. When I woke in the morning there was no more pain. It was then that I decided to become a shaman."

* * *

For many Americans, Shamanism is not a foreign concept. In fact, Shamanism took off during the 1960s counterculture movement and is now a fixture among New Agers seeking spiritual solace. You can join shaman workshops from Honolulu to Hoboken and in today's virtual world, hopeful shamans can even sign up for on-line courses, paid with Visa or Mastercard.

The ancient version of Shamanism, I soon learned, predates just about every temple and holy book on Earth. Dating back to the Neolithic period (7000 to 10,000 years before Christ), it was a faith that grew from necessity. The belief in spirits required a mediator, someone of high social standing that could enter the spirit world and negotiate on behalf of humans for abundant crops, a safe journey, luck in battle or good health. Filled with peril, a lifetime of experience was needed to successfully negotiate the spiritual planes.

The belief system rose independently across parts of Eurasia and Africa, but its growth was seen most significantly in Central Asia. The dawn of more organized religions threatened Shamanism but in some cases the two merely blended into one. In Tibet, most notably, Buddhism was forced to mix with the native Bön faith, resulting in what we now called Tibetan Buddhism, or Lamaism.

Shamans with their spirits in tow were among the first peoples to cross the Bering Straights into the Americas. Shamanism traveled to Japan and mixed with Shinto. It went to Finland where the tietäjä, a figure equivalent to the shaman, still practices today. In Mongolia, Shamanism existed even before the Mongols became the dominant ethnic group. Its longevity has shaped their core and imbued them with a deep sense of respect for nature, Mother Earth, and the elements.

Shamanism remained widespread in Mongolia until the end of the 16th century, when the Mongol leader Altan Khan invited an army of Tibetan monks to Mongolia to convert his people. Shamanism retreated to the most impenetrable forests of northern Mongolia as new laws were adopted to weed out the faith. Rituals involving sacrifice were condemned, practitioners were punished, and the Shamanic *ongons* (idols) were burned. Shamans were murdered or fumigated with burning dog feces. But the Buddhists found that some harmless Shamanic rites, such as worshipping nature and the eternal blue sky, were too difficult to eliminate. In the end, many of these rites were adopted by Buddhists.

The last links to the old faith were smashed again when the Communists took over in the 1920s. Rather than fumigating the shamans they just shot them or sent them to prison work camps in Siberia.

Democracy allowed for the return of shamanism. Its popularity grew rapidly. Old folks turned to the shamans in search of health remedies; entrepreneurs sought advice on improving their business-es; herders asked for the return of lost cattle; and students went to the shamans in hopes of scoring better results on exams. Soon conferences and ceremonies were held and modern Siberian Shamanism took shape.

This new Shamanism was fused with both communist and demo-cratic principles of equality, with re-worked ideology that avoided offending other religions. Shamans and scientists worked together to develop *Tengrianstvo* (Russian for Tengrism), which shifted the focus from the shaman (priest) to Tenger (heaven), bringing it closer to Christianity and the belief in a God in heaven that oversees and designs all. The scientists insisted that the new approach would draw a wider, more liberal audience, helping to bring Shamanism out of the Dark Ages. The shamans, however, had little contact with the outside world and, without books, less bargaining power at the conference table.

"The shamans started to believe that the academic scholar was more respected. He became the model," said my anthropologist friend Laetitia. "The shamans started confirming their own prac-tices with the scientists, as if something written in a book must be true. Now the scholars are teaching the shamans as a way of holding onto traditions that don't exist anymore. Maybe the traditions only existed in the mind of an old Soviet folklorist. They try to freeze the culture. What they don't understand is that shamanism is not dogmatic, but always changing within a frame created by the individual shaman."

A few weeks after the Altargana Festival, I was back in eastern Mongolia's Bayan Uul, a small enclave of Siberian log cabins and larch forests. There I found a dozen people engaged in building a new monastery. They were busy whacking logs apart, sawing planks and hammering boards. An old lady with gray streaked hair tied in a long braid ordered me to sit down for *suutei tsai* and biscuits.

"Sit, sit, drink, drink," she commanded.

The male laborers, including three monks, stopped their work to ask familiar questions.

"How old are you?"

"I'm twenty-six."

"That's very young. Where are you from?"

"America."

"Oh, you have good democracy in your country. What is your name?"

"Michael."

"Aha! Michael Jordan."

"No, Michael Jackson."

"Hey, Jackson," they said, missing the joke, "Do you drink vodka?"

"No." There was a shaking of heads.

"Do you smoke?"

"No."

"Are you married?"

"No."

"You don't smoke, you don't drink, you're not married. What's wrong with you?!" the older one asked.

"Are you a missionary?" asked one of the monks, attempting to reconcile such puritanical behavior.

"No, I am not a missionary. I work for Montsame."

They didn't believe this either. When I first came to Mongolia everyone mistook me for a Russian. Now that the Russians are all but gone, and with the missionary numbers rising, I was frequently asked this question.

"I am Jewish actually." A look of confusion.

"It's another religion, you know, Israel?" I said helpfully.

They discussed this among themselves. "Jews are clever," one announced.

"Thanks," I said. "And you? Are you red or yellow Buddhists?"

"Yellow," said one of the older rough-hewn men, throwing a thumb in the direction of his half-built temple. "Dalai Lama."

"What about Shamanism?"

"Oh, we all believe in Shamanism too, but we are Buddhists. Did you see a shaman?" he asked.

"You should see Tsereng," the old lady chirped before I could answer.

"Who is Tsereng?"

"Tsereng is the fat old shaman of the mountain," she said, extending her arms out in front of her, as if supporting a huge imaginary belly.

Tsereng sounded like a man of great importance, and the builders were eager to send me to him. They pointed toward the mountains. Their directions would have been perfect, if I had a horse. There are no street addresses in Mongolia—there are hardly any streets. Looking for someone would be a matter of wandering about and asking his neighbors. Instead I headed for the road out of town, dropped my backpack in the grass, pulled out a dusty copy of Edward Abbey's *A Season in the Wilderness,* and waited for a lift. After one car left me in a cloud of fine Siberian silt, I resorted to the

Tibetan style of hitchhiking and set up a road block of boulders to ensure the next car would stop.

As the hours passed and the sun headed toward the horizon I could see an emerging dust storm. It was a bullet-gray van blazing up the road, madly zig-zagging at breakneck speed. At the last moment the car skidded to halt in front of my rock barricade and I peered inside. The back of the van was full of goods from a Russian trading market: beer, sausages, soda pop, fabric, clothing, tires, petrol cans, cheese, boots, green apples and canned fruit. The occupants of the cab, just in from the border, flung open the doors and fell out of the car. The driver staggered around in the dust, tripped over himself, and dropped to the ground in a heap. The other passengers were in a similar state.

A woman inside the cab soberly and sternly pointed to an open bottle of vodka. The driver shook off my offer to drive—he felt as comfortable behind the wheel as he did in the saddle despite his mile-high blood alcohol level. I really didn't mind. After sitting in the dust for four hours I was just happy to be back on the road.

We sped down the open road, swerving around divots and flying over bumps, our cargo sliding to and fro. We shared a bottle of Ochikov. The directions to Tsereng's home went something like, "Go over two passes, around a bend and over a bridge; then go west up a valley for a few kilometers. . ."

Still, it was hard to keep track, and after I realized we must have gone too far I asked the driver to stop at the top of a hill. We all fell out of the car again at a large *ovoo*—a pile of stones sacred to Mongolians and shamans in particular. The *ovoo*, found on just about every pass across the country, is a meeting place for the nature spirit that presides over the pass or nearby mountain. It is *de rigueur* for travelers who pass an *ovoo* to walk around it three times, adding a stone to the pile on each pass. This shows respect for the spirit who grants safe passage.

We walked around the *ovoo* and the driver brought out his bottle of Chingis vodka from the front seat. He poured a swig into a cup (actually the light cover on the ceiling of the van) and tossed the vodka skyward, a gift for the sky god Tenger. He poured again and passed the cup around until there was no alcohol left. The bottle joined a dozen other beer and vodka receptacles on the *ovoo*. A variety of other offerings lay at its base: old car parts, horse and cow skulls, bits of torn money, dried cheese, and a crutch. This debris is not considered refuse. They are gifts to the spirits.

After toasting the gods, the driver hugged me, tried to kiss me and then demanded that I visit his home in Choibalsan City. He ordered the woman to give me some food and I was left with a huge slab of ham, some cheese, a loaf of bread, and a half-liter of Ochikov beer. Mongolians appreciate rough travel and know what it takes for a traveler to get by.

They sped off down the other side of the pass, and I was left alone in the tall grass under a blazing sky. The summer sunsets at this latitude last an incredibly long time and the whole world seemed washed in orange light. It was too late to look for Tsereng so I ambled off the road and pitched my tent in the grass.

As I sat there, feasting on my meal of ham, cheese and beer, I watched the stars come out one by one. They sparkled like Christmas lights against the black universe. Because of its high elevation and lack of urban light, Mongolia is one of the best places in the world to stargaze.

The planet Venus, or Tsolmon, stood out brightly above the horizon. This planet is the source of comets and meteors, which are said to be war arrows launched in battle. Venus is usually painted on the shaman's drum along with the Great Bear constellation, as a way to channel power. Another group of heavenly bodies, the Pleiades, are considered a group of spirits associated with the creation of the first shaman.

According to a Buriat legend, Ulgen Tenger, the leader of the 55 benevolent western Tengers, created mankind. He gave them a life free of disease and trouble, which angered the ox-headed Erleg Khan, the leader of the 44 malicious eastern Tengers. In retribution, Erleg Khan sent disease and sadness to humans. As more and more humans grew sick, the western spirits held a conference in the Pleiades to determine what should be done. After much debate, they sent an eagle to cure the sick as a shaman might do. The eagle flew down from heaven but found that it could not heal—it had been created by the eastern spirits and could not speak the human language. The bird retreated to the Pleiades and described his problem to the Tengers.

They deliberated again and advised the eagle to mate with a woman. He returned to Earth and made love with a beautiful woman resting under a tree. Their son became the first shaman. Because of his divine origins, the shaman had fantastic powers. He could perform amazing feats and travel around the Earth like a bolt of lightning. His pupils were equally talented, and some grew arrogant. The Tengers did not like to see their power infringed upon, so they challenged Hara-Gyrgen, one of the most renowned shamans. Ulgen Tenger stole the soul of a girl from Hara-Gyrgen's clan, and her body was left almost lifeless. Hara-Gyrgen traveled to the upper world in search of the girl's soul, which he found in a bottle Ulgen Tenger had capped with his thumb. The shaman turned himself into a bee and stung the god on the neck. When the Tenger slapped at his neck, the shaman swooped into the bottle and came out carrying the trapped soul back to safety.

Ulgen Tenger was furious. He decided to punish the shaman for his hubris. Hara-Gyrgen was forced to spend eternity jumping up and down on top of a mountain. When the mountain is worn away, Ulan Tenger declared that the power of the shamans will be lost forever. Up to now, it is believed that the shaman is still jumping. Since the mountain is shrinking, the powers of the shamans are not as strong as they once were; their ability to communicate with the spirits is lessened and humans cannot understand some of their songs.

With these romantic visions dancing in my head, I slipped into my little green tent and slept soundly.

The following morning I hid my backpack in the tall grass and set off in search of Tsereng. I was tired of lugging all my gear so I took with me only the essentials—a camera, notepad, pen, and Mongolian-English dictionary. I wandered about the yellow hills for a couple of hours, lost and thirsty, wishing the shamans' spirits would carry me to their fat mountain healer. Then I saw a horseman trotting up a nearby path. I waved him over. The horseman was wrapped in a purple *del* tied with a yellow *buus*. Bright eyes glared out from under his heavy eyelids. He was on his way to town to sell yogurt, stored in a metal jug lashed to his back. Seeing my exhaustion, he dismounted, sat in the grass, and unsealed his stock of fresh dairy. He plucked a weed from the ground, dipped it into the container, and flicked drops of the cream in all four directions as an offering.

Yogurt is not the first thing that comes to mind when wanting to quench one's thirst, but in this case, nothing could have been better. It was thin and sour, yet contained a freshness one can only appreciate when drunk from a metal bucket in a grassy field. I thanked the nomad for his generosity and told him I was lost en route to Tsereng. He pointed down the valley to a homestead.

"Tsereng Bo," he said.

Upon arriving at the homestead, I was able to see that Tsereng Bo (*bo* means shaman) really wasn't that fat. He had a paunch but compared to the folks I'd seen in Branson, Missouri, Tsereng was a veritable swimsuit model. He wore a red silk shirt that fell over his belly and sported a gray handlebar moustache on his weathered and shorn head. A clump of whiskers grew from a large mole on his cheek. His eyes narrowed when I introduced myself, as if he was staring into my soul.

The old shaman lived in an idyllic golden valley, with a small lake surrounded by hills dotted with pine trees. His large wooden house

was impressive and had corrals and stables for the animals, now out
to pasture. Tsereng even had his own on-site Buddhist temple—the
fat shaman was also a fat lama.

Tsereng was not alone. A group of people in city clothes were
milling about, as well as a dozen children in Buriat *dels*. A Japanese
tourist was there too, taking photos. There appeared to be some
kind of ceremony going on. When it started, the tourist pulled me
aside and informed me that I would need to pay proper respects to
Tsereng Bo. This included giving Tg5000 ($5), a bottle of vodka
and a silk scarf called *khadak*. Realizing that I had come unpre-
pared, Shinji, my new acquaintance, happily donated the required
items for my benefit.

As it turned out, Shinji was not a tourist at all. He was an anthropologist on a field trip to document the life of Tsereng. I had arrived
at the right time—a weekend festival was in full swing. Shinji said
he had known Tsereng for several years and told me the old shaman
once welcomed all visitors. A European woman even became a shaman under his tutelage. But since then Tsereng has mastered the free
market economy and no longer had the free and easy schedule of
his younger years. For meetings he now charges $5; pictures would
cost a hefty $12.

Tsereng accepted my gifts with a cursory glance and placed the
vodka bottle on his altar, joining it with the other "spirits." We were
sitting in his "shaman temple"—a small *ger*-shaped structure with
benches for visitors, and colored wall pictures of the shamanic spirits. Like the Buddhist pantheon, they appeared in a variety of forms:
horrible monsters, gentle angels and wizened prophets. Tsereng's
paraphernalia—masks, drums, bells and cloak—hung behind him.
A table full of butterlamps and monetary offerings was at one end;
my gift was added to the pile. Underneath was an array of animal
parts: legs, shoulders, ribs, and the grinning head of a goat that had
been sacrificed the night before.

Tsereng leaned back on his orange throne and answered my

questions with terse gruffness. He was clearly not interested in giving interviews, but I had paid my $5. After some introductions, I asked about his profession.

"I am shaman!" he barked. I slunk back into my seat.

"Yeah . . . But weren't you trained as something else during the communist era?" I thought it a fair question, since monks I had met were often happy to tell me of their careers as mechanics or truck drivers during communism.

Tsereng, however, did not want to dwell on the past. He described briefly how in his youth he had been arrested and jailed twice for practicing Shamanism—once for five years and another time for two. His life outside prison had been equally difficult and he had never earned anything from the communist-era. There was no free education, training or benefits. Democracy, he said, was the best thing that had happened in his life. Because of it, his home now doubled as a sort of retreat center-cum-pilgrimage site, an impossible dream just a decade ago. But while conceding that democracy had saved him, Tsereng and I knew that it was Shamanism that would protect him in the long run. As a secret forest-dwelling religion, Shamanism would forever guard him behind a veil of mysticism.

The interview had gotten off to an awkward start and had only gone downhill from there. His mind seemed pre-occupied, answering my questions briefly or not at all. He didn't seem to notice when I thanked him and slipped away to the back of the Shaman Temple. Staring blankly ahead—as if already in a trance—Tsereng called upon his blind assistant to proceed with the next order of business.

Some people had come up from Choibalsan to seek advice and blessings from Tsereng Bo. With my meeting adjourned the blind shaman announced that a ceremony was to begin straight away. The visitors sat on wooden benches and stared in awe as Tsereng began his ritual.

Warm sunlight passed through the open hole in the roof, illuminating the dust particles inside the *ger*. Despite the heat, Tsereng hauled a huge black cloak over his shoulders; it was decorated with bits of colored cloth and metal bars that acted as armor during the dangerous trip to other worlds. These bars are also said to absorb energy, as a magnet would, to power the cosmic ride. Tsereng closed his eyes and began to beat his drum. The pudgy blind assistant shaman rang a bell. The song they chanted sounded so much like that of a Native American, we could just as easily have been on a Hopi Indian reservation.

The music continued for some time and no one said a word. Tsereng swayed to the rhythmic beat as he fell into a trance. Another man burned juniper branches and waved the smoke around the room, hoping to attract spirits. Then the crowd started to react.

"*Hurai! Hurai!*" they chanted. "*Hurai! Hurai!*"

"There are spirits here," whispered Shinji as the songs grew louder.

The spectators, dressed in street clothes and dels, arched their backs and fingered their prayer beads. Occasionally they extended their arms and waved their cupped hands, drawing hiimori into their body. Some were busy writing questions on scraps of paper. Then they chanted all at once.

"*Hurai! Hurai!*"

All the hollering, drumming and background chatter gave the small wooden shack the feel of a Sunday church revival. The quietest person may have been Tsereng. Shamans sometimes make the sounds of animals as they travel between the worlds—growling like a bear or cawing like a bird as the spirits of these animals enter and guide them. Our shaman was silent but beads of sweat rolled down his face. When he started to twitch and jerk a man moved behind him to break a possible fall. While Tsereng's soul journeyed across the spiritual planes, the ceremony occasionally stopped for questions to the spirits. The spectators would be called to kneel before Tsereng while one of the younger shamans read out the questions.

"I have a pain in my liver," one elderly woman had written.

"You should treat yourself with natural herbs and say prayers to the spirits every day," the *ongod* said in a gruff voice through Tsereng.

"My business is not doing so well," another paper read. The spirit asked what kind of business he was involved in.

"I have a restaurant in Choibalsan," the man told Tsereng "But we don't get many customers."

"The spirits are stopping customers from coming to your restaurant, you should make on offering to the sky when you get to work each day," the *ongod* said. The restaurateur returned to his seat and recorded into his notebook what the spirits had announced. As I watched this I thought of Indra back in Ulaanbaatar. She was a Buriat like these folk and also a strong believer in the occult. Despite her business-like exterior, Indra, more than anyone else at *The Messenger*, had a predilection for the superstitious. She watched the astrological charts, checked her horoscope, and consulted the lamas. Even little things, like getting a haircut, had to be done on the "correct day" as appointed by the spirits. Dressed in her neatly pressed black skirt and silk blouse, I had a hard time imagining her here among them, but I guessed that in the right mood, anyone could be taken in by the spirits.

Sometimes prospective shamans came to Tsereng for training. At the time I visited him, there was a man from the Buriat Republic in Russia taking a shaman's course, his third degree (there are 13 in total).

Ayush, a middle-aged construction worker, was thin in body and wore a trim moustache on his sullen face. His beady eyes, set below a streak of matted hair, remained fixed in blank stares. His smile revealed gaping holes where teeth once stood; those that remained were capped with gold. He showed almost no emotion at all, and when it was his turn to speak he did so in a nervous and mumbling tone. Ayush firmly believed he had psychic powers, and had received training from a shaman in Russia. But his teacher died after the first course, since then he had been developing his skills under the tutelage of Tsereng Bo.

"Tell me about your powers," I urged as we sat on logs eating a dinner of noodle soup prepared by Shinji's wife. Ayush spoke, or rather mumbled, a mixture of Buriat and Russian that made him very difficult to understand. The Buriat language is similar to Mongolian, but has a heavy accent and some different words. The "S" is replaced by "H," so that *"Sain bain uu?"* ("How are you?") becomes *"Hain bain uu?"*

"One night in 1984 I was drinking vodka in my home," said Ayush. "Suddenly on the TV I saw a beautiful woman, like a spirit. I asked her questions and she told me about the future of my friends and family. But you know what?" he said, pausing for effect. "The TV was off."

"How many cups of vodka had you drank that night?" I asked, a little suspicious.

"Then in 1989," he continued, ignoring my question, "a similar situation occurred. I was sitting in my living room with the TV off when it suddenly flicked on and showed a conference of the "sky deities." There was a paper being printed out, like a fax, but in those days we didn't know what fax machines were. The fax said that I should become a shaman, and join the other shamans of the world who live everywhere, even in San Francisco and Mexico."

Those around the circle nodded in wonder.

"What did your family think?" I asked.

"Oh, at first my wife was nagging me; she said I was a foolish drunk. But then the things I said started coming true," his face brightened a little with that. "My friends and family started to believe me but then people decided they didn't like to hear the future, it was always so gloomy; so I stopped."

"Then why did you start pursuing Shamanism again?" I asked.

222

"I still believed in my powers," he said, "I couldn't turn my back on the spirits, so I continued to study for myself. Anyway, people shouldn't be afraid or mad at me. It's not *me* making these predictions. *It's the spirits.*"

That night Ayush was going to summon the spirits and request permission to attain the third degree. Tsereng was exhausted and retired to his shaman *ger* for a long sleep. This time the blind shaman led the ceremony. The sun had gone down and it was getting dark, now was the time when the spirits would be most active.

The clouds, a wispy shade of pearl-gray, turned darker until the sky was ebony black all around. There was no moon. The area was illuminated by a raging bonfire, which lit up the spectator's faces with flickers of orange. A crowd of people had gathered to watch. Some were the folks who had come up from Choibalsan City; other Mongolian tourists had traveled from neighboring villages.

"We came here to watch a shaman ceremony," said one man, sounding uncannily like the same visitors who had come from Denmark or Canada or Spain. "There aren't any shamans in our village so I thought I would take my family to see one."

Another man named Altangerel, whom I recognized from the Altargana Festival, squeezed onto the bench next to me. His huge Buriat *del* smelled of mutton grease. He was a swarthy old character with a big bald head and child-size glasses that were lashed together with frayed string. He carried a large staff decorated with feathers.

"Enjoying your visit?" I asked.

"Oh yes. We have lots of shamans in my village but Tsereng Bo is the only one I really trust when I need my fortune told."

"So you came here for your fortune? What was it?"

"Good news. The spirit advised me to sell lots of sheep this year, as the price will be higher than usual. Tsereng predicted I would have good fortune and health because I respect the spirits."

Meanwhile, Ayush was having no luck with his spirits. With instructions to run around a grove of trees (a little bigger than the size of a basketball court) until a trance was induced, he set off on a jog. When the trance came he was to climb the highest one, the *toroo*, in order to contact the Tengers. As the shaman ascends the nine rungs of this representational World Tree, he sings a song of praise to the spirits and at last will fall into a state of ecstasy—induced by the beating drum and shouts from the audience.

"When does Ayush climb the tree?" I asked Tsereng's son and financial manager.

"Only the spirits can decide that, it may take all night," he said seriously, although at the time I thought he was just being facetious.

Ayush, decked out in his Shaman's costume, ran diligently around the trees in a pair of Adidas track shoes. A dozen Buriat children came skipping after him, singing a repetitive nonsense rhyme that went "*Ah hey, yo hey minge ho . . . Ah ya mahe minte go . . .*"

The children were dressed in their *dels*—blue for the boys and purple for the girls—and some had long silk scarves tied to their little peaked caps. The boys and girls, running through a forest with songs on their lips and innocence in their hearts, made me feel as though I had descended into a child's fairy tale.

The blind shaman continued to pound his drum as Ayush ran round the trees. But as the hours wore on, Ayush grew tired. His run became a stagger as blisters swelled up on his feet. His clothes were soaked with sweat. When he stopped, an old woman fanned him down with a rag as if he were a prizefighter. Soon he got up to run again.

The stars changed their positions in the sky, but there seemed no end to Ayush's running. The crowds drifted away. They trooped into a nearby barn that served as a shelter for the pilgrims. Meanwhile, the children amazed me—not a single complaint crossed their lips. It was well past 2am but they continued to skip and sing after Ayush, pushing him forward with their shoulders, possessed by their *utha*, their extra soul.

"Ah hey, yo hey minge ho . . . Ah ya mahe minte go. . ."
"Ah hey, yo hey minge ho . . . Ah ya mahe minte go. . ."

Ayush stopped occasionally and stood below the tree; his hands clinging to its branches and his head hanging. He panted and trembled, but couldn't fall into a trance. Was it his fault or the spirits'? Meanwhile, poor Ayush ran and ran and ran.

At one point, a vodka cup ritual was organized. Someone filled a cup with vodka and tossed it aside, cup and all. Ayush circled the vessel and prayed to it, beckoning the spirits to join him. This didn't work either. Ayush resumed his running.

"Ah hey, yo hey minge ho . . . Ah ya mahe minte go . . ." the children sang.

I fell in and out of sleep all night long, awakened occasionally by the drumming or the chants of little voices rising out of the wood and into the broad arc of stars. I could not tell how much was a dream and how much was real.

Finally the sky faded into a dim blue oblivion that marked the morning. I rose and found the participants milling about like zombies. Ayush had failed to climb the tree. Tsereng was roused for advice. Everyone guessed that the spirits hadn't come because he was missing.

Informed of the night's events, Tsereng fell groggily out of his shamans' *ger*, and elected to resolve the matter by way of the cup ritual. He would flip a cup in the air, and being guided by the force of Tenger, if the cup landed upward, Ayush could receive the degree. If it landed downward, he could never progress beyond his current level. As I saw it, Ayush's hopes, and four years of study, were now up to gravity.

As it turned out, the cup landed upwards. Ayush wore a little smirk that for a brief moment made him look a touch enlightened. It seemed illogical to complete such a complex and esoteric ceremony with a simple solution. But Western logic is of little use in these spirit-dwelling forests.

At one time I thought that the shamanic cult could take off in Mongolia, a country longing to rediscover its historical past. But as I walked back to the main road to await a vehicle that would take me back to Ulaanbaatar, I realized how Shamanism was not destined to become an urban faith. It could not compete with the Christian-Buddhist rivalry brewing in the capital. It was destined to exist only amid the vast wilderness where it was born.

~ 15 ~

OVER THE MOON CUCKOO

In the heart of the Gobi Desert is a sacred place called Dulaan Khar.
During the dark depths of winter, the argali sheep and wild moun-
tain goats descend to this place to seek shelter. But no herder would
dare to set his ger in such a holy place.
—from "The Desert Dreamer," November 3, 1999

SO STARTED THE MOST BIZARRE STORY ever published in *The Mongol*
Messenger. The first time I picked up the article I could hardly get
through the first few paragraphs before I was lost in its mystic desert labyrinth and cadenced religious references.

"Bayarmaa, what is this? I can't make heads or tails of it! Who
wrote this?!"

"I translated it out of *Önöödor,* see," she said, holding up the
newspaper. "Somebody named Dogmid wrote it."

A deadline was looming and I had no interest in trying to deci-
pher Dogmid's religious ramblings. Since the author did not work
at Montsame we couldn't ask for any clarifications. The fact that
nobody asked Mr. Dogmid if we could reproduce his story was ir-

relevant. The concept of intellectual property rights did not exist in Mongolia. Thus when we were short on material, Indra would pick stories out of the daily papers and assign them to Bayarmaa for translation.

"Well, we've got a deadline to beat in the morning. Can you PLEASE give me something I can understand."

Grudgingly, Bayarmaa pounded out another story, which allowed me to sit on the wild mountain goat story until I had time for a proper read of this strange tale. For the moment, getting the paper out on time was our number one concern, and it wasn't going to happen if I had to spend half the night languishing in lyrical obscurity.

A couple of weeks later, Bayarmaa and I found the time to sit down together and dive headlong into the story we had tried so hard to ignore. With the original copy of the text in one hand and an English-Mongolian dictionary in the other, Bayarmaa navigated our way through the story. Only after we finished did I finally start to appreciate what a wonderfully mysterious yarn it was.

The author of the article depicted the life and times of Danzan Rabjaa, sometime painter, playwright, healer, lover, songwriter, statesman and social critic. It was suggested that the monk, living in the early 19th century, was an alcoholic womanizer with serious psychological problems.

The article contained curious anecdotes and tidbits of information: that Danzan Rabjaa owned the head and skin of a Mongolian Yeti (something like an abominable snowman); that he built a European-style bathroom where he and his disciples could wash away layers of Gobi dust; that when foreigners tried taking a picture of him, the only image that appeared in the photo was a black outline of his body.

Danzan Rabjaa, according to the newspaper article, was not entirely sane. The signature quote ending his poems was, "Drunken Rabjaa has gone mad, drunken Rabjaa is shouting!" By sequestering himself for weeks on end in caves or his doorless *ger*, he earned the moniker Dogshin ("Terrible") Danzan Rabjaa.

The monk seemed to have acquired almost mythical status in the Gobi, where legends and stories about him are still passed down through the generations—not unlike Robin Hood or Jesse James. He became so popular, in fact, that a museum dedicated to protecting his legacy recently opened in the provincial capital Sainshand. I was still keen to learn more about Buddhism, and this strange monk proved so fascinating, that I decided to visit the museum.

Sainshand lies ten hours away by train from Ulaanbaatar. I didn't bother much with packing. I had become very Mongolian in the way I traveled. In the past I always left home with a huge backpack full of clothes and other junk, but since my trip to Tsereng Bo, when I had shaken off the yoke of my worldly belongings, I decided to leave everything behind except the journalistic essentials. I had it in mind—like the nomads who traverse the steppes with nothing more than a bag of rock hard *arul*—that I'd just pop into a *ger* for the occasional cup of *airag*.

The train car was nearly empty but I shared a compartment with a small man in a gray suit whose legs, when he sat down, were not long enough to reach the floor. He introduced himself as Batbayar, a thirty-year veteran employee of the Mongol Bank branch in Sainshand. He was returning to Sainshand after attending a banking seminar in Ulaanbaatar. As we got acquainted, the train jolted to a start and we were off to the desert.

By late evening the train made its halfway stop in Choir, a wreck of a town on the edge of the Gobi that had once served as a secret military base for the Soviet army during the Cold War. The purpose of Choir (and two other bases in Mongolia) was to act as a front line barrier against any invasion from China. That event never occurred and when the Soviet Union ceased to exist, the bases were abandoned. They now lie in ruins—stripped to the bone by Mongolian scavengers. The foundations of Choir are today as bizarre and mysterious as any ruins from antiquity.

The runways, once prized by the Soviet air force, are still there. While I wouldn't go so far as to call them "geopolitically strategic" somebody surely saw value in them. There were even rumors that the United States had secretly test landed F-14s on them. True or not, we may never know.

After a brief stop to allow 11-year old vendors to board the train and sell *buuz,* we were off again. As the train clanked forward in the winter night, Batbayar and I talked and the conversation eventually wrapped its way around to Danzan Rabjaa. When I told him of my interest in the old monk his face broke into an excited smile.

"Yes, I know of him. Everyone in Sainshand knows Rabjaa."

I asked for his opinion on the matter and he said that during the communist days Rabjaa was not highly regarded—people seemed to think of him only as a debauched drunk. They enjoyed his poetry however, so his books were still read. He was a sort of Jim Morison of the steppes.

"What did he write about?"

"Oh, nature, love, race horses—those sorts of things. But some of it was critical. He criticized the Manchus and the aristocrats and sinful lamas, anyone really," Batbayar said.

"Do you still think of him as a drunkard?"

"Oh, no! Not anymore," he was shocked at the idea. "Now we recognize Rabjaa as a great thinker and a leader. In the past, we couldn't follow him so closely because he was a monk and Buddhism was banned. But now we can do whatever we want. Some people even rebuilt his monastery."

Batbayar said the monastery was an hour away from Sainshand and I thought I might go there. He also told me to find a man known as "Museum" Altangerel, who would know a lot about Danzan Rabjaa. "He is the one you want to interview."

* * *

The Danzan Rabjaa Museum, a former bank building (Batbayar's old stomping grounds), had been redone to look like a Buddhist temple. A miniature curved roof and an overhang decorated with dragons had been tacked onto the building like Lego pieces. On arrival I found Museum Altangerel, huddled over a chipped radiator that gave off just the slightest hint of warmth.

The black leather jacket he wore covered a body more suited to a wrestling ring than a museum. He seemed to be in his mid-forties and actually looked a little bit like Danzan Rabjaa, who loomed behind him in a wall painting. The museum was small, dominated in the middle by a wax statue of Rabjaa. All around were little trinkets, Buddhist statues, sutras and paintings. The artwork had recurring images—scorpions and swans predominated. Human bones were another popular motif. Altangerel recounted how Buddhist monks favored bone for its spiritual quality. Craniums of learned lamas had been made into cups and drums. A string of beads was fashioned from the skulls of 108 monks. The femur of an 18-year-old virgin had been formed into a trumpet. Even Danzan Rabjaa's bones were on display, encased in a glass jar like a science experiment.

I found more haunting displays inside a case that held Buddhist treasure mangled during the 1930s purges—singed sutras and mutilated deities. One statue of the Buddha had been pierced from behind with a bullet hole, shot during the ransacking of the temples.

"These are the previous incarnations of Danzan Rabjaa," said Altangerel, pointing to a wall that held a row of neat, cartoon-like figures. Rabjaa was the fifth (out of seven) Mongolian incarnates of the *Gobi Noyon Khutagt* (Lord Saint of the Gobi). The Mongolian lineage was preceded by 33 Tibetan and Indian incarnations. The first supposedly lived in Tibet about 2,000 years ago. These incarnations were believed to be a product of Yansang Yidam, a Buddhist deity embodying wizardry, power and genius. His portrait also hung on the wall—a monstrous creature with four legs, six arms and three snarling faces. Sinners were portrayed dying in agony under his stubby feet.

The incarnations appeared to me like a cast of super heroes—each one with special powers and qualities. Some could fly, stab themselves without injury or walk through walls. Others were beggars, herbalists or equestrians. One had long wild hair and was shown wielding a knife, while another sat peacefully in the lotus position. Paradise, depicted as a great green landscape with a deep blue sky and cotton clouds, surrounded the incarnations. Hellish creatures were also to be found in the paintings; dogs and birds feasting on the organs of live humans.

I asked Altangerel if he had the names of each incarnation. In response, he opened up one of the display cases and lifted out an old book bound with moldy leather. He opened it and flipped through flimsy handwritten pages, until he reached the right one, and skimmed down the squiggly Mongol script for the names.

"Danzan Rabjaa wrote this," he said. "It's on Chinese paper." It was the first museum I had visited where the exhibits also served as reference books. He went down the row of paintings and listed the names of each incarnation.

At the end of the section stood a display case with dozens of little playing-card sized drawings of figures in various sexual positions. Compared to the skilled hand that had so lovingly made the incarnate paintings, these were crude and childlike. Altogether they were an informal manual for eroticism—rather risqué artwork for a 19th-century Buddhist holy man, I thought.

"Rabjaa wrote that sex opens up the 108 veins of the body," Altangerel explained as I hovered over the pictures. "It was part of his Buddhist meditation."

Because Danzan Rabjaa belonged to the Red Sect (Kagyupa) of Buddhism, his views on sex and drinking were more liberal than the conservative Yellow Hat (Gelugpa) monks, who followed the order of the Dalai Lama. Mongolian monks, moreover, had their own interpretations of the Red Sect and tended to bend the rules even further.

Monks also misconstrued the true meaning of Tantra—often featured in artwork as two deities locked tightly in naked embrace—as a means for achieving pleasure. Some refer to it as "tantric sex," though this term seems to exist only in heavy metal rock songs. There actually is no sex in true Tantra. In later stages of meditation a practitioner may take a consort but only as a vehicle to advance his or her spirituality. The encounter should only happen once or twice, and while the man enters the woman, in Tantra, it is the woman who enters the man—in the spiritual sense.

Danzan Rabjaa may have missed that point, as legends tell of his lascivious behavior with a whole harem of women. Separating fact from fiction in this arena, however, is tricky. Altangerel assured me that most of those stories were merely myths.

"A lot of people have the wrong idea about Danzan Rabjaa," he said, "because there are so many legends about his magical powers and the women who lived with him. Actually, they were just students. He did a lot to educate women, and treated them as equals in his classes."

Altangerel, clearly impressed that I was taking notes, invited me to get some lunch. We went across the street to a grubby restaurant and ordered bowls of *suutei tsai* (milk tea) and *khuushuur* (mutton pancakes).

I bit into one and a river of grease cascaded onto my plate. Altangerel slurped up the contents of his *khuushuur* in the proper way with a mighty "shoooop!" Tucking in a second meat pancake, I asked him to tell me about the martial arts weaponry I had seen in the museum. Chinese throwing stars, daggers and swords seemed a curious addition to a museum dedicated to a monk.

"You know Kung-fu?" he asked, lifting up his hands in mock battle pose. "Danzan Rabjaa was a Kung-fu master."

"Did he ever fight anyone?"

"Well, yes. One time while traveling in China some bandits rode up to his caravan. They demanded money and women but Danzan Rabjaa refused. Instead he leapt down from his wagon and slew seven or eight of the miscreants with throwing stars and his bare fists." The story had Altangerel beaming with satisfaction. "One of the people in the caravan was a student from Japan. He was so impressed with the martial arts display that he gave Rabjaa his samurai sword."

Altangerel appeared to be a walking Danzan Rabjaa reference book. I asked him how he had become qualified to speak on such an obscure topic.

"I am the seventh generation curator," he said. "My ancestors have been taking care of Danzan Rabjaa's relics for nearly 150 years. You see, after Rabjaa died he was mummified and placed in a special temple. All his artwork and writings were also kept safe. The person who took care of those things was Balchinchoijoo. He was my grandfather's grandfather's grandfather. After he died the title of *takhilch* was passed to his son. It has been going on to this day."

I put down my *khuushuur* and looked up the word *takhilch* in my Mongolian-English dictionary. The exact definition was "monk in charge of the objects used in sacrifices." Clearly, Altangerel was no ordinary museum curator.

"Danzan Rabjaa is part of my family legacy. From a young age the *takhilch* begins to study Rabjaa's plays and learns how to care for his possessions. I learned from my grandfather. He taught me to read traditional script and Tibetan, both necessary to understand Rabjaa's poetry. But because it was during communism, we could not do this openly. He did not want people to know that I studied this. I was like a secret child. I could not go out to meet people and when others came over, I had to hide in the *ger* where we hung the meat. Come, I can show you our family tree."

Back in the museum, Altangerel dusted off a tube-shaped case covered with peeling camel hide and brass emblems. He released the latches and pulled out an old handwritten book that was bound

234

with frayed string. Each turn of a page marked years of his family history.

"This person," he said, tapping his finger on the thin paper, "is Khökh Taij. He was a writer and a teacher. His father was Suren Galda, also a writer. And his father was Batmönkh Galda, yet another writer."

Altangerel continued to tick off the names and occupations of his aristocratic ancestors and I wondered how far this family tree stretched. He said his copy was last updated in 1872, but the first ancestor listed was born in 1614. This fascinated me. Altangerel was a little piece of history himself—a man of princely blood who still protected the legacy of a mystic saint. My "living element" story angle was playing out better by the moment.

I met Altangerel and his son the next morning in front of the museum. We planned to take a ride to Khamaryn Khiid, Altangerel even brought a bag of food for the journey—a thermos of milk tea, some fried bread and the ubiquitous snack foods of Mongolia: sugarcoated peanuts from Vietnam and Disco cookies from the Czech Republic.

Before leaving I made a quick call back to *The Messenger* office to check on things. This was only a long weekend trip, but I wanted to make sure everything was on cue with the paper for my return on Monday morning. Amarbat answered the phone and had good news. Indra and Narantuya had been in the office that morning to write up a story and Undrakh was coming in later for translation duties. It was snowing, he added, and cold.

My conscience free, I paid the operator for the call and dashed out of the Sainshand Telephone Office (like a post office but for telephones, found in all Mongolian towns). I was only halfway into the jeep when the driver gunned the engine, sending the vehicle bounding off the pavement at the end of the main street. Upon leaving the town, all that lay before us was an endless sea of snow. Tiny mountains, just visible on the horizon, appeared like ship's sails. I

235

could see how the old man Rabjaa could lose his mind out here. The wilderness seemed completely lifeless until two gazelle jumped out of the snowy hills and bounded alongside our jeep.

As we rolled over the plains, interrupting vultures in the midst of a carcass brunch, I asked Altangerel how Danzan Rabjaa was chosen to be the fifth Gobi Saint. He said he had to preface the story with a description of Jamyn Oidov Jampts, the fourth Gobi Saint. Jamyn, well known as a dynamic healer and meditation man, lived at Khashant Monastery, not far from modern Sainshand. One day he was called to Erdene Zuu Monastery to save it from a plague of mice that had been chewing up the building's internal framework. The monks were desperate for a proper prayer seminar and believed the famed Jamyn Oidov Jampts was their best hope.

Always willing to oblige, Jamyn agreed to help, quickly mounted his horse and headed for Erdene Zuu. Once he arrived the extermination prayers began at once. Following hours of prayer, meditation and fumigation with a special powder called *zai,* the mice began to flee Erdene Zuu. The monks celebrated with a feast where Jamyn drank a tremendous amount of *airag.* After becoming sufficiently drunk, he went for a walk to observe the horses of Erdene Zuu. On his meanderings, Jamyn was introduced to the son-in-law of the Manchurian Emperor, a Mongol prince recently posted to Erdene Zuu with his new bride.

Repulsed by the monk's drunken ramblings, the prince immediately waved off Jamyn Oidov Jampts and ordered him away. He suggested that the monk sober up and stick to studying camels rather than speak so much of horses. The offended Jamyn then cursed the prince for marrying into a Manchurian family, calling him a traitor. Name-calling soon turned to punches and the fight ended only when Jamyn delivered his knife into the prince's chest, killing him on the spot.

This did not bode well for the saint and he was sent to Peking for "consultations." Jamyn, however, knew full well the fate ahead of him. In Peking he bought a horse for his assistant Jintu Gonchig and urged him to carry on the legacy of the Noyon Khutagts by leading the search for the next incarnation.

"After the fourth saint was executed, Jintu rode his horse back to Mongolia and traveled across the Gobi for several years, searching for the fifth Gobi Saint," Altangerel said. "He couldn't go back to Khashant Monastery because the Manchus burned it down in revenge."

One day, Jintu saw young Rabjaa with his father at a festival; the boy was about six at the time. His father introduced them as *badarching*—homeless wanderers who made their money by singing. Jintu, impressed with Rabjaa's voice, laid out a selection of objects and asked the boy to pick one. He reached out for the rosary that had once belonged to the fourth Saint, and then blurted out, "that horse is mine too."

"Jintu believed he had found the right boy and selected him as the fifth Saint. Rabjaa went from rags to riches," Altangerel explained. "They gave him the finest clothing and the best education in Inner Mongolia. He built Khamaryn Monastery when he was just 18. At that time it was huge—there were temples, a library, a museum, quarters for the monks and even a theater where Rabjaa put on his plays."

We drove over a knoll to come upon a cluster of buildings that appeared like a winter mirage in the vast, empty landscape. A parking sign, speared into featureless field, led our driver to a halt. Nearby was a squat yellow building with a metal roof painted pine green. It looked typical of the miniature temples that had mushroomed across the country over the past ten years. A white stupa stood in front of it and, although there was no fence, there was an oddly-placed gate that appeared suspended in the snow. A boy, urging forward his obstinate camel, paused for a moment to consider the jeep. This was the great Khamaryn Monastery.

At the turn of the 20th century there were dozens of golden-roofed temples and hundreds of monks here, but Choibalsan's pogrom insured that nothing would remain. In 1938 a detachment of troops stationed here executed 160 monks, jailed 300 others and turned all the buildings to ash.

"That is where the drama theater used to be," said Altangerel, pointing to a spot in the sand where I could barely make out a stone foundation. The article in *The Mongol Messenger*, the one that led me here, alleged that the structure was three stories tall and that the "acoustics were so good that people on horse and camel back could hear the singing from the rear of the theater."

The idea of camel-borne nomads watching melodrama in the desert struck me as peculiar, and I asked what sort of theater Danzan Rabjaa put on. "The Life Story of the Moon Cuckoo," Altangerel said, was the monk's masterpiece. There were different versions of the play but the longest could take up to a full month to perform. The play was actually an adaptation of an earlier work done in 1734 by a Tibetan writer, but Rabjaa Mongolized the names and events to match the 19th-century Mongol lifestyle.

Altangerel gave me a plot summary. It describes the mirrored lives of a young Indian prince named Nomun-Bayasgalant and his wicked servant Laganaa. The two spend their childhood as friends, the bond between them strengthened by an angel who shows them how to animate the bodies of deceased animals. But in adolescence Laganaa grows increasingly jealous of Nomun-Bayasgalant and conspires to take the throne.

One day as the prince and servant walk by a river, the latter suggests they cross to the other bank where a secret garden holds delicious fruit. The prince thinks it's a good idea but is certain his father would not allow him to borrow a boat to get there.

"No matter," says Laganaa, "We can animate these cuckoos." He reveals two dead birds, conveniently stashed in his pocket.

Leaving their own exanimate skins on the shore, they fly to the garden and are lost in its wondrous pleasures. While the prince is preoccupied, Laganaa flies across the river again and hops into the prince's body; then tosses his own exanimate body into the river. Disguised as the prince, he returns to the palace and launches a terrifying purge. Buddhism is crushed and the principal queen is banished from the castle to be replaced by Laganaa's lover.

"The story ends in disaster," Altangerel surmised. "The prince must remain in his cuckoo body and teach Buddhism to the birds as Laganaa runs away from the palace after his plot is exposed."

Karmic principles have obviously led to the demise of the characters. In a previous life, Nomun-Bayasgalant and Laganaa had been rival kings; the suffering witnessed in the play is the result of sins committed in a previous lifetime. While such Buddhist references swallow up much of the play, there were other underlying themes—namely, the subtle mockery of the Manchurian royalty and the petty Mongol aristocrats who served them.

The play caused such a scandal that the monks of Khamaryn Monastery barely dissuaded the Manchus from burning down the theater. It also gave Rabjaa unique status as a social critic, precisely why Mongolians found him so endearing.

I followed Altangerel toward the little temple. Even before we entered, I could hear the rhythmic beating of a drum mixing with the discordant crash of cymbals and the bellow of conch shells. We struck the snow off our boots with wooden rods left on the front steps, and ducked through the narrow doorway. Inside, six stone-faced monks sat huddled over faded sutras, chanting in Tibetan. One old woman wrapped up in a purple shawl rocked back and forth on a bench. She moved her lips in quiet, repeated prayer:

"*Om! Mani padme hum . . .*" ("Hail! Jewel in the lotus").

Altangerel, his son and the driver went through the usual motions; round the temple once, making a brief stop in front of the altar to deposit some tögrögs and bow before the deities. When the ceremony ended, Altangerel introduced me to the head monk, a big man with black sideburns and thick glasses. He gave me his business card. One side was printed in English:

Khamaryn Monastery
Dush
Head Lama
Tel: 221

The three-digit number was for a phone back in Sainshand. There weren't any phones at Khamaryn Monastery, or electricity for that matter. The entire town consisted of about ten families, two cars and 5,000 head of livestock. "Please come to my *ger* for lunch," said the old lama. "My wife should have it ready soon."

There was a clothesline outside Dush's *ger*. The sweaters, shirts and pants that hung on it were frozen solid and icicles dangled from the cuffs. A mangy black dog with yellow spots over its eyes barked as I approached.

"*Nohoigoo!*" I said. ("Go away, dog!")

Dush let us into his *ger*, which was very warm and had me stripping off layers of clothing. A child on the floor played with his collection of sheep anklebones—a multi-purpose toy that serves as dice, tidily winks, building blocks and jacks. Dush's wife was smashing up a tea brick with her hammer. She scattered some of the tea dust into a wok of boiling water, poured in milk and a few tablespoons of salt for flavor.

A cabinet in the *ger* displayed a collection of family photographs and Buddhist relics. A small wooden box caught my interest. It contained little cloth sacks tied with string. "Medicine," said Dush, "from plants we collected."

Altangerel claimed Rabjaa was a "great healer," and I asked Dush if he was employing the same methods as his 19th-century counterpart.

"Danzan Rabjaa had a great collection of medicinal plants that he collected from the desert or bought from traders; but he could also heal the sick using his spiritual powers. Everyone respected him for this," said Dush, sending a pinch of snuff up his nostrils.

"What sort of spiritual powers?" I asked.

"Well, one day a man rode to Rabjaa's tent and called out for help. Rabjaa invited him inside and the man said his child was very ill. After hearing the symptoms, Rabjaa went outside with his flint-lock and aimed it in the direction the man had just come from. He shot the gun and a big plume of smoke rose into the air. 'Go now. Go home to your family. Your child is better,' Rabjaa said.

"The man rode his horse home and when he arrived he found a gaping hole in the *ger* wall. But at least his son appeared happy and healthy. The man asked his wife what had happened. 'I am not sure,' she said. 'We were just sitting here and suddenly the wall collapsed. Then our son vomited pus and now he is better!'"

"So you see, usually a gun can shoot just one kilometer, but Danzan Rabjaa could shoot his sixty kilometers." He appeared quite serious, as did the others. I asked if it were a true story.

"Perhaps so. Danzan Rabjaa had great powers. But of course, we herders like to tell stories, so maybe this one was just made up," he chuckled. "You will have to decide for yourself."

I later read other stories detailing Danzan Rabjaa's supernatural skills in a book that Altangerel gave me. He could turn water into vodka (clearly an important skill in Mongolia), travel hundreds of miles in mere seconds and predict future events. Even at the moment of his birth he "glowed like an angel."

Caves near Khamaryn Monastery are said to be the inspiration for Rabjaa's miracles. We made our way to them through mud-washed ravines and gravelly earth, accompanied by a monk called Enkh-jargal. The caves were mostly notches along the walls of a shallow canyon made of red volcanic rock. There were supposedly 108 caves, a significant number for Buddhists, representing the 108 imperfections of man. One or two were big enough to fit half a dozen crouching monks.

Enkhjargal, a truck driver who turned to the holy life in 1990, ducked inside one and whispered a few terse prayers on our behalf. Then, when I pointed my camera at him, he posed for me, his hands clasped in supplication. I asked if he felt some spiritual connection to Danzan Rabjaa.

"I greatly believe in the spirit of Rabjaa and I have been here since 1990. I think one day his incarnation will come again. We wait because he is famous in Mongolia and all over the world," he said. Then, speaking half to himself and half to me: "Bless me God because our teacher has 23 magic abilities and is clever in politics and the arts. He has the ability to turn water back to the mountains from whence it came, Lord."

Altangerel noted that in the old days a monk might retreat to a cave for 108 days of solitary prayer and fasting. Food would be brought to him each day in a wooden cup and slid underneath the wall by an anonymous gloved hand. Upon finishing his meal, the monk would thrice scrape his cup on a rock before returning it to the daylight. By about day fifty, the cup would be completely scraped away, and the monk would spend the remaining 58 days without food. (The power of his meditation keeping him alive).

Monks occasionally went mad this way; a few had died. But those who came out of the experience alive and sane were believed to have undergone a major spiritual transformation. After a few days of rest, his peers would sit beside him and read sixty cartloads of Buddhist texts, which he would "easily memorize." When that was over, the enlightened monk was ordered to levitate small Buddhist relics to prove his worth.

"Danzan Rabjaa could read a sutra and used the power of the words to push his arm through the cave walls. He could also balance objects on beams of light," said Altangerel matter-of-factly.

The days of self-immurement are over but Dush said his monks occasionally visit the caves for prayer. Inside the biggest cave was a table that held Buddhist statues, bits of cloth, dusty sutras, a pile of money and an incense burner. A photograph of the seventh Gobi Saint—a square-faced young man in a dirty *del*—also rested on the table. This saint, Altangerel explained, was executed by the communist government in 1931. His demise marked the end of the line for the Gobi Noyon Khutagts.

The caves served another purpose. When the communists overran Khamaryn Monastery in 1938, Altangerel's grandfather Tuduv used them to hide chests full of Rabjaa's artwork and belongings. He scattered 64 crates around the region that summer and there they stayed until Altangerel unearthed half of them in 1990, providing enough relics to open the museum. And so, after sixty years of communist oppression, the cult of Danzan Rabjaa was again up and running.

"What happened to the other thirty-two crates?" I asked.

"Oh, they are still out there," he said, nodding toward the desert. "If I dig them up now I wouldn't have anywhere to store or display the artifacts. Plus it's dangerous. Our museum isn't well protected— no alarms. It's safer just to leave them buried. I am the only one who knows the location of the chests, no one can disturb them."

As thoughts of digging up buried treasure entered my head, Altangerel led us toward the top of a bluff and a rock formation with a hole in it.

"This is the representation of a woman's uterus," he said. "If you climb through the hole it is like being born again and all your bad elements will be cleansed." We all squeezed through the hole, except Altangerel who was too big to fit.

Further down the bluff we entered a stony ravine. Jumbles of brown rock stood around us, smoothed clean by the occasional floodwaters that rushed through here in the rainy season. The noon sun created enough heat for us to take a short walk without becoming numb from the cold. The sandy ground crunched beneath our feet as we explored the caves and miniature plants struggling to survive the harsh winter. As can often happen to Gobi Desert visitors, we soon discovered a dinosaur bone poking out from the earth.

Roy Chapman Andrews had no idea that he would find dinosaur bones in Mongolia. He went there in search of the origin of mammalian life—believing a theory that Europeans and North Americans had originally spread out from the heart of Asia. He ended up uncovering one of the largest repositories of dinosaur fossils in the world.

I saw a great bone beautifully preserved and outlined in the rock. There was no doubt this time; it was reptilian and, moreover, *dinosaur* . . . the dinosaur bone was the first indication that the theory upon which we had organized the expedition might be true; that Asia is the mother of the life of Europe and America.

Andrews made several trips to Mongolia in the early 1920s, collecting plant samples, big game trophies, dinosaur skeletons, and dinosaur eggs—the first ever seen by Western scientists. Andrews delivered part of his plunder to the Mongolian Scientific Committee, packed the rest in crates and sent them to New York where the collection amazed the American public.

Andrews made his last trip to Mongolia in 1925, the year the country closed to Westerners. In 1990 the government re-opened the country to Western paleontologists and many visitors have followed the ghost of RC Andrews to the famed Flaming Cliffs of the Gobi. I met one such hopeful Englishman named William who had gone to the Gobi with a group of scientists, and, paying them off, returned with eight boxes full of dinosaur bones that he passed out to friends at parties.

"Don't worry," he said when I protested. "They are all over the place down there, as plentiful as cow shit!"

* * *

On our way back to Sainshand we passed two rock cairns on top of a knoll. Altangerel called it the Breast Ovoo, a sacred place for women to pray. As we drove away, he spoke of restoring the monastery to its former glory. After ten years it had regained only two temples and eight monks—it seemed a long way to go, but Altangerel was optimistic.

"Danzan Rabjaa predicted the decline of Buddhism; it was part of the great cycle of life. But he also said there would be a revival. Some day we will have many temples here, many lamas . . ."

Altangerel said the people of Sainshand donate around $4,000 a year. But this wasn't nearly enough for Altangerel's dream. The next step, he said, was to build a tourist camp.

"People will come from all over the world to learn about the life of Danzan Rabjaa. I can take them to his birthplace, the mountain temple of the third Saint, the caves . . . Maybe do some camel trekking. Foreigners like to do that sort of thing."

Only about forty tourists came in the past year, but Altangerel was sure the numbers would pick up with proper publicity. We discussed the potential for such an ambitious project and he showed me a brochure for the area. There were a few fuzzy pictures of wild horses and Danzan Rabjaa's art. "Plus, it's very convenient to Ulaanbaatar. Just ten hours by train!"

We enjoyed the museum late that evening, sipping *suutei tsai* supplied by Altangerel's daughter. He was busy digging through his storeroom to show me uncatalogued items. Researching and labeling it appeared to be a lifetime project. But he had something like ten brothers and sisters and I wondered why they weren't helping. Weren't they too the descendants of Balchinchoijoo?

"But they don't have *the* birthmark," Altangerel explained. "You see, the *takhilch* (protectors) must have a special birthmark to indicate he is the right one. All former *takhilch* had a special birthmark."

"Where is yours?"

He stood up, removed his jacket and lifted his sweater. There in the middle of his back was a beer-coaster sized birthmark, the biggest I had ever seen. This immediately reminded me of traditional Asian symbolism. For example, when the Dalai Lama is selected as a child, he must display certain symbols to prove that he is the correct incarnation. Unusual birthmarks are one such symbol.

"Whoa," I said, taken aback. "What about your son? Does he have a birthmark?"

"Of course! When he was born I turned him over and I saw this."

He called over little Altan-Ochir and swung him around. He lifted the boy's shirt and sure enough, there on his back was a light-colored birthmark about the size of a silver dollar. The boy, slung over his father's knee, flashed a shy smile and his green eyes lit up. The cult of Danzan Rabjaa was sure to survive in them for another generation.

AN OUTING TO INNER MONGOLIA

The land swelling with natural riches, producing nothing, in need of everything, destitute and suffering from the world's cataclysm: that is Mongolia.

—Ferdinand Ossendowski, 1922

I HAD NEARLY GIVEN UP HOPE. Despite having traveled around Inner Mongolia over the past four days I had yet to meet a single ethnic Mongol. Finding Inner Mongolians in Inner Mongolia was like searching for a Sioux Indian in Sioux City; there just didn't seem to be any left.

Indra had warned me. Although she had never been here, or knew anybody that had been here, she was confident that Inner Mongolians had become extinct long ago. Amarbat said that if I did find any there was no way that I could communicate in Mongolian, and that I'd better brush up on my Chinese.

Yet I remained optimistic. The Lonely Planet guide said that there are three and a half million Mongols in Inner Mongolia, swamped of course by 21 million Chinese, but still a sizable population. I'd just have to get out of the cities. They'd be out on the steppes, tending to their livestock, as Mongols do.

After a 750 mile train journey from Ulaanbaatar to the Inner Mongolian capital Hohhot, I continued east by public bus. This was the Khar Desert, a desolate expanse of plains and ravines once known for its banditry. At a lonely bus station along the highway I fell into conversation with a young couple that had just arrived from Beijing. The boy, whose disheveled suit was about three sizes to large, described how he and his girlfriend had ridden for two days and nights on the trains to see their parents in nearby Bayan Khot.

"Bayan Khot? Those are Mongolian words! It means 'Rich City!'"

"Really? I had no idea," the Chinese boy said in reasonable English "I knew it was Mongolian, but I didn't know what it meant."

"Are there any Mongols there?"

"I don't know any personally, but I am sure that some live there," said the boy. "They have a monastery."

"With Mongolian monks?"

"Yes, I think so. But why do you want to meet them?"

"Well, I have been living in Outer Mongolia for the last couple of years and . . ."

"Two years in Outer Mongolia!" he gasped, cutting me off. "You like grass, eh? Ha ha." Two sets of yellow teeth clacked together as the couple broke down in hysterics.

As I restrained myself, the girl, aloof until now, assured me that if I went along with them I'd meet some Mongols. Bayan Khot was only an hour and a half away by taxi and we agreed to share the ride.

One thing I had on my side was timing. Tomorrow was Tsagaan Sar, the Mongolian lunar New Year celebration. I knew that if I were to find any Inner Mongolians, my best bet was in the local temple.

The scrubby grass around the village soon gave way to the empty desert. About an hour into the journey, we passed a section of the Great Wall; crumbling and chewed up by centuries of weather and marauders. The road shot right through it, into the ancient lands of the Mongols. Meanwhile, the Beijingers were slumped in the back of the car, sleeping on each other in a heap of polyester clothing.

At one time, all of this had been central to the great Mongol Empire. When their influence waned, this part of Mongolia was the first to fall into the hands of the Manchus when their armies rose in their early 17th century. The eastern and southern Mongol lands became subject to the new Manchu Emperor in Beijing, who named them "Inner Mongolia," because they were close to the capital. The as yet unconquered northern territories were called "Outer Mongolia."

At the time, Outer Mongolia was divided into eastern Khalkh and Western Oirad clans and both put up stiff resistance to the coming Manchu threat. Eventually, both were defeated and incorporated into the Qing Empire, which ruled until 1911. It was during the Qing Empire that vast change swept across Inner Mongolia. Hundreds of thousands of landless Chinese moved there during the 18th and 19th centuries, making the Mongols a minority in their own land. Having been converted to Buddhism—and their soldiers turned to lamas—they were powerless to stop the waves of immigrants from plowing up the steppes. Outer Mongolia, meanwhile, was left relatively untouched and spared the influx of Chinese migration.

In 1921 the two Mongolias were further severed when Outer Mongolia sided with the Soviet Union. A border between the two was established, cutting trade ties, cultural links and family relations. The chasm between the two widened further with the Sino-Soviet split in the early 1960s. The border became a heavily militarized zone as Russia and China prepared for war.

Later, the Cultural Revolution would hit Inner Mongolia like a bombshell. Temples were ransacked, monks slaughtered and civilians disappeared in the night. Somewhere between 23,000 and 50,000 people had died and roughly 800,000 were jailed and tortured. No one knew the exact figures.

Today, many Inner Mongolians secretly long for freedom. Vocal support for such a plan, however, is virtually silent under the blanket of Communist China. When there is dissent, it is dealt with swiftly and harshly—many Mongols are currently serving time in Chinese prisons for political reasons. Their hope for any sort of recognition is muffled by a mighty government and a lack of voices.

Over the past 50 years, the urban areas of China have undergone a significant overhaul. From the village to the city, it was the same everywhere: the bulldozers went in, leveled everything that was old, and built anew. This started in earnest in the 1960s and designers were influenced by the Soviet model for town planning. Wide boulevards and square housing blocks decorated with white bathroom tiles are the dominant feature. Apparently a close relative of Mao had run the tile factory and is now held accountable for transforming a nation into an open air lavatory. Bayan Khot had not escaped this, yet the surrounding mountains and crisp blue sky gave it a hint of charm. However, its proximity to the Gobi was worrying as sand blown in from the desert seemed to be slowly consuming it.

My Beijing companions directed me to the monastery. The temples were deserted, save for one ancient looking caretaker, hunched over a cane and dressed in a peasants' outfit.

"*Sain Bain uu?*"

He looked up with bleary eyes. His wrinkled brow and hollow cheeks were burnished dark by the sun.

"*Sain. Sain bain uu?*" the old man replied with a toothless smile.

At last! A Mongolian!

I told him that I was glad to finally meet a Mongol in Inner

Mongolia. He stared blankly for a while and then closed his eyes. I thought he'd fallen asleep until finally he spoke.

"*Margash*," he wheezed, "*Mongol chuut irekh. Tsagaan Sar bain aa.*" ("Mongolians will come tomorrow. It's a holiday").

Right, I'd just come back in the morning for the New Year's festival. I extended my arm and shook the caretaker's skeletal hand. I promised to return and waved goodbye.

Any doubts I'd harbored about meeting Mongols eroded the next morning when I found about forty people milling in front of the main temple. The old caretaker was not among them but I recognized them as Mongols—their round, pudgy faces and wide smiles giving them away. I sidled up to the group and began speaking. An unknown foreigner conversing in their native tongue momentarily distracted them from their prayer routine. I introduced myself as a journalist from Outer Mongolia, and, when the commotion died down, they invited me to watch the service.

We went inside the main temple where about 25 more Mongols sat on wooden benches, fingering their prayer beads, while a dozen resonant monks chanted in Tibetan. I circumnavigated the hall in a clockwise motion with the other worshipers and placed a few yuan on the dusty, deity-strewn altar. I heard later that Inner Mongolian monks are more skilled in Buddhist theology than their Outer Mongolian counterparts. And for good reason: Chinese communism had banned religion for less than twenty years. In Outer Mongolia it had been banned for nearly seventy. But I was also told that this temple had only one monk under 50 years old. Apparently the authorities allow a new monk in only when an old one dies—a marked contrast to Outer Mongolia where the monk population is young and flourishing.

When the service ended a circle of worshipers, curious about Outer Mongolia, latched onto me outside the temple. They wanted to know about the weather, the number of livestock, and what the capital looked like.

"Ulaanbaatar is not so big," I said. "Really just a village compared to Chinese cities. It's quiet, not too many cars, and not a lot of flashing signs. In the countryside there are a few small towns but it is mostly open grasslands. People still live in *gers* and ride horses. They live much like their ancestors did . . ."

I stopped short when I saw a touch of longing well up in their eyes. I had not seen much of Inner Mongolia, but from what I could tell, it was definitely not a good place for Mongols to hang around, much less live in. Cities were polluted and their surrounding grasslands plowed up and ravaged. They had been dissociated from the traditional nomadic lifestyle and this seemed to have a damaging affect on their psyche.

It was like speaking to housebound ancient mariners who missed the sea. They implored me for more news, so I went on to describe the political climate; recounting the demonstrations of 1990, the elections, the recent string of government failures and the murder of Zorig. They knew nothing of it, only that Bagabandi was the president. Recent news events pertaining to their own country likewise drew blank stares.

"Did you know that the Karmapa Lama escaped Tibet and fled to India?" I asked, touching on a topic hot in the Western media. There was much shaking of heads and the news sent them whispering. The only reports they received from Tibet were the Chinese government-sanctioned stories of hospital, school and road building. In their eyes everything was all well and good on the plateau. It made me wonder how far into the 21st century the Chinese government could shelter its people from the world. For a country so eager to jump on the globalization bandwagon, it seemed only a matter of time before the information age would catch up with the 1.3 billion people who lived here.

A squat fellow in a brown sweater introduced himself as Surtalto and invited me to his home for a Tsagaan Sar feast. I accepted and took leave of the others, trudging down the hill in a blizzard that seemed to come from nowhere. He said he was a doctor and that his wife—at home cooking up the meal—was a doctor too.

Surtalto pointed me down a muddy alley, and we ducked through a wood fence and into his yard. It was well laid out with a small garden and a sort of birdbath, but what caught my eye were the wood shelves pushed against his house—all filled with colorful and oddly shaped rocks. Quartz, agate and opal specimens gleamed in the afternoon light. He opened the glass door to his living room and I stepped inside to find even more minerals, each properly labeled in Chinese, Tibetan and Mongol script. The house looked like a small museum of geology. Surtalto introduced me to his three teenage children and his wife Narantuya, a plump woman who smiled broadly and then scurried back into the kitchen to tend to her stove.

On the far end of the musty living room, there was a large cabinet crammed with old medical dictionaries and textbooks on Mongolian history and culture. There was a small study-cum-laboratory attached to the living room. Shelves here were filled with jars of mysterious content; roots, powders, liquids and perhaps organs, all of a different color and consistency. Surtalto was clearly no ordinary doctor.

"We practice traditional medicine," he said, passing me a book with medieval-looking medical drawings. "There is a hospital of traditional medicine in Bayan Khot; we have about 40 doctors."

I asked him who his patients were and he said they were all Mongols, many of whom hailed from the countryside and different villages. The Chinese, he explained, have a hospital of their own. As I flipped through the yellowing pages of a medical manual, Surtalto lit up a cigarette.

"Where do you get all this stuff?" I asked, pointing to the rocks and jars and books.

"From all over really; people from Taiwan and Hong Kong bring most of the rocks. We crush it up and make medicine." He let a big cloud of smoke into the room. "Sometimes I'll get rocks on my own and sell them. I have one that is worth 4,000 Yuan ($490). Recently my daughter went to southern China to collect rocks. She wants to go to university so she studies medicine with me."

The daughter smiled shyly from her position on the sofa and I asked Surtalto about the jars.

"A lot of the potions are from Tibet, India and Nepal." He took one of the jars off the shelf; it was labeled in blocky Tibetan script. "Crushed deer antlers, powerful aphrodisiac. And this," he pointed to another, "is bear blood. Very good for a headache."

As I leaned forward for a closer look, I pondered the legal dangers of owning and importing such rare items. "You can buy as much as you like?" I asked.

"Oh yes, in China such items are very popular, we can make medicine from almost anything."

Judging from his large rock collection, I had to agree. I had never heard of making medicine from stones but Surtalto seemed to be making a good living. While I perused his eclectic collection, food was placed on the table. It was certainly not the Mongolian fare I had grown accustomed to Ulaanbaatar. This was Inner Mongolian cuisine, the same type that Westerners eat at restaurants back home, right down to the gurgling hot pot. Narantuya brought out dozens of little platters until the table could hold no more. They contained a delectable and diverse variety of egg, meat, vegetable, fish, chicken and peanut dishes—the Inner Mongols had clearly fused their diet closely to that of the Chinese. One plate had what appeared to be *buuz,* but when I bit on it there were vegetables inside. I described to them the Outer Mongolian Tsagaan Sar and they were enthralled with the idea of devouring an entire sheep.

The dinner conversation weighed heavily on life in Outer Mongolia. I described my experiences there and showed them a copy of *The Mongol Messenger.* I kicked myself for not bringing Montsame's traditional script newspaper—they would have been able to read it. They couldn't read *The Messenger*, but they enjoyed the pictures and I tried translating the headlines. They bombarded me with questions, but I was not qualified to discuss the development of Outer Mongolia's traditional medicine trade. Surtalto surprised me, however, when he said he had been to Ulaanbaatar in 1990. He recalled how bad things were then.

"The economy is still weak, but better than before. At least the days of ration tickets are over," I said. "Now Mongolia is just struggling to find its own way."

"Life is not so bad here," he said suddenly, comparing the Inner and Outer Mongolias. "We have shops and jobs; things are not so expensive."

His home was modest but comfortable. Surtalto did appear to be doing okay for himself. Indeed, most of the people from the monastery looked fairly well-to-do by Mongolian standards.

"But we don't like China," he added with a little laugh, his family smiling at this. "We may be well off but the Chinese and Mongolians have never gotten along. You see, we had to give up our freedom." When I had trouble with his accent he took my pen and drew a picture of a little stick figure kowtowing to another stick figure.

"But life is not so bad," he said again. "As long as we follow the rules the Chinese don't bother us. I knew someone who joined a pro-independence movement in 1989. He was arrested and sentenced to 15 years in jail. We know what our limits are." He shrugged his shoulders. "Well, there is nothing else we can do."

I was glad that Inner Mongols existed (contrary to popular belief in Outer Mongolia), but I didn't like the idea of living in an occupied country. I tried to imagine myself as a silenced minority agonizing over the loss of my territory. Like anyone, the Inner Mongols really just wanted to be free. No matter how wealthy the Inner Mongolians became, they could never buy back their homeland. It was not unlike what the Plains Indians went through in 19th-century America, or any number of peoples fighting to recover land today, including Chechens, Kurds, Tibetans and Palestinians.

Of course, the Chinese see things differently. They allege that this land, as well as Tibet and the Islamic province of Xinjiang, have always been theirs, and have gone to great lengths to justify their claims. As for Inner Mongolia, the Chinese explain that since Chingis Khan ruled China he was therefore a "Chinese Emperor." Thus, they assert, all Mongol lands automatically became Chinese when he took them over. This reason is extraordinarily self-defeating as it suggests, from another point of view, that the Mongols are still the legitimate rulers of China!

When it was time to go, I left a little donation for the family rock collection—a polished red stone I had found in the Gobi while visiting Khamaryn Monastery. Despite its apparent worthlessness, Surtalto gave it an honorable place on his mantle. He walked me to the station and while I waited to buy a ticket to Yinchuan, he appeared from a shop holding a package of food.

"Here, this is for your trip," he said. "Very healthy." The plastic package was filled with a dried fruit called Ningxia Wolf Berry. There was a product description on the back.

> The Ningxia Wolf Berry is world famous, it is ruddy in color, thin in skin, thick in flesh, less in seed and sweet in taste. Regular usage may resist cancer, protect liver, create sperm, nourish energy and blood, make vision clear, brace up the whole system and prolong life. It is the best health care product

"Eat this. Very good for making love," he said, giving me a thumbs up. He then waved goodbye from the sidewalk, as the bus rolled away and Bayan Khot vanished in the snowfall.

I had found my Inner Mongolians. They had preserved themselves, albeit underneath the veneer of China. They understood well their place in society and seemed resigned to their fate. Outnumbered as they were, there was no alternative. But there was another place I hoped might act as a sort of Shangri-La for Inner Mongolia. I didn't know what to expect from Ejin Horo, but was optimistic that it just might be a little island of ancient Mongolia within China.

Ejin Horo has long been recognized as a Mecca for Mongols seeking spiritual solace. It was, after all, home to the Chingis Khan Mausoleum. The Mausoleum, a three-domed palace-like structure decorated with garish blue and gold tiles made a curious sight amid the vast acres of surrounding farmland. Out in front, there was a rather dramatic bronze statue of Chingis atop his horse. There were gardens, a huge *ovoo* topped with blue silk scarves, and imperial-looking tents; at first glance it was very impressive.

It was also empty. I stumbled upon a round glass structure that vaguely resembled a *ger*, but was really a restaurant. The cavernous room was vacant, save for a table full of thickset men playing cards in their winter overcoats. They looked like Mongols.

Indeed, they were Inner Mongolians and claimed to be Dark-hats—the legendary Mongol tribe responsible for the preservation of Chingis Khan's cult. They were also caretakers of the adjoining hotel.

The Chingis Khan Mausoleum was actually a misnomer. Since the warlord's grave has never been found, it is certainly not there. The actual grave is probably somewhere near his birthplace in Khentii Aimag. Legend has it that after his death in 1227, Chingis Khan was borne back to Mongolia and buried in an unmarked grave, along with horses, concubines and the plunder of 20 kingdoms. To ensure secrecy of the location soldiers slew the grave diggers. Then when the soldiers returned to Karakorum they too were put to the sword.

The Mausoleum at Ejin Horo was actually created centuries ago not as a burial place but as a place to protect the possessions owned by Chingis—his saddles, clothing, bows, knives and other objects dear to him. His grandson Khublai Khan was responsible for founding the cult. Khublai designated that the relics be placed inside eight tents, which became known as the Eight White Ordon (*ordon* means palace).

The Darkhats set up a code of honor for the Ordon and pilgrims were required to follow the customs when they arrived. Over the years the Darkhats grew wealthy from the pilgrims who attended ceremonies and left offerings.

The tents, unharmed for centuries, came under threat as the Manchu Dynasty fell into disarray in the early 20th century. War refugees and fighting in the area put pressure on the Darkhats and some of the relics were destroyed or stolen in the confusion. When peace returned the Darkhats were able to restore what was lost; and the Ordon were again up and running.

There are very few accounts of foreigners who made it to the Eight White Ordon, but the famed Mongolist Owen Lattimore reached the site in 1935 and wrote extensively about his visit. Lattimore came at a time when the tents still served their original function, as a place of worship for Mongol devotees. He and his Swedish companion Torgny Oberg were called upon to pray as the Mongols did. Lattimore recorded his thoughts:

"A herald announced us as pilgrims from far away who had come to pay respect, sacrifice and worship, and a man standing on my right took the lamp from me, placed it on the altar, and then we made three more prostrations—a total of the holy number of nine. I was never more interested in my life; but even while absorbed with the effort to remember every detail I could not help chuckling at the idea that Torgny, the son of missionaries, was prostrating himself in this heathen ritual and just as much fascinated by it as I."

Lattimore completed six rounds of the wine offering and then drank until the great bowl was empty. "There was no ritually fixed number of drinks; we just finished it. The quantity of the thin sour liquid dazed us a little—it needed all my strength to raise the vessel—but it was not powerfully heady," the American wrote.

The last phase of the ritual was the meat offering. After the flesh of a recently killed sheep was offered up, the herald announced the names of the pilgrims in alliterative, cadenced verses. Following worship at the various sites, the pilgrims were finally brought before two sacred white camels. "They were thin and grinding their teeth in the cold... they wore soft halters of twisted silk of the imperial yellow. We plucked a tuft of the white wool from one camel, and we had completed the ritual."

Lattimore arrived just in time to see the relics. In 1939, Kuomintang troops confiscated the chest that supposedly held the khan's remains. Twenty years later the communists got hold of it, and Mao's Red Army abolished the Darkhat administration. An institution that had lasted over 700 years had suddenly vanished. Although the Darkhat were gone, pressure still mounted to return the chest, and in 1954 it was brought back to Ejin Horo.

Then, curiously, the Communists announced they would build a permanent mausoleum for the relics. It seemed that the Communists were playing up to the disgruntled Inner Mongolians, but there was more to it than that; the Chinese were engaged in a propaganda campaign, hoping to draw the severed province of Outer Mongolia, back to China.

The offering ceremonies, however, were still banned, and the relics were treated as museum pieces rather than sacred objects that needed special attention. This sapped the life from the Chingis cult. But the worst was yet to come. In 1966, Mao's Red Guards destroyed the building and most of the relics inside. The building was used to store salt until the mausoleum was restored in 1979. Darkhats were invited back to care for the "shrine" and restore the lost relics. Very little remained, but the protectors did return to the site and have served there ever since.

I went walking around the grounds and it didn't take long to realize this was not the Shangri-La I had been searching for. Unlike Lattimore, I was treated to neither ritual nor feast. Instead I studied the various Chinese interpretations of Mongol culture. At the mausoleum, the jokey artifacts propped up inside the tents might just as well have come from the gift shop. The building was glossy and sterilized, like a giant toy just unwrapped from its box. And the minder who was assigned to spy on me was a far cry from the Chingis-worshiping Darkhat who might have been responsible for the sacrificial slaughter in days long past.

The shrines, temples and sacred sites of Outer Mongolia were always enlivened with discordant color schemes, jumbles of dusty relics, an aroma that dated back centuries, and most importantly symbolic rites. The sacrificial slaughter of livestock, the tokens left on altars, and the drinking of wine had come to an end. But by contrast, the new "mausoleum," was nothing more than a scrubbed-down theme park, and I wondered if the Darkhats really appreciated their role as token custodians and tour guides.

I returned to the Ulaanbaatar a few days later with fresh eyes. All along I had wondered why Mongolians had been so appreciative of Russia and even grateful toward Stalin. But my Inner Mongolia experience made me realize what life would have been like if the Chinese, rather than the Soviets, had controlled their country. For the first time I understood why the Mongols were so grateful to those oppressive Russians. Without them, Mongolia might not exist today.

~ 17 ~

WINTER OF DISCONTENT

THE WHIRL OF THE HELICOPTER BLADES blew a cloud of snow into the air, forcing the family of herders on the ground to shield their faces. The giant passenger carrier touched down in the box canyon and ejected its supply of foodstuffs, clothing, Members of Parliament, journalists, foreign aid workers and the US ambassador. Everyone sank past their knees into the powder-white drifts. We waded through the snow to the family's *ger*, wedged below a rocky precipice, and ducked our heads as we entered the dimly lit shelter.

"After the biggest storm," the herder told us, "we had to climb out through the skylight because the door was blocked with snow."

The man and his solemn-faced family had been trapped on this mountain for six weeks after deep snows blocked roads and passes. They were just one of many families trapped in the wilderness, cut off from nearby villages that offered food, communication, supplies and relatives. We had come here to find out how bad the situation was and what the aid organizations could do. When the Ministry of Defense asked for journalists to come along, Ariunbold dispatched me to cover the story for *The Messenger*.

261

It was obvious that the family was coming down to meager rations, but how many others were there? The idea was frightening and this was only November. The winter up here in the Khangai could last another six months.

"We didn't have time to make winter preparations so we have already run out of fodder for the animals. Our animal dung won't last much longer either," the man said as we sat around his stove. His wife, I realized, was exhausting her precious supply of dung to keep us warm.

"It is a very difficult time," the old woman said while poking a metal rod at the embers. "My son has brain damage and he sometimes loses consciousness. This is the worst winter of our lives."

We passed out some of the goods we had brought, including flour, rice and knee-high felt boots, donated by the Finnish Red Cross. They posed glumly for a news photographer before we left. "They will be fine," one MP promised as the helicopter blades spun back into action. "We Mongols are resourceful!"

The helicopter, a massive Russian-built craft that resembled a flying submarine, lifted high into the sky and accelerated north over spiky peaks and wide white plains. Our craft was a sort of transport vehicle with an open hold. We sat on benches along the side and kept our luggage on top of the 2,300-gallon gas tank. The chopper's reliability was dubious. Indeed, one year later this very helicopter would crash, killing nine passengers, including journalists, a Member of Parliament and UN workers.

On the horizon we could see only a hint of civilization. We touched down near a collection of shacks and sagging fences, and peered out the portholes as a crowd of people came toward us, their garments flapping in the wind. Tiny children in *dels* caked with camel gob tried to keep up with the crowd. They looked like the ragged and frozen refugees from *Dr. Zhivago,* with threadbare coats and scarves dangling from their bodies. When the metal hatch of the helicopter was propped open, they rushed to peer inside.

"When will the roads be opened?" they asked. "When will the food come through?"

The residents of Gurvanbulag had not seen outsiders since the middle of September and their supplies had almost run out. Wood and petrol reserves were nearly depleted. Supplies of rice, vegetables and flour were being doled out in rations. They had been reduced to total isolation, living (literally) off the fat of their herds. They were in the midst of the *zud*, a fearful word that loosely translates as "winter of great severity."

Bayanhongor, the province we were visiting, was not the only area plagued by the white *zud* (when heavy snow prevents livestock from reaching the grass underneath). Snow had blanketed much of central Mongolia. The far west of the country was facing the threat of black *zud*—a drought. In Dundgobi province, herders had lost their grasslands to a biblical plague of field mice. All across Mongolia the *malchin* (herders) were in a state of panic.

As the helicopter blades ground to a halt, we stepped into the snow to unload sacks of flour and rice, plus boxes of warm clothing donated by charity organizations. The supplies were hardly enough to support the village, though the gesture came with words of support from the Member of Parliament who represented this district.

"The government is paying attention to the situation and foreign organizations are working with us. I urge you to have strength together," the MP said to his constituents.

They circled around us, prodding for news about family members trapped in the mountains or those who had made the dangerous *otog* (trek) with their livestock over the passes to the habitable valleys of Arkhangai. The provincial governor told us that up to 40,000 livestock had been evacuated from the area; only the strongest men had made the *otog*, and their status was still unknown.

"The trail to Arkhangai is lined with animal corpses," a burly man announced. "Every ten or twenty meters you can see one."

"Were you able to reach your family?" I asked.

"The only car we have is broken, and there is no petrol anyway," he said, pulling his wool hat tight over his head. "We wanted to get them using horses and camels. But the snow is too deep. It's too risky." He turned to the governor, "Can't we clear the road by pulling a big pipe behind a tractor?"

"We tried that but it didn't work," the governor answered. A bulldozer or snowplow would have worked wonders, I thought, but the closest one was half way across the country in Ulaanbaatar. The others crowded around, each wanting to tell their story into my outstretched microphone.

"The people are very cold and their spirits are low; some are suffering from frostbite and others are hungry," one man said. "We have all been sitting at home, just listening to our radios, hoping that someone would come."

"Do you have electricity?" I asked one man.

"I had already forgotten about that place," he said, motioning toward a defunct electrical station. "We have nothing; no hospital, no medicine, no way to reach our relatives. And our salaries have not been paid for months!"

I wondered why our delegation had not been dispatched weeks before. Only now, with the province on its knees, had any response been made.

"We thought the snow would melt," the Defense Minister admitted as we scrambled to re-board the helicopter. "We realized it was a crisis when the blizzards hit again in October. Every time we tried to clear the road, it snowed again."

The helicopter lifted into the air and flew over what looked like Antarctica, until we reached another village where we would spend the night.

The mayor of Jargalant met us at the helicopter and directed us toward his office. We sat on wooden chairs, still in our huge winter jackets, and watched our breath by candlelight. Suddenly, we heard the distant hum of the power station and the lights flicked on. The mayor, hospitable as he was, could not let the government officials and the US ambassador sit in the dark, and had ordered that the power station be turned on just this once. As a solitary bulb swayed overhead, he briefed us on his snowbound village.

"We began to evacuate the herders in the first week of October; they were sent to an area without snow called Little Khalkh Lake. But this place is not prepared for winter—there are no shelters or dung to burn, so it will be very difficult. We have contacted Arkhangai province and made requests for wood; they have agreed but we have no trucks to collect it and the roads are impassable. We need money to purchase supplies and pay salaries."

The Minister of Finance folded his arms and spoke up. "The money allotted to you was already sent to the Bayankhongor Governor's office; you should have received a portion of the Tg24 million ($22,300) we sent."

Eyes turned to the governor, who looked rather nervous. "We are delivering the funds a little at a time," he said sheepishly.

"We have not received anything yet," the mayor retorted. An eerie silence followed.

"There is no budgeting," the ambassador whispered.

We could only hope it was a budgeting error, I thought, noticing the shiny silver belt buckle and new *del* that the governor was wearing.

"Since you have many goats, we can provide a loan," the Finance Minister said helpfully, and perhaps trying to save the governor from further embarrassment. "Your *soum* earned Tg112 million ($104,000) from cashmere sales last year. We can issue a loan that will be repaid after the goat combing season."

A murmur arose as the officials discussed a loan package. When they were finished, the governor, mayor and finance minister were shaking hands and pitching back shots of vodka. Neither realized there would be no cashmere in the combing season. The goats that provide it would be dead by then.

* * *

When the meeting ended we gathered around a large table and enjoyed a feast of meat and potatoes. The warmth of the plate thawed my fingers, which had gone numb from the cold. After the meal, we were escorted across the road to the theater where the community had assembled for a town meeting.

The delegates sat in two rows on the stage while locals squeezed inside the tiny wooden hall. It was standing room only and some remained in the hallway, craning their necks for a view. The MP representing the area stood at the podium and gave a rallying cry for his constituents. "Your relatives in Ulaanbaatar support you, the government supports you, and I support you. But most importantly, you must support yourselves! You must work hard! The times have changed. Now all the property and animals are yours, so you will decide your fate. The times will get harder, but I implore you not to give up."

The audience looked on in silence, perhaps coming to terms with the fact that communism was indeed over. The social safety net was gone and they were on their own. Ulaanbaatarites had figured this out long ago, but out here, in the high Khangai Mountains, the unforgiving hand of the free market economy had not yet fully shaken the people from their long socialist slumber. Maybe the *zud* would.

"This is not a *zud*," one elderly man called out with a moue of displeasure. "This is worse than a *zud*; this is a complete disaster! Your government has not delivered on its promises. All this time they say, 'wait, wait and our country will improve.' But the situation gets worse every year!"

More hands shot up. The government was blamed for everything from the high price of petrol to personal health problems. "My sons are up in the mountains; they took rice, flour and sugar to their *gers* but I have not seen them for weeks. I heard that one of their rice sacks fell off their cart and someone found it," an old man said while leaning on a wooden cane.

266

In his monologue he cursed the system: "Government assistance does not usually go where it is supposed to go; it should be monitored better!" And searched for sympathy: "I have kidney problems, so I went to the doctor and he prescribed four kinds of medication, but the medicine was so expensive. Lots of things have gone up in price so I think we should decrease the price of ALL items..."

The crowd began to grumble, urging the man to reach a conclusion. Then the mayor interrupted with a request to the US ambassador, asking if his government would fund the construction of a direct road to Ulaanbaatar to increase trade for the village. Standing up, the Ambassador said America was indeed putting money into road construction, but couldn't promise to fulfill the mayor's specific request. Then the Minister of Finance stood up and encouraged everyone to invest in solar panels for their *ger*. They were expensive, he told them, but would pay off in the long run.

Finally the session ended and the crowd shuffled into the darkened streets. I followed them outside and stared into the void of space. Soon my chin was frozen. I flicked on my flashlight and noted that the mercury in my keychain/thermometer had bottomed out.

"We're in for a long winter," I said to myself. "A long winter."

The helicopter flew us back to the capital and our small delegation parted ways; back to our offices and news agencies to type up reports about what we had seen. It was a different world in the city, and we felt safe from the disastrous winter bearing down on the countryside. But in a *zud* year, even urban Mongols are affected, and those last days of autumn carried ominous signs of what lay ahead.

The first indication of trouble came a week later when I was at the Mercury Market buying groceries. The price of meat, I noticed, had doubled.

"Mal bakhgui," a butcher told me. ("There are no livestock")

At the office, Bayarmaa lamented that her family could no longer afford to buy meat—all they had were flour and potatoes. Thousands of other families faced a similar crisis and medical workers warned of illness if so many people's diets were affected. Just as worrying were the psychological challenges of being cut off from countryside. Because so many people were stranded in the mountains without any contact to the outside it was impossible to know the status of friends and relatives. Some co-workers who had relatives in *zud* areas had not heard from their family in six weeks.

Next came the strange prophesy of Dashbalbar, the radical Parliamentarian and poet. Rather out of the blue, he checked himself into a hospital one day, announcing that he had been poisoned by the KGB. He predicted his own death, saying that the nation was to blame and would suffer for it. People scoffed. Another one of his public relations stunts, they said.

One month later, Dashbalbar was dead. His sudden demise seemed like just another loop in the emotional roller coaster that Mongolia was enduring. There was talk of a nationwide curse and monks were called upon to recite healing prayers.

In the days after Dashbalbar's funeral, the last of the autumn leaves blew across the dark streets of Ulaanbaatar. I also felt a sort of impending doom and slept fitfully. Then, just to cap off my own private struggle to comprehend this seasonal affective disorder, a mini-tragedy of sorts occurred at my apartment building. Asleep early one morning on my pull out sofa I was startled awake by the sound of gun shots. I leapt out of bed and looked outside to see a dog killer picking up his prey and loading it onto a truck. Mongolia, you see, does not bother with dog pounds. Instead, municipalities dispatch marksman to patrol the streets and shoot stray dogs—they get one dollar per mongrel.

The dog killer climbed back in his truck and lumbered around the corner. Moments later there were more gun shots. I dressed quickly and went downstairs. There by the gate, my trusty doorman was sobbing over his dead dog. Without apologizing, the dog killer slipped back into his truck and drove off. Mongolia, which for me had always seemed such a well-meaning place, suddenly felt cold and callous.

At the office, each of us tried reconciling our collective depression in different ways. Indra kept busy by helping her son Sambuu fill out applications for a study abroad program. Mongolians like Indra were desperate to get their kids out of the country for work and study opportunities and had mastered the art of the grant application. Just about everyone I knew who spoke a modicum of English had been treated to study abroad trips in recent years. As luck would have it, Sambuu's scholarship application was accepted and he was off to Budapest for his freshman year at the Central European University.

The others were busy too. Amarbat went on a trip to Zavkhan, his first time back to his homeland since leaving six years earlier. Narantuya had been selected by a Danish aid program to attend a one-week journalists' seminar in South-East Asia. And Bayarmaa was in better spirits: we suspected that she had a boyfriend though she always denied it.

Me? I worked. Boring as that may sound I never found the work dull. I had cobbled together several freelance writing jobs and kept busy pitching story ideas, writing and shooting photos. That winter, the zud was the main story to sell and the work seemed endless. I found it easiest to write at night so in the evenings I'd barricade myself in the office, tune into the World Service on the BBC and tap at my keyboard. When the computer overheated and threatened complete meltdown, I'd shut down the office, wrap myself up under a dozen layers of clothing and dash down to the Khan Brau, Ulaanbaatar's most popular watering hole and late night meeting ground for young expats.

One night, while listening to a BBC program on the upcoming worldwide Millennium celebrations, I decided to enliven things up at *The Messenger* with a special Millennium issue, highlighting a thousand years of Mongolian history. If nothing else, it might lessen the depressing news that we were spilling out week after week. Chingis Khan and his marauding descendants featured prominently and were central to our story and readers' poll on the "Most Influential Mongols." It goes without saying that Chingis was number one. Among contemporary figures, S. Zorig snuck in at number five, while Mongolia's first and only cosmonaut, Gurragcha, secured the number ten spot.

"Mongolia established the greatest land empire of the Millennium; we went all the way to Europe!" Davaajav, the Foreign News Editor, said triumphantly.

"What will you do to mark the occasion?" I asked.

"I have a tradition on December 31 to stay home with my family. My children and grandchildren come over and we make a toast with champagne. Then I drink an entire bottle of vodka by myself."

Another journalist, Nyamsuren, who was half the size of Davaajav, boasted that he planned to drink two bottles of vodka, in honor of the Millennium.

"Mongolia accomplished a lot over the past 1000 years, so we ought to celebrate," he said. "We helped to found great civilizations when Chingis encouraged the East and West to meet. The Moghuls in India, the Golden Horde in Russia, the Yuan Dynasty in China— they all descended from us. But I think the most important person of the Millennium was Karl Marx; he showed humans the best way to live."

I asked him what he thought was in store for Mongolia over the next 1000 years.

"I think that by the next millennium there won't be any more Mongolia. By then it will be under the care of the United Nations, like Kosovo," he said.

"Kosovo?"

"Mongolia is already starting to disappear. Over the last 800 years we have been losing parts of our country." He was, of course, referring to the time when the Mongolian empire included most of the Asian continent. Yes, it had shrunk significantly since then!

Amarbat and I walked the icy streets one day to collect people's opinions on the past and future of Mongolia. As expected, several people followed up on Nyamsuren's Karl Marx comment—a great many people called Lenin the Man of the Century, and some considered the fall of communism the most significant event.

We asked one local woman who she thought was the most influential person of the Millennium. She ruminated for a moment and finally said she could not decide between Hillary Clinton and Princess Diana.

Another man cast his vote for the Dalai Lama. I asked him which one and a look of confusion spread across his face. "All of them," he said, "*the* Dalai Lama."

We also met some of the fortunetellers that milled around outside Gandan Monastery. I approached one man wearing a scarlet-colored *del*. We sat next to him on plastic stools and asked what was in the cards for the coming century.

He showed me a stack of old Manchurian coins, then closed his fist around them and shook vigorously. Revealing the coins, he spread them across the palm of his hand and studied their alignment for a moment.

"Life will be peaceful for the next five years, but then Mongolia will become more dependent on Japan and China," he began, pointing at two of the coins. "Then in the sixth year there will be a great battle between the countries that want to take Mongolia. The Russians will come to defeat our enemies because they have always defended us. I just hope that there will be a person like Dashbalbar who will stand up and defend our country!"

Good old Dashbalbar, I thought, as onlookers shook their heads in somber remembrance. The fortuneteller peered at his coins again while the crowd hovered around us. "Mongolia will need great leaders in the future, but there will never be a rebirth of Chingis

Khan. Chingis was Chingis and that's that. But any man who uses his philosophy will succeed," he declared.

The theoretical rebirth of Chingis Khan had become a big media event of late when several lamas announced that his reincarnation had been born in September. Happy parents who gave birth to sons in that month boasted that their newborn would one day be a great leader. It wasn't until later that I learned that the origin of this prophecy was not from Buddhism, but 16th century France—the Mongolians were quoting Nostradamus, who wrote in quatrain X, 72:

> The year 1999, seventh month,
> From the sky will come a great King of Terror:
> To bring back to life the great King of the Mongols,
> Before and after Mars to reign by good luck.

The reason that "seventh month" was translated to September and not July was simply because the Asian calendar pushes everything forward by two months.

We turned to Badarj, another fortuneteller, for a second opinion. He opened up an old, worn out sutra, rocked slowly and mumbled to himself. Finally he set his book down and made some predictions.

"Chingis' reincarnation was born on September 9," he said, "and in the year 2800 a 15-year-old Chingis Khan incarnation will lead Mongolia. He won't fight a war, he will just lead."

"All right, the year 2800 is a little way off. How about the more immediate future? Any predictions for the coming year?"

"The year 2000 will be marked with a great earthquake and many horrible diseases, then Mongolia will be destroyed and there will be no nation. All humans will be infected with a terrible plague and all the crops will die. It will be the end of the world!" He lifted his sutra to show us and drew his finger across the words.

"At least that is what it says in this Tibetan book. But if that doesn't happen," he assured us, "Mongolia will be a nice place to live."

The coming Armageddon had me determined to celebrate New Year's Eve in style. Mongolians don't make much fuss out of the New Year, mostly because they have their own New Year in February. But expats living in Mongolia often go out and celebrate. In fact, expats adhered quite closely to their national celebrations, and since I had friends from almost every European country, I got to know their holidays quite well. Every June, for example, the local Brits celebrated the birthday of Her Majesty Queen Elizabeth II, and every July the French diplomats celebrated *l'occasion de la fete nationale* (Bastille Day). Both events were suit-and-tie affairs and the only difference was that the French served better cheese.

The American embassy put on a huge BBQ for the Fourth of July—grungy Peace Corps volunteers, pseudo-intellectual aid workers, and scores of prim missionary families rubbed shoulders while munching on long-awaited cheeseburgers. At Halloween, kids from the International school would turn up in costumes at the US Embassy for tricks or treats. Christmas parties were usually organized at restaurants. Meanwhile, the tiny Jewish population (there were about seven of us) celebrated Pesach at the home of an Israeli family who lived in a *dacha* outside town.

In addition, Daniel, the Cuban chef at Millie's, put on a bimonthly "Salsa Party," in honor of his homeland. In the midst of all this, there was no lack of house parties to celebrate birthdays, departures or lesser known provincial celebrations like Koninginnedag (Queen's Day in the Netherlands) when our Dutch friends made us consume orange colored food and alcohol. The epicenter for numerous such events was the apartment below mine, occupied by a darling Scottish lass named Ishbel. I could tell when something was afoot down there when thumping music drifted through my orange floorboards. Wandering downstairs I'd inevitably find bleary-eyed Commonwealth volunteers dancing to Oasis, with the occasional Scottish clog if they were up to it.

Mongolians didn't get involved with such events, let alone the Millennium. As I began the countdown to 2000, friends and colleagues spoke of staying at home with family.

A few days before December 31, City Hall broke with tradition. The mayor ordered all shops and offices to be decorated with tinsel for the New Year. Ice sculptures were commissioned for the Children's Park. Stout men dressed up as "Father Winter" (aka Santa Claus) were dispatched into the streets to greet children. A tall pine tree was propped up in Sükhbaatar Square and trimmed with lights and ribbons. In the span of a day, Ulaanbaatar metamorphosed from its usual grumpy winter gray to a kaleidoscope of holiday cheer and color. Regular work slowed down as the news agency went on early holiday by turning their last work day of the year into a vodka-fueled office party.

I tuned in the BBC World Service around 6 pm on December 31, 1999. Hour by hour, the announcers described the celebrations: first the quiet ceremony in the Kiribati Islands, and then the mayhem erupting in Auckland and Sydney. Mongolia was just a few hours behind.

Down at the British Embassy I found most of the expats who had remained in town. British school teachers, German bankers, Scandinavian aid workers and a small contingent of diplomats were sipping cocktails and eggnog.

"Are *you* still here?" each one asked the other upon entry. Only the most dedicated or lowest-income foreigners had stayed for the holidays. Everyone else had gone home or flown to warmer climates.

Looking for something a bit more uplifting, I later walked down to Sükhbaatar Square with Baigal, a girl I had been seeing for the past couple of weeks.

Baigal was a quiet but curious girl, a self-effacing botanist, with a round baby face and beautiful almond-shaped eyes. Like many urban Mongols, she was only one generation removed from her nomadic past—her mother had come from a nomad family in the Khangai Mountains. She said her father didn't know his ancestry; his parents had died when he was young and he had grown up in the state orphanage. They were the transitional generation, from the countryside to the city.

Baigal and her siblings symbolized the new generation of young people who had grown up in Communism but swore by Democracy (Gen-D, as I called them). One sister was working in Budapest, a brother was in Korea, and a second brother was studying to be an engineer.

Baigal and I conversed mostly in Mongolian, definitely not a romance language. There were moments of hesitation, and times when we had to sift through my Mongolian-English dictionary, but somehow we managed.

Hand in hand, we walked down Peace Avenue toward the snow covered Square. Bright lights from the surrounding colonnaded buildings twinkled in the winter light as we made our way to Sükhbaatar's statue. We found a few of my foreign friends, lingering about, each bundled up in puffy Day-Glo down jackets that made them look like a rack of billiard balls. We stood there, shifting back and forth on our feet, drinking icy beer, until we heard a small explosion overhead. The Sükhbaatar Square Christmas tree, trimmed with decorations, lights and apparently faulty wiring, was on fire. By 11.30pm the fire had extinguished itself and most of the crowds drifted away.

The night was starting to look like a bust. Mongolians, it seemed, had little interest in the European New Year, and I became resigned to an early eve.

"Let's go to the park," said Baigal. "Maybe we'll find people there."

I was in a state of doubt. But she grabbed my hand and led me through the snow and cold, past the gates that led to the park, toward a frozen pond where kids went ice skating.

The scene in front of us made my jaw drop. It was absolute bedlam around the pond, an ocean of humanity drunk on adrenaline and Chingis Khan vodka. Every man, woman and child—bundled up against minus 30°F temperatures—was jostling, laughing and singing in the winter night.

Ten minutes before midnight, sparks started to flare up all around; and then a huge pyrotechnic display erupted all around us. Never had I seen such an incredible (and close!) display of fireworks. It felt like a rocket attack and for ten solid minutes its glow transformed the plaza from night to day. The crowd, now completely crazed, surged through a line of police and down to a frozen pond where a stage had been set up for entertainers. Down the icy slope they went, and once on the pond it was every man for himself. I grabbed Baigal's hand and we skittered across the ice with the others. Circles formed, champagne bottles were popped, bottle rockets fired horizontally and chaos brewed under a Creamsicle sky. As I introduced the idea of the New Year's kiss to Baigal, men riding shaggy ponies and dressed like Chingis Khan's soldiers appeared on the ice and waved banners. Huge wooden teepees were lit and bonfires raged around us. At some point during those 15 minutes of madness, the clock struck midnight and the Millennium was on its way.

The euphoria from the Y2K celebrations lasted for several days. My colleagues returned to the office refreshed and for a while everyone was in better spirits. There was even mild relief that the over-hyped Millennium Bug did not strike, and our power stations still hummed into the night. But as the days of January passed, the harsh reality of a Mongolian *zud* began to settle in again. Temperatures dropped across the country, in some places down to minus 45°F. Teachers' salaries were being withheld and another strike loomed. In the Government House it was politics as usual, with parties bickering and another government on the brink of collapse. But the news from the countryside showed that beyond our secluded valley lay a far worse state of affairs.

In late January the herds started to die off, succumbing to the cold and lack of fodder. By early February they were dying *en masse*. The steppes were littered with the corpses of cattle, horses, sheep and goats. Herders reported finding their animals' stomachs filled with dirt, stones and litter. There was nothing else for them to eat.

Pictures published in local newspapers of animals piled in mounds made my co-workers cry. In Mongolia, camels, sheep, horses, goats, cows and yaks are food as well as property. From these animals, the nomads can produce clothing from the hides and wool. They use the dung as fuel to heat their homes. And in a barter economy, animals can be used just like cash—they are traded for clothing, foodstuffs, tools, and motorcycles. Mongolia's livestock are the wealth and pride of the nation, and the devastation of the herd is like a death in the family. By March the losses topped one million animals.

Meanwhile, a Russian energy producer shut down, cutting off power to the western provinces. Springtime wildfires raged out of control in the northeast. Grasslands in non-*zud* areas were quickly depleted when thousands of refugee animals were herded in from disaster-hit areas.

The crisis taxed the national psyche. A report by the United Nations said depression was slowing work production and leading to illness. I even saw this at Montsame, where my co-workers stared at their typewriters in an exhausted daze.

By April the animal death toll had reached two million and the numbers were still rising by 300,000 per week. Reports came into Montsame that some depressed herders had committed suicide.

"Spring is the worst time for the animals. They are exhausted from the dust, wind and hard winter. People even die more often in the spring—it's just natural in Mongolia," said Batjargal, a livestock specialist I interviewed one day. He blamed the government for its lack of preparation and said the plan now was to let all the weak animals die to save the healthy ones.

Aid workers who had been to the countryside were coming back to the capital with frightening tales. The roads they drove on were littered with the bleached bones of animals, their flesh picked clean by rapacious scavengers. The national mood was different from what I had witnessed in November, when everyone had the energy to help a neighbor in need. Now it was death that hung over the scattered *gers* and it was everyone for themselves.

The herders needed an early rain, but it never came. Just as the Mongols had always told me, *"Havariin tengershig busgui"* ("The spring sky is like the tempestuous emotions of a young girl"). In April, melting snow flooded valleys and drove people from their homes. Dust storms and snowstorms ravaged towns and blew *gers* apart. People were lost in whiteouts and found frozen solid. The winds tore roofs from buildings and knocked down miles of power poles and towers (helped along, no doubt, by thieves who stole the nuts and bolts that held them down).

Ulaanbaatar was not spared. My co-workers and I used to stand on the balcony at *The Mongol Messenger* and watch the dust clouds roll over the city with terrifying speed. Those caught outside were forced to find shelter in doorways. Windows rattled and broke, shutters and doors slammed, debris was tossed across the city. This was authentic Mongolian weather. Friar John of Plano Carpini described it with eloquence when he visited in the 1200s.

"The climate is very intemperate, as in the middle of summer there are terrible storms of thunder and lightning by which many people are killed, and even then there are great falls of snow and such tempests of cold winds blow that sometimes people can hardly sit on horseback. In one of these we had to throw ourselves down on the ground and could not see through the prodigious dust. There are often showers of hail, and sudden intolerable heats followed by extreme cold."

* * *

While Friar John spent his spring in Mongolia out in the elements, my memories of spring 2000 were of the empty city—empty offices, empty streets, and empty shops. People's thoughts also seemed empty, or preoccupied. They stayed at home as much as possible—as though the city was under quarantine. Baigal and I would go to restaurants and be the only patrons, or we'd walk Peace Avenue, joined only by a few beggar children. The feeling of death seemed not far away.

Just when it felt like Mongolia could handle no more of this, the country was struck by the dreaded foot-and-mouth disease. Vast sections of the Gobi, bordering on China, were quarantined and hundreds of animals died within in a few days. The army dispatched troops to enforce the quarantine, locking down whole cities and towns.

There was no logical explanation as to why so much bad luck had befallen the country at one time. I did wonder if Badarj the fortune teller really knew something that we didn't. Whatever the cause of the problem, Mongolia was at its wits end.

~ 18 ~

THE SUMMER RAINS

"SUMMER IS LIFE," sang Bayarmaa with one of her classic, mile-wide smiles. She twirled around in a circle allowing the summer rains to pelt her face.

"How about you Amarbat?" I asked. "Don't you love this, everything is turning green!"

"*Zavkhan-shig*" ("It's like Zavkhan") he managed, reminiscing of his old countryside homeland.

"With the exception of all that!" I said, pointing to the giant city of Ulaanbaatar below us. From up here, the WWII memorial atop Zaisen Hill, we had a perfect view of the city below. In an almost overnight change, the summer rains had turned the entire valley from a dusty spring brown to a gorgeous summer green. Perhaps, if you turned in the right direction or blotted out the city with your hand, it may have vaguely resembled one of Zavkhan's untouched valleys.

We had each brought a can of Cass beer and toasted the summer rains that were cooling off a city suffering from a severe heat wave. Spring, which had brought so much despair, had turned to summer and now the depleted pastures were given a breath of life. To be sure, the countryside had been crushed by the *zud,* but the nomads had begun the process of rebuilding their herds.

"Erool Mendiin Toloo," ("To your health") I said, raising my can of Korean beer to Amarbat and Bayarmaa. As the rain soaked through our clothes we drank in silence while a rainbow strutted its way across the valley before us.

All this was a good sign, and it brought a much needed attitude change to the entire city. In part this mood swing was attributable to the upcoming elections. Mongolians love their elections and are enthusiastic voters. Turnout at the polls is often over 80 percent. Election Day, in fact, has become something of a national holiday, in part because after four years of misery, voters are finally able to oust their most hated politicians.

The 2000 election appeared to be over even before it started. The opposition MPRP had the clear lead while the various democratic parties were in absolute disarray; their coalitions collapsed and their ranks scattered. Hoping to distance herself from the chaos, Zorig's sister Oyun broke from the Democrats and formed her own party, Civil Will. She teamed up with the Green Party to form a new coalition; their motto was "environmentally friendly and politically clean," revolutionary concepts for Mongolian politics.

Oyun's breakaway party started a trend of sorts, as other hopeful politicians registered their own parties and alliances. Each built new identities with bold promises and guarantees. The Mongolian Party for Tradition and Justice, for example, announced it would annex Inner Mongolia from the Chinese if it were voted into power.

Some parties sounded so similar it was hard to keep track of them. Ballots offered: the Mongolian Social Democratic Party (MSDP), the Mongolian New Social Democratic Party (MNSDP), and the Mongolian Democratic New Socialist Party (MDNSP). Like a scrabble board, everything hinged on a single letter. Eager to carve out an identity, the MNDSP announced that that the MSDP had "sold their souls to the devil."

Most Democrats realized that they had no chance of winning in their old constituencies so they just went carpet-bagging in other provinces. The prime minister that had lost his job over the 1998 bank scandal, Elbegdorj, changed from Bayankhongor to Dornod, a district in eastern Mongolia. He announced that he was looking for a place that would offer him "a challenge," as if the *zud* in Bayankhongor had not been challenging enough. Among other candidates who doubled as out-of-work prime ministers was Narantsatsralt. He had replaced Elbegdorj in January 1999, but only lasted in office seven months, voted out of office following a shady privatization scheme that appeared very profitable for himself and the Democrats. The list of Democrat candidates also included one fellow being investigated smuggling cars and another being investigated for murder. No one ever accused them of not being a colorful lot.

Few Democrats put much effort into their campaign, realizing that they would lose no matter where they ran. Instead they prepared to clear out their desks at the Government House, awaiting the inevitable.

In May, about a month before the election, I took a field trip out east. I was visiting Choibalsan, a relatively large Mongolian city (population: 45,000) that survived on contraband trade with nearby China. The big export items that summer was marmot pelts and gazelle meat—both animals were being hunted ruthlessly on the steppes and I was there to meet environmentalists to discuss the problems.

Smuggling, however, took a back seat when election madness erupted and rolled into town. By some bizarre coincidence, five of the six biggest political parties arrived on the same day to promote themselves, each arriving in a motley caravan of SUVs, Hum-Vees, trucks and jeeps that carried their supporters, security staff and privately hired rock-and-roll stars.

The biggest show in town had to be the New Socialist Party, which led by a reclusive multimillionaire businessman turned politician named Erdenebat who ran a construction company called Erel. That fateful morning, while sitting outside my hotel, I watched somewhat stunned as the New Socialists arrived in eight brand new SUVs. I put down the book I was reading and watched as a gaggle of badly dressed KGB look-alikes got out of the cars and escorted Erdenebat inside the hotel as if it were the Kremlin. A group of his officials waited outside, trying to make themselves look busy by relaying messages through walkie talkies.

"Might I be able to get an interview with Mr. Erdenebat," I asked one of the officials, a man with a crisp three-piece suit and a fireplug physique.

"Sorry, he doesn't give interviews," the spokesman said. "But you can come to our concert. We brought Hurd!"

Mongolia's biggest rock and roll band arrived a few moments later. They were followed by two Erel trucks that proceeded to unload metal poles, planks of wood and a bevy of workers in blue suits with "EREL" printed across the back. Within an hour, a stage was set up in the town square.

Rock was still a fairly new genre in Mongolia but it seemed that Hurd (which means Speed) had figured it out. Their music sounded a little like the Scorpions, but their lyrics were purely Mongolian, complete with praise to their mothers, the blue sky and the wild horses. They looked like rock stars ought to look—long hair whipping about, tattoos branded on their arms, multiple piercings. The lead singer vaguely resembled Anthony Kiedis. But being the country's most popular band by no means guaranteed them a big money record deal. In order to stay afloat they had to sell the name of their group to Erdenebat. They were now called "Erel Hurd," which would be like Bono calling his band Forbes U2.

When the concert got going the band appeared on stage in motorcycle racing jackets, which they zipped off to reveal yellow and blue "MDNSP" T-shirts. The crowd, some of them nomads fresh off the steppes, stood in bewildered silence as Hurd rocked Choibalsan. Few seemed impressed with the show of power.

"These people don't care about us, they just want money. They come here with their cars and trucks and music, then after four years they will be even richer. So where does that leave us?" one spectator asked me as the band members wailed in the background.

At the end of the show, the lead singer screamed into the microphone, "VOTE FOR THE MONGOLIAN DEMOCRATIC NEW SOCIALIST PARTY!"

When it was over, the band loaded its gear into the bus and Erdenebat jumped into the lead SUV. The entire cavalcade marched out of the city as quickly as it had arrived. The dust settled back onto the streets and the people of Choibalsan returned to their affairs as if nothing had happened.

There were a few changes at *The Messenger* when I got back to the city. First of all, we had a technological upgrade. Indra had cut a deal with a local electronics distributor who sent us a much needed Siemens computer in exchange for advertising in *The Messenger*. At first its primary purpose was to keep idle journalists occupied with Solitaire and Tetris. Eventually, Amarbat put it to use for book keeping and advertisement design.

Staff changes were equally significant. Baatarbeel, our number three journalist, had somehow made it to Japan where he found work at a fish packing plant. Then Undrakh and Narantuya left us to start a competitive English newspaper called *Mongolia Today*. Because of this exodus, we were forced to move to a dingy little room across the hall. The windows faced a courtyard that contained a huge metal garbage bin that burned continually, sending toxic fumes into our office. I was furious at having to move but my protests to Mr. Amarsanaa fell on deaf ears.

We also acquired a new editor. Maidar was a wire thin, bespectacled agronomist with neatly trimmed hair and a penchant for crimson-colored sweaters. Ariunbold was given the new title "Commentator," appropriate, given his predilection for opinionated news reports.

The change in leadership was a blessing. Ariunbold was never keen on making management decisions or giving orders. The entire time I had been here he had given me free reign over editorial matters and I had rarely met any opposition when it came to the final layout. There had been occasional set backs. My front page coverage of topics such as the visit by the Bogd Lama or adventures of Alan Parrot had proven very controversial and very nearly cut short my career at Montsame. Whenever the rest of the staff or Mr. Amarsanaa worried about my interest in such topics, Ariunbold was asked to step in and "read" the paper before it went to print. This would usually last for two or three issues and then it was back to business as usual. Ariunbold seemed relieved when the heavy burden of editorial blame was lifted from his shoulders and he made good on his promise of producing more content for the paper.

But Ariunbold had other reasons to come to work. Summer had also brought a new love interest. Dolgoo, the woman he was dating, was 15 years his junior and worked at the translation desk across the hall. Their flirtations had gone on for some time, it was clear that this was more than a fling. Ariunbold's estranged wife, who now lived in Chicago, left him in charge of raising their son. With luck, Dolgoo might be willing to become part of a new blended family. (Months later they would indeed get married).

At first there was concern that the loss of three hardened news veterans would cause added work for all of us, but as it turned out, the work suddenly became easier. We were a leaner, meaner team, with less bureaucracy and inner office-squabbling. It took some time, but finally I had the staff I wanted: One reliable journalist in Indra; a hard working translator in Bayarmaa; a diligent administrative assistant with Amarbat; fresh production out of Ariunbold; and an editor who understood the importance of management and public relations.

Coming to work was more fun, and it didn't matter that Maidar had never spent a day in journalism. He was moonlighting as the manager of a greenhouse. He didn't attempt to disguise this and said he would only come into the office when his tight gardening schedule allowed. At the office, his angle on the marketing of the paper was scientific. To earn revenue, he thought we should set up clubs and charge membership fees. "The *Mongol Messenger* Chess Club," and "The *Mongol Messenger* Horticulture Club," he assured us, would make the paper more accessible to its readers. But I had to break the news to him that the "*Mongol Messenger* Tourist Camp" just wasn't going to pan out.

Editorial content was mostly left up to me with consultations from Indra. But Maidar did ask that I leave open page eight for one of his colleagues, a scientist named Erdeni, who agreed to contribute a series of articles. All summer long our subscribers were introduced to Erdeni's "Super Unification Theory," which, he said, was the first and complete "answer to the great Universal question."

"Waste no more time on current theories, concepts and models which will never end with a Universal Theory. It would be much better to be promptly conversed into my faith," he wrote in an article titled "Erdeni Completes Einstein's Dream." Erdeni's answer to the universal question was too lengthy to detail here—it took him a whole book to explain it. The book, however, never really got off the ground, so The *Mongol Messenger* continued to run his scientific theorems. Here was one that I could not hope to explain:

Hindu Period = Age of Earth;

$$\frac{\Phi\pi}{4} = 1 + \frac{lg\ 33\ \sqrt{\overset{1000}{Hindu\ Cycle}}}{10}$$

With the Super Unification Theory becoming a permanent fixture on page eight of The *Mongol Messenger*, Gyatso the Australian monk gave us yin to counterbalance that yang, and filled up page seven with a string of columns dedicated to the Buddhist's answer to life, the Universe and everything.

Change was in the air not only at *The Messenger*, but across the entire city. Because politicians thought that they could buy votes, many spent their campaign allowances on community improvement projects in their electoral districts. Ambitious politicos filled potholes, mended fences and painted buildings. Erdenebat from the Socialist Party erected basketball courts in every capital district. Clearly Mongolia needed an election every six months just to keep the country in shape. But the visual enhancement didn't last long. People stole the wood off fences to burn in their stoves. And the inevitability of road deterioration took its toll—newer and bigger potholes appeared.

The élan that had come with the start of the campaign had waned significantly; and the major sentiment among Ulaanbaatar residents was that the political campaign was breaking the country's back. The money used to finance the various projects came from bank loans that no one expected to be returned. Although the city was looking better, a bank crisis loomed.

While the economy slumped, there was a feeling of early triumph in the MPRP camp. Meanwhile, the Democrats were scrambling to rape the system before they were kicked out of office. Reports of corruption were increasing and private entrepreneurs were losing their shirts. Eddie, my friend from Pizza De La Casa, often ranted to me about the ongoing troubles when I'd stop by his restaurant.

"Have you noticed how *bad* it has all become?" Eddie asked me one day, while serving up hot pizzas and cold cokes. "The economy is bad, people are bad. Everyone has lost hope. All the businesses are complaining about corruption. Tax officials come into every shop and restaurant and act like Mafiosos. They eat our food and take whatever money they want! I blame the Democrats. They know what is happening and they are profiting from it. They are just taking what they can get before they lose their jobs."

As it became clear that the MPRP would win, foreign investors and diplomats grew wary of what might happen when the "communists" took over. To allay their fears, Enkhbayar called for an interview with The *Mongol Messenger* a few days before the election.

Enkhbayar, a square-shouldered and patient man, represented the moderate faction of the MPRP. His liberal views were likened to Tony Blair's Labor Party, perhaps because Enkhbayar himself was educated at northern England's Leeds University. His English was flawless and he had spent a long career as a translator, turning Mongolian epics into English and Charles Dickens into Mongolian. He was progressive enough as to hire a well-heeled Dutch consultant named Tjalling to manage his foreign contacts.

Enkhbayar was the mastermind behind the MPRP's recent transformation from a party with extreme leftist elements and an aging hierarchy, to a youthful and progressive tour de force.

I entered his office, we sat opposite one another and he immediately began speaking into my microphone. He cut down the opposition and spoke on a broad range of issues including the preservation of Buddhism, the need for an environmental clean-up, the importance of completing IMF and World Bank economic reforms, the stoppage of illegal privatization and, lastly, his vision of increasing the birthrate. He had certainly done his homework, but I wondered how much of it was just lip service.

"We want to make government's role more active in business and social issues. We want to solve problems like poverty, street children, the *zud,* and unemployment," he told me, indicating that tighter controls were on the way. Some feared this prospect; others welcomed it.

On Election Day I joined a group of likeminded journalists and we hired a driver to take us to polling stations in the countryside.

"It must be around here somewhere," said Bayarmaa, who was working as our translator and guide for the day. We were searching for a *ger*—no ordinary *ger* but one of the voting *gers* that were set up for the nomads to spare them going all the way into the villages.

After an hour of searching the green hills, we lurched down a steep slope and spotted a Naadam Festival in the distance. Stopping in a grassy plain we heard the distant songs of children on horseback.

"*Giinnggooooo . . . Giinnggooooo . . .*" the small jockeys chanted. "*Giinnggooooo . . . Giinnggooooo . . .*"

"What are they singing?" I asked Bayarmaa as we walked closer.

"There words are meaningless; they make the sound to pacify their horses," she said. "It will make them run faster."

Suddenly they were off, galloping away to the cheers of the crowd. When the horses disappeared behind a knoll, the elderly men regrouped into circles—chatting and refilling their empty bowls with fresh *airag.* Pretty girls in bright *dels* gossiped shyly and powdered their faces amid the clouds of dust. The photo opportunities were excellent and Greg, the photographer in our group, managed to send pictures to his Tokyo office on a satellite phone.

"Where are we?" he asked. "I've got to put a dateline on these pictures."

No one seemed to know for sure as the nomads around us offered a variety of names. We settled on "Grassy Plain, MONGOLIA."

Waiting for the ponies to return, some wandered over to a *ger* that had a Mongolian flag rising out of its smoke hole. Inside the neat little tent, three portly women were passing out ballots. A couple of elderly election observers exchanged snuff bottles and handed me one as I found a spot on the carpeted floor. The nomads entered respectfully, greeted the officials with handshakes and traditional compliments, and voted without fuss.

My informal *ger* exit poll tested many of my assumptions about this country that had become my second home. Some, for obvious reasons, didn't want to tell me who they had voted for. Others said they had voted for the MPRP. One girl who was voting for the first time said she had picked the former communists "because everyone else is voting for them." None I spoke to had voted for the Democrats.

"Why not?" I asked the girl. "What's wrong with the Democrats?"

She looked at me strangely, as if the question was too obvious to ask.

"They have acted badly," she said, her smile fading away. "Who would support them?"

My phone rang early the next morning. It was Joe, one of the journalists in from Tokyo to cover the elections. He had stayed up all night to get the results.

"Huh, they won what?" I said into the phone, trying to make sure I was really awake and hearing him correctly.

"Seventy-two seats," said Joe, now repeating himself. "They were popping champagne bottles at 6am."

"Are you serious?" I couldn't believe it. How could they (the MPRP) have won all but four seats?

"I wouldn't lie about this," he said.

Within minutes I was at The *Mongol Messenger* office, where I found Bayarmaa. Her face was pale and her eyes held a glint of fear.

"What are we going to do!?" she said in a panic. I think she seriously thought the gallows were going to be out in Sükhbaatar Square—ready to hang all Democrats in preparation for a Stalinist future.

"I am afraid!" she said with a nervous laugh.

We quickly got the election tallies and read that the only new MPs outside the Revolutionary Party were Oyun (Zorig's sister), Erdenebat (from Erel Company), the former PM Narantsatsralt and an unknown independent candidate from Khövsgöl province named Gundalai. I later learned he was the owner of Ulaanbaatar's most famous strip club, the Attila Bar.

People on the streets shared Bayarmaa's reaction. Everyone expected the MPRP to do well, but not *that* well. A look at the breakdown, however, showed that the MPRP had only won half of the popular vote (the conservative half). But the other half of the votes had to be shared among the many Democrat candidates that had entered the fray. Just as Ralph Nader had taken away valuable votes from Al Gore, so had the Mongolian liberals essentially canceled each other out by running against one another.

At the office, Indra, a long time supporter of the Democrats, congratulated the MPRP winners over the phone without delay. Journalists flew into action. Vodka bottles mysteriously disappeared from desks. The mere idea of the "communists" returning to power was enough to get the country running again, and perhaps scared a few into action. Four years of parties, scandals, chaotic money grabs and lawlessness seemed to have come to an end overnight. I wondered how long it would last.

While the MPRP celebrated, the Democrats gave up power in silence. In keeping with elections over the past decade, the transfer of power would be a peaceful one. "On Judgment Day, Mongolians delivered a punishing lesson to the people they had once trusted," Ariunbold wrote in his commentary for *The Messenger*. "The Democrats were crushed by the mighty fist of the people—giving the young Democrats a four-year sentence to contemplate their crimes."

"We think it's okay," said Moogie, pouring over the results at his desk in the Foreign News office. "They Democrats were too reckless, what this country needs is a good old dictator to straighten everything out: now Parliament will finally get something done!"

The four-person opposition certainly had its hands full. When the new Parliament opened two weeks later they sat quietly in their seats and, when a vote was counted, looked helpless when 72 arms shot in the air around them.

The MPRP wasted no time in getting down to what they do best. A feeling of stability and fatherly authority dawned on the country after several subtle incidents. I first noticed it at the national Naadam where the usual pre-pubescent rap acts were replaced by a military band in Sükhbaatar Square. The brass band was called back for more concerts in the weeks to come.

At night the national radio station dipped into the archives to play thundering renditions of the old Soviet songs.

"Moskvaaaaa! Moskvaaaaa!," boomed from my radio.

Other catchy tunes included "Teacher Lenin" (My teacher's teacher! Lenin is the best leader!), "Cosmonaut" (Did you have a nice journey, brother cosmonaut? Did you stop to meet the moon and sun?), and my personal favorite: "My Book" (an entrancing children's rhyme that describes a boy's love for a recently purchased picture book).

In between the ballads, a stentorian voice would read old folk tales. It all culminated patriotically at 11pm sharp with the playing of the National Anthem. Since bars and clubs had been ordered to shut down early on strict government orders, the streets were empty by the time I left the office.

"This was what Mongolia was like when I was young," Baigal reminisced one Saturday evening as we walked down a solemn Peace Avenue. We had been seeing each other for six months and this had become a familiar walk. Normally at this time of night we'd find neon lights flashing and young people stumbling in and out of bars. "It was quiet, like tonight. There was nothing to do except go home, make dinner and go to bed."

Although Baigal had supported Oyun, and would have been content to live under Democrat rule, her parents had sided with the elder generation and voted for the MPRP. Over *buuz* one night at her *ger* out in the suburbs, Baigal's mom admitted she had chosen the MPRP mostly because the Democrats were "too young and inexperienced."

"We gave them a chance," she said, disappointed like so many others.

Meanwhile, in the Government House, the new ministers ordered a crackdown on all unpaid debts. The four year grace period had ended and it was time to pay up or go to prison. Enkhbayar (who was selected as Prime Minister) personally cancelled all countryside Naadams so the *malchin* could begin winter preparations. State employees who supported the Democrats were sacked and replaced by MPRP members (Our Amarsanaa was displaced by a squat hardliner named Baasansuren). The number of journalists allowed into the Government House was restricted. Some of the Yellow Press tabloid newspapers were shut down. And then, in an incident that created an outcry from the Democrats, Bat Uul was jailed for three weeks and interrogated by detectives still on the hunt for Zorig's killer.

"We are outraged and condemn the actions of the MPRP, which is launching repression in a well-trained manner, rather than starting its program pledge of free education and medical services," said a statement from the Democrats.

Despite these developments, the market economy showed promise. It was encouraging to watch new businesses opening, largely with the help of a revamped banking sector that was finally able to give out reliable loans. It was shocking to see Ulaanbaatar-style shops and cafés popping up not only in aimag centers like Choibalsan and Ölgii, but in one-horse villages out in the hinterlands. Progress and authoritarianism—just what the voters had ordered.

From the revamped economy to the hard line culture in our offices, Mongolia appeared to be moving in two directions at once. But more surprises lay in wait. The next story to catch our fancy involved a visit by a large delegation of Russians coming to Mongolia to put on a cultural fair.

More than 140 wrestlers, businessmen, Bolshoi ballet stars, folk singers and magicians arrived in Ulaanbaatar for the event. The merry band of Muscovites sung, danced and performed. For the first time in many years, Russian flags fluttered over Sükhbaatar Square.

Moogie and I went to the Russian Cultural Palace to watch the performances. The packed house was ecstatic. Eyes were misting up as the Master of Ceremonies recalled red letter dates of historical importance between the two countries. Many hoped that Russia was returning for the "eternal friendship" that had been temporarily displaced when the Soviet Union collapsed.

"Russia is like a sleepy wild grizzly bear that can't wake up," a patron told us. "If we compare Russia to a person, he is just a child trying to find his way—coming to Mongolia to learn things and get in touch with himself." We turned the microphone on his friend, who compared Russia to the Titanic—a sinking ship that was trying to use Mongolia as a "life raft."

The festival presaged the arrival of Russian president Vladimir Putin who swept into Mongolia in November under KGB-style secrecy. It was the first time a Russian leader had set foot in Mongolia since Breznev arrived 26 years before. His visit was a patriotic one—he laid a wreath on Sükhbaatar's statue and another on the Mongolian-Russian war memorial overlooking the city.

"A Mongolian proverb says 'first help your friend and then get help from him.' Russians will always remember the 'Revolutionary Mongol' tank brigade, the 'Mongol People warplane squadron' and the food aid Mongolia granted during the Second World War," Putin told Parliament. "There is nothing that can separate us... and the new Russia is open to any political negotiations and talks with Mongolia—an independent and sovereign country."

As ties with Russia strengthened, some ghosts of Mongolia's communist past won a reprieve. I learned this at the Moscow Days festival during a chance meeting with the son of the former Communist dictator Yu. Tsedenbal.

The dictator's son, named Zorig, was a skinny middle-aged man in a wrinkled blue polyester suit with large, floppy lapels. As the child of a Mongolian father and Russian mother, his youth was divided between Ulaanbaatar and the Black Sea, where his parents went on long holidays. Then, in 1984, he was banished to the USSR with his parents.

"There was a *coup d'etat* against my father organized by the KGB and its allies in Mongolia," Zorig told me. "My father even died in exile. But thanks to democracy, I can come back to my homeland."

Zorig had recently received a Mongolian passport, started taking Mongolian language lessons and made the fateful decision to live in his "native land." He had moved to Ulaanbaatar a year earlier; the mayor had been courteous enough to give him an apartment. He even ran for Parliament under the Party for Civil Will (but finished in dead last).

As we discussed the thaw between Russia and Mongolia I asked if sentiments had also changed toward his father, whose regime had been hated by so many. Indeed, Zorig said that a fondness for the Tsedenbal-era had been mounting. A museum dedicated to his father was being readied, as were books, a documentary film about his life and a statue that would be placed in a prominent downtown location.

"One goal of the Academy of Tsedenbal," he said, "is to write his biography, his real biography, with both positive and negative sides."

After wishing Zorig good luck, Moogie and I headed back toward Montsame together, over the Selbe River and past the University. On the way he conceded that despite the failings of the old system, it had its merits. For this reason Tsedenbal's mistakes were being forgiven.

"Tsedenbal provided us with a good education and health system. He cultivated a European style in Mongolia," Moogie said as we passed through the Parliament gardens. "He moved us away from feudalism toward an urban lifestyle, which was good. Before that time all Mongolians lived in *gers*. Eleven people in one *ger*, can you imagine that Mike? The oldest child was 18 and the youngest was two, and their parents were screwing right there! It was barbaric!"

His eyes searched the ground as he mused for a moment.

"Of course, we had to give up our culture. Even Chingis Khan's name could not be mentioned because we Mongols destroyed Moscow. The Russians did not want to hear about those days. So we just tried not stepping on their toes. But it was okay, because we received culture from the modern world, the European world. Tsedenbal liked Mongolia and I think it was good that he is being rehabilitated."

"Plus!" he said slapping my back. "There are a lot of young motivated people in Mongolia." He was talking about himself now. "They are strong-willed and have good skills. They are the children of Tsedenbal!"

Moogie was proud to be part of the Tsedenbal generation. If there was any doubt that the public was dissatisfied, it ended in October when the MPRP won another resounding victory in local elections. They gained 552 positions while other parties only won 113. With the local areas, the Great Hural and the President's office in MPRP hands, Mongolia had become a virtual one party state. Just like the good old days.

~ 19 ~

WHERE EAGLES DARE

I WAS SO CAUGHT UP IN THE OTHERWORLDLY POLITICS of Ulaanbaatar that at times the rest of the country lay in a sort of dreamy fog. But I knew I would be leaving the country soon and was determined to make one more trip to the countryside.

I had been thinking about visiting the eagle hunters. Even before coming to Mongolia I knew that the Kazakhs in the western part of the country used eagles like weapons, training them to hunt for fox, wolf and small game. I had read an article about them in a travel magazine long ago and had always wanted to join the hunt.

With the help of Indra—who had always assisted me when it came to extending visas, buying plane tickets or otherwise organizing writing trips—I bought a return ticket to Bayan-Ölgii and packed my North Face bag with the heaviest winter gear I could pull out of my closet. Baigal watched in bemused silence, unsure why I wanted to go to the most remote corner of the country in the dead of winter.

As I had done on my previous trips, I lined up a friend to fill in for me at *The Messenger*. Dan, a PhD student researching health in

297

Mongolia, agreed to help at the paper in exchange for beers when I returned home. In the past I'd sub-contracted English teachers to take over, and always regretted it. The job was always more stressful than they imagined. Dan was an experienced writer and spoke decent Mongolian. I knew he'd be able to handle it.

With the paper in safe hands, I laid out my plans to Ariunbold and the others, and asked if any of them had tips for locating these eagle hunters. I should have known better. It was like asking a New Yorker the best place to watch a Texas rodeo. Ariunbold did suggest, however, that I make a stop in Ölgii City. There I'd find Shinai, the local Montsame correspondent, who would help with arrangements for my onward travels.

Fresh snow dusted the runway ahead of my Antonov propeller plane. Settling into a frayed seat, I listened to the soft voices around me speaking in Kazakh. I felt like I'd already left Mongolia. Suddenly the propellers roared into action and the tiny metal plane buzzed down the tarmac, lifting into the sky with a slight shudder. I peered out the small porthole and watched the urban sprawl of Ulaanbaatar disappear into a hazy void. Wrinkled brown hills, streaked with snow inched under us as we traveled west for a thousand miles. The hills grew into snow-capped mountains as we neared Ölgii and the plane touched down on the dirt runway, kicking up a plume of dust.

Ölgii is the provincial capital of Bayan Ölgii province, a remote area of jagged peaks, deserts and glaciers, bordered on the northwest by Russia and the southwest by China. It is a special province designated as a "homeland" for the Kazakhs that live there. This unique status, designated in 1940, ensures that Kazakh language (belonging to the Turkish Qipqak family), culture and customs are preserved in tact.

Numbering around 100,000, the Kazakhs first arrived here in the 1840s to graze their livestock during the summer, returning to Xinjiang in the winter. Nineteenth-century Muslim rebellions in Xinjiang forced them deeper into the mountains, and many stayed for good. Like the Mongols, they remain nomadic, moving their large felt *gers* to high pastures in summer. But Kazakh *gers* are larger than the Mongol variety, and retain less heat, so in winter they retreat to villages comprised of small adobe homes.

The airport in Ölgii consisted of a single concrete hovel. A throng of locals had amassed outside, waiting to see who had come home. Waiting outside in the winter chill, shivering in my down coat, I searched unsuccessfully for my luggage. When I asked the attendant where my bag had gone he said it never made it on the plane but would arrive on the next flight—two days from now. I wasn't going to complain just yet, given Mongol Air's safety record I was simply glad to have arrived in one piece.

Carrying just my daypack, I caught a taxi into town and checked into the local lodge in time for lunch of mutton stew and steamed bread. The hotel management took a DIY approach to customer service. When I asked for a thermos of hot water to wash up the matron pointed to the kitchen and told me to boil it myself.

Having settled into my room I went looking for Shinai. The search did not last long and we were soon getting acquainted in his office, a tiny, disheveled room located above the Post Office. Shinai, who had worked as a journalist in Ölgii since 1963, was a skinny man with rheumy eyes and bushy, gray brows. He wore a brown tweed blazer and threadbare pants. Forty years worth of dusty newspapers crammed the room. He shared the space with another journalist who helped him produce a Kazakh-language newspaper called *Jana Omir*. I asked him what sort of news he had reported on lately.

He pondered this for a moment, seemingly unsure if anything newsworthy had occurred of late, but finally remembered the biggest story of the year: the "45-day cleanup."

"What's that?"

"The new governor has ordered a 45-day purge for the entire province. We have to pay off our debts and clean our offices and homes. We have to come to work sober. We must repair fences and paint our houses. Herders are supposed to clean out their livestock stables. It's all very good-spirited," Shinai said, leaning back in his fragile wooden chair.

"What if you don't do those things?"

"We'll be fined, or maybe lose our jobs."

It was a very communist thing to do; ordering people to sober up and clean up their houses or face retribution. But why not? Civic well-being made good sense. I hadn't been around that long, but from what I could see, the Kazakhs were a hard-working, business-minded lot. Shinai likewise appeared very dedicated to his job, but I asked if he every got bored or lonely out here. It had been closed off from the world for a long time.

"During the communist era," he explained, "we knew nothing of the world. We never saw *The New York Times*, or any other newspaper from the West. We did read some Western authors though. I like Bernard Shaw, Jack London and Ernest Hemingway. Have you read Farewell to Arms? Such a brilliant story!"

I was ashamed to admit that I had not.

"People got their news from our paper, *Jana Omir*," Shinai continued. "It was a great newspaper. We had many employees and we published two issues in a week. There were eight pages, four in Kazakh and four in Mongolian; but now it's very small and we only have two workers."

He showed me a copy of *Jana Omir*. It was written in Cyrillic. The Kazakhs used to write in the Arabic script, but like the Mongols, submitted to Soviet pressure and gave up their traditional writing long ago. Above the banner, it said "1941" and I assumed that this was when this edition had been printed. It was yellow, grainy and shoddily laid-out. Hand-drawn lines divided the stories.

"It's a very old one, from 1941," I commented.

"No, no. It's this week's edition. It says *"printed since 1941."* Come, let me show you what happened to our press."

Shinai led me outside and we walked through a fence to a concrete wreck of a building. A chained guard dog with dred locks snarled at us as we peered though the broken windows. Inside, huge iron printing presses lay in deserted rooms. The gray machinery was stripped and bits of metal lay scattered about the floor.

"This was the printing press."

Shinai explained how the printing press began to disintegrate after funds for maintenance ran out. It eventually stopped running and all the *Jana Omir* writers lost their jobs, except two. Now the newspaper is typed up, glued together and photocopied onto grainy yellow paper.

"It's not like it used to be," said Shinai wistfully. "Now we have nothing. *Odriin Sonin* (Daily News) hasn't paid me in six months, I don't even have a typewriter. Montsame has promised to send me a computer, but they haven't. When you go back can you ask them to send me a computer?" he pleaded. I promised to speak to my bosses at Montsame but cautioned him not to get his hopes up. The agency was broke, I told him, and was struggling just to pay wages.

Later that day Shinai pointed me toward the market, where he said I could find anything I needed for an expedition, including a ride into the mountains. I entered alone, passing through the market stalls, avoiding barking camels that spit in the dust. Inside I found myself rubbing shoulders with bearded old men haggling for fat-tailed sheep. I peered over tables where rough-looking characters threw away their money on card games.

"How much will you pay?" asked one man. He wore sunglasses on his face, a baseball cap on his head and a massive Golden eagle on his arm. The eagle fluttered its great wings a little when he lifted the bird to my face.

"Cheaper, cheaper."

"I don't know," I said, rather unfamiliar with the dynamics of the raptor trade. "How much you asking?"

"Fifty dollars." A silence befell the crowd around us.

"That's okay. I am just looking today."

"You don't want that bird," another man whispered into my ear. "Sick, no good. Look at the way its head and wings droop. Very sick, no good."

I had to admit the eagle, draped over its handlers' arm like a wet towel, did not look like the fighting powerhouse needed for hunting. "Come, come," the man said. "I'll show you a good bird. Very healthy, strong."

Kwat, as he called himself, didn't look like an eagle hunter. His trench coat and derby made him look like a Chicago gangster from the 1930s. He led me along the Khovd River until we reached his adobe home, set behind a wooden palisade. He unlocked a shed in his yard and when he opened the door I heard the sound of wings flapping and feathers ruffling. I stooped to enter and when I stood up was face to face with a Saker falcon.

"Doochin myang," said Kwat. Forty dollars.

"Where did you get it?" I asked, slightly alarmed and a little saddened to see a captured Saker that was likely to either die or be sold to an Arab smuggler. I had sudden flashes of Alan Parrot kicking the door down to apprehend us. Kwat looked down and shifted his eyeballs back and forth a few times. "Mountains," he said vaguely and swept his hand across the bluffs towering over the city.

"Yes, of course. But I really can't use a falcon now. Sorry."

"Khorin myang," he offered, slashing the price in half in sudden moment of desperation. He listed the falcons' finer qualities. It would retrieve fish, mice and rabbits, he promised.

"No, really. I wouldn't be able to get it back to America. They would confiscate it at customs. But thanks."

"Just take it back to Ulaanbaatar," he pleaded. "You can use it there."

Use it in Ulaanbaatar? Did he think I was going to train it to deliver *Mongol Messengers*? He brought the flustered falcon off its perch to soothe it with his hands, sensing my apprehension about the deal.

"Why don't you stay at my house; I am good guy. What food do you eat? Do you drink vodka? Come inside, rest and drink," he said, urging me into his home.

"Really Kwat, thank you for everything. But I am just looking for eagle hunters. Any idea where I might find them?"

"Yes, eagle hunters. First we drink," he said, sitting me down so that he could retrieve a bottle of vodka from his cupboard. We toasted to the Kazakhs and after a couple of shots he settled down. Vodka: just the fluid to get the cogs rolling.

Kwat understood why I didn't buy his falcon. He recognized my inexperience in falcon care, but was resolved to help me find a ride into the mountains where I could meet genuine hunters. The village of Tsengel, he said, was the best place, and I ought to look out for old man Yasiin.

I thanked him and slipped away, back to the market to arrange a ride to Tsengel. Before leaving town, I called Dan at the office. The paper would be going to print after the weekend and I was anxious to know how he had fared.

"Hello"

"Dan? Hey, it's Mike."

"Mike? I can barely hear you."

"Yeah, I am at the telephone office in Ölgii. Bad connection. How are things at the paper?"

"We're okay. But I think I pissed off Amarbat. He wanted all the editing done today so he could finish the layout. I'll have to come in over the weekend to tidy up some stories."

"How are the others?"

"Indra's been going to the Government House everyday and says she is writing something for Monday. Ariunbold has been busy playing blackjack on the computer. That's about it. Oh and there was a translator across the hall, I think he was some kind of a playboy . . ."

"That would be Batbayar."

"Yeah, he comes into the office every night with a bottle of vodka and tries to wrestle with me! I can't get any work done!"

"Yeah, I know what you mean. But don't lock him out because the door is jammed and you'll just end up locking yourself inside!"

"Thanks for the advice."

"No problem. Hey, I gotta go, somebody's knocking on the window here. I'll see you in a couple of weeks."

Click.

Tsengel was a small collection of adobe homes with an unpaved main street that looked like the set of Spaghetti Western, complete with a school, town hall and a handful of shops that sold sacks of flour, clothing and boiled sweets. Its population was hard to pin down. In summer it's mostly empty as the herders take their *gers* and flocks to the mountains while in winter it houses around 5000 people. Besides Kazakhs, around 1500 Tuvans live here, somewhat divided from the Kazakhs by cultural differences and language.

Yasiin was not hard to find. He was the only Yasiin in Tsengel and this was the sort of town where everyone was on a first name basis. As Kwat had indicated, he fit the mold of the eagle hunter. He had a shaggy, weathered face with rheumy eyes, bushy sideburns and a five-day-old beard. He wore battered leather boots that came to his knees, torn cotton pants, a black padded vest and a green jacket with a broken zipper. He walked with a gait formed by years in the saddle of his trusted horses. I looked around Yasiin's yard and sure enough, there, amid the sedate livestock and ragged children, sat a massive eagle on a wood perch.

"This is Aselbek; she is the best bird I have owned. Last year she caught a hundred foxes," Yasiin said proudly.

I would later notice that every hunter I met called their eagle "the best they had ever owned." Avoiding offense was tantamount as much superstition surrounds these regal birds. Good eagles, the hunters believed, will bring a family fortune and pleasant health while an ill-tempered or "unlucky" eagle would bring financial problems or disease.

I asked Yasiin if he would take me on a hunt and he seemed happy to oblige. We first went into his home for *suutei tsai* (milk tea) and preparations. Out here they add a dollop of butter to their tea, which, they say, will keep the body temperature high.

As Yasiin slipped into his huge black cloak, he told me he grew up in Tsengel but left for Ulaanbaatar in 1958 to become a tractor driver. After ten years he returned to Ölgii to crush rocks at a mine. But he lost his job in the 1990 economic collapse and had no alternative but to resume his former life as a herder.

"I now have three hundred animals," he boasted. "Life is different now, but not necessarily better. We have our freedom, but no security. One day we could disappear and no one would know or care."

Another hunter suddenly banged the door open without knocking. Khuantai, the local ranger, had come over to say he would join our hunt. Word had apparently gotten round of my arrival. Khuantai was a throwback to the days of medieval lore. He was in his mid-30s, had a pale rectangular face with orange whiskers and light-colored eyes. A rare smile revealed two big gold teeth. He was stoic and hardy, a square-jawed warrior of the steppes, and an "Aimag Lion" who made it to the final round of the provincial wrestling championships.

As we sat and drank tea I did some name dropping, asking about other eagle hunters Kwat had told me about and suggested I meet. Where was Taikhun wintering? And had Wadkhan finally sold that tractor of his? Taikhun, they said, was wintering about 15 miles to the west, and I could visit him if I wanted.

"Wadkhan is out by the lakes, it's very far. But you can't hunt with him anyway."

"Why not."

"A few weeks ago his eagle went after a wolf. One of its talons was bitten off. Wadkhan won't hunt again this winter unless he buys another eagle."

"Holy Shit! How could an eagle kill a wolf?"

Yasiin demonstrated how the eagle tries to grab the wolf by the muzzle with one claw and the chest with the other. Then it gouges out the wolf's eyes with its beak. The blinded wolf is then an easy target for a hunter with a gun. If there are two eagles, one will try to dig its talons into the spine, paralyzing the wolf.

We set down our cups of tea, bundled into heavy clothing, and headed for nearby mountains; Yasiin and Khuantai riding shaggy ponies and me following on foot. Their hooded eagles rested on their arms, maintaining balance as the horse bounced forward. The scene looked wonderfully barbaric. The horse sported a shaggy coat, an uncut mane and a tail so long it brushed the ground. On top sat a man dressed in clothes fashioned several Chinese dynasties ago. The hunters scanned the mountains for prey and searched the snow for tracks. Transportation, brains and weapon melded together in this crack hunting unit.

Hares darted in front of us as we trudged up the sandy slope. But we would need to hunt from the ridge. Unlike the smaller hawk and falcon, eagles must hunt from up high. They are too big to fly and cut quickly up a hillside. They glide slowly from above, outwitting and out-powering their prey.

We reached the rocky ridge and peered over the snow-lined valley below. There, down in the flats, we spotted a hare. Yasiin whipped the hood off his eagle. She saw the rabbit at once and expanded her huge wings. A moment later Khuantai released his eagle. They glided silently like heat-seeking missiles. The hare saw its predators and launched into a dead run across the snow. Then Yasiin's eagle folded up her wings and sped forward like a rocket. She reached out to snatch her prey but missed and was stranded on the ground. Her talons were tethered and she could not take off again. (This made it easier for Yasiin to retrieve his bird but also meant the attack was a one-shot deal). Seconds later, Khuantai's eagle arced toward the earth with her wings outstretched. She also missed. The hare would live another day. I thought this might be a rare event; two eagles missing the defenseless hare. What was the success rate?

"Rabbits are fast, which makes them hard to catch. Foxes and wolves are easier, but there aren't as many as there used to be," said Khuantai. Fox and wolf numbers, I knew, have fallen off drastically in recent years, the result of increased poaching by urban cowboys out on weekend hunts.

We had no luck that first day and the second day was more of the same, except that several other eagle hunters had joined us. The sub-zero temperatures and white out conditions never fazed them. They chatted and laughed; they followed fox tracks and debated where prey might lie. They smoked cigarettes but ate nothing. At first I thought their patience was superhuman. But I realized that their appetite was naturally adapted to the harsh climate. They lived as their ancestors had for thousands of years, making do in this barren land.

After the hunt I settled back inside Yasiin's home as the hunters crowded in for tea and *bortzig* (fried bread balls). Yasiin's wife, bent over at the waist after years of domestic servitude, doled out cups of tea and started to prepare dinner. After the meat was prepared it was placed in a large wok and left to boil for over four hours. It was like Thanksgiving dinner every day. I would sit in Yasiin's home, chatting with his visitors while eyeing the pot of food. When the dinner was finally ready, his wife piled the sheep parts into a bucket and set them on the table for the men to eat.

After all hands were carefully washed, Yasiin said a short prayer, reached into the bucket and began pulling out slabs of meat. The most honored portion was the rubbery flesh off the skull. Under the flickering light of a solitary bulb overhead, Yasiin hacked off pieces with his buck knife, slipping one into his mouth and depositing the next into the tub for anyone else to eat. The meat was tough and the flesh from the skull rubbery, but as a hot and filling meal it served its purpose. Then Yasiin's wife set down a plate of food scraps on the floor where she and her daughters ate their meal. I eyed this scene with suspicion.

"Why is your wife eating on the floor?" I asked Yasiin.

"Kazakh tradition," he said, "Like our Muslim cousins to the west."

Like all the other nights, this one was bitterly cold. After the fire in the stove died down, the temperature fell rapidly to minus twenty degrees. I would lay curled up in a ball in my sleeping bag, trying not to think about the cold, but quietly praying for daylight.

The third day was equally frustrating. When would I see a kill? No one was hunting the fourth day so I moved further into the countryside. I had a driver take me further west to the home of Taikhun, an hour's drive away in an empty U-shaped valley. We stopped in front of two mud homes at the base of a mountain. There was nothing else around but desolate wilderness. I paid the driver, my last link to civilization, and he sped off down the dirt track.

I knocked on the door.

"Uhhh . . . *Salemetses,*" ("hello" in Kazakh), *"Taikhun bain uu?"* ("Is Taikhun around?" in Mongolian)

There were three women inside; two young and one old. They didn't speak Mongolian.

"Taikhun?"

They pointed toward the mountains. I nodded, smiled, and they let me inside where I took a seat on a cushion. Surely, I thought, they must be alarmed by the unannounced appearance of a total stranger. But in their stoic way, they just continued their chores. Dung was collected and added to the fire. Fresh *bortzig* was fried in oil. The room was tidied.

I took note of their decorations. Three wolf pelts, a mounted owl and fox skins gave it the mark of a hunter's home. On a dresser I inspected old black and white photos: relatives gathered in front of a *ger*, a man on his horse with an eagle, and the ubiquitous family portrait in Sükhbaatar Square. Contrasting this solemnity were felt carpets and wall hangings, each with dazzling floral designs, spirals and psychedelic color schemes.

An hour later I got up to stretch my legs. I opened the little door in the atrium, stepped outside, and saw the dark shape of a horse, a man and an eagle. The sun shone brightly behind the man so that all I could see was the outline of his shoulders and fox fur hat. The sight startled me so much that I stumbled backwards, tripped over the threshold and fell backwards into the home. Taikhun had returned.

Taikhun, old and wrinkled like a peanut shell, dismounted. I introduced myself and mentioned that I had come from the United States, by way of Ulaanbaatar, to see a genuine eagle hunt. He considered me with his blue eyes, fingered his stringy goatee and invited me inside with a gravely voice. We ate *bortzig,* slurped tea and listened to one another's story.

Taikhun was an amazing old fellow with a shaved head and just enough teeth to tear apart a leg of mutton. He had sired eleven children and 32 grandkids with more on the way. It was comforting to know that these harsh mountains could nurture a man for 70 years, keeping him sharp enough to hunt on a daily basis.

His sons Jantimeer and Midet returned later after a long day of herding sheep. We exchanged pleasantries as one can only do with nomads—briefly and with little emotion. A solitary candle provided our evening light. Taikhun's wife silently spun camel fur into yarn. A baby lolled and cooed on Taikhun's lap. Orange faces whispered. There seemed little need for conversation out here. Outside the wind howled and the stars shone brightly in the sky like so many diamonds.

We hunted for two days, trudging out into the snow each morning with high aspirations and our warmest clothing. The mountain behind Taikhun's home was silent but every so often we could sense movement, a fox or a wolf, upon its rocky slopes. Taikhun's eagle, named Khana, was ever on the alert but the prey always seemed one step ahead of us, and despite our efforts we came home empty-handed each time.

We had our closest encounter late on the second day. Standing atop a ridge, Taikhun spotted a rabbit and whipped off the hood covering Khana's head. Immediately she spotted her prey and launched into attack mode. I held my breath as Khana sped forward. Alas, she was simply not fast enough, missing the rabbit by mere inches. Clearly frustrated at this she lunged after the rabbit. Although her talons were tied she managed to take flight again, this time spotting new prey. With her killer instinct, she soared back toward the ground, heading directly toward a black shape sitting on a rock—a baby goat.

Taikhun gasped while Midet started to run. And then Khana was on top of the goat, pecking and tearing at raw flesh as the animal let out sickening mews of agony. Midet scrambled over the rocks.

"AARRRGGHH, RRAAARRR . . ." he called, shooing the eagle from the goat.

She finally released her grip and Midet sent the goat limping after its panic stricken mother.

"That was the neighbor's goat," mumbled Taikhun under his breath.

Two days later I found myself back in Tsengel. It was evening and a neighbor named Kavai decided to slaughter a yak in his home. He invited his hunting buddies to help out. Khuantai slit the beast's throat and the group set to work. Two or three families joined in and piece by piece they hacked up the carcass into small portions. Kavai's wife cooked up a platter of meat and served it to the guests.

The whole process typified life in Tsengel. Kazakhs did not do things by themselves. All the families were interlinked and little could be done without the help of a friend, cousin, brother or neighbor. I had watched them team up to shoe horses, load logs onto trucks and repair jeeps. Even if it wasn't their personal project, it was their duty to assist. Communism had died but communities remained closely knit natural work units.

The dinner conversation was lively, fueled by shots of Russian vodka. I told them about Taikhun's eagle attacking the goat and they roared with laughter.

They asked about the animals in America and I launched into a long list. An armadillo was a bit hard to explain (a cross between a turtle and a pig, I said) and they were flabbergasted at the size of a grizzly bear.

"Do you eat bear?" they asked.

"No, not in California. Do you eat bear?"

"Of course, if we can find one. The meat from a bear will feed a family for a month," said Yasiin. They were dismayed that I could not tell them the number of livestock in America. So I told them about aquatic life, describing lobsters, seals, crabs, shrimp, fish, sharks and whales. They were shocked to learn the size of a whale. I tried to relate, explaining that a whale might feed a village for a month.

Then they spoke of eagles—the eagles that they had caught and trained, their many adventures in the mountains, eagles and wolves battling each other to the death.

"Do you have eagles in America?" they asked.

"Yes, it's our national symbol. But ours has a white head."

They argued that no eagle had a white head, that it must be some other bird.

"No, really. We call it a bald eagle. But there aren't many left. Many have disappeared because of overcrowding and the destruction of their habitat."

They weren't impressed. Kazakhs, they said, live in harmony with nature. It's the only way they can survive. It was the sort of answer I expected. I had met enough rural folk to realize they were the keepers of Mongolia's natural environment. They had too much at stake—livelihood, home, health and their souls—to let their land be devoured by urbanization and the whims of politicians.

Another two days passed and all I had to show for my hunting efforts was numb feet and weakened optimism. I thawed out in the evening but still had no feeling in my toes. A hideous blister formed on one foot and Yasiin popped it with a sharpened bone fragment. I slept poorly with nightmares of eagles circling around me and pecking my eyes out. Morale for this mission had reached a low ebb.

The hunters said they weren't going out for the rest of the week so I told Yasiin I would return to Ölgii the next morning. By 10am my bags were packed and a car was on its way to pick me up for a return ride to Ölgii. It was disappointing not to have seen a kill but I was not going to winter here. Yasiin came into the house and I thought he was going to tell me the jeep was ready to go.

"Let's go out for one more day of hunting. Kavai and Kadal are already heading toward the mountains," he said with wide, excited eyes.

The answer was no. I had had enough of mutton and tea; enough of freezing, sleepless nights; enough of families staring at me for long hours while I scribbled notes into my journal. The only problem was that I didn't know how to turn them down.

"Okay, give me two minutes," I said.

There was no horse for me, so I stumbled along after them, my camera dangling from my neck and the crisp air biting my cheeks.

We went up the mountain as usual and saw a couple of hares. "Please let your eagles go, please catch a hare" I silently begged them. Their eagles stayed on their arms and we pushed further up the slope. When I reached the ridge they were already off their mounts, peering over the edge of the rocky cliffs. Kadal tipped rock. Yasiin made screeching sounds. Nothing. We moved on.

I followed close behind as we marched around a rocky outcrop. The hunters stopped their horses as we approached the next cliff. All dismounted. Yasiin and Kadal crept to the edge with their eagles and crouched low to the ground. Kavai stood with his eagle to their right a few feet away. He tipped a rock down the slope.

All at once, I saw the hunters eyes grow wide. They shouted in unison and the three eagles rose simultaneously. Two flew directly down the slope and one, strangely, off to the right. The hunters roared and waved their arms. Further below, about one hundred feet down the slope, I saw it; a small golden fox, glowing in the morning sun. It stood still on the edge of a rock, paralyzed with fear. The two eagles flew side by side, their combined wingspan over 12 feet wide. Four yellow talons extended forward. Nanoseconds later, the eagles bounced off the slope like basketballs and soared back into the sky. Like a scene out of National Geographic, I saw the silhouette of an eagle soar into the sky with the fox beneath it in its talons. It was a sight I will never forget.

The hunters roared again and threw up their arms as if they had just thrown the winning pass in the Super Bowl. Then they leapt on their horses and charged recklessly down the slope—standing in their stirrups and whipping their horses. We reached the fracas of feathers, wings and beaks to find the eagles clutching the fox in a death grip. The hunters reached in to separate talons from flesh. What emerged were two maniacal raptors and one dazed and bloodied (but still living) steppe fox.

Yasiin grabbed the fox by the tail and placed it on a rock, tempting his eagle, the one that had veered in a different direction during the attack. The eagle eyed the fox from above, flew down from its perch, and made a perfect two point landing on the "bait." It stood there with a death grip on the fox, literally squeezing the life from its body. The suddenness of the kill was terrifying, yet seemed more noble than using a gun.

The proud hunters posed stoically for a picture with their trophy, and then Yasiin strung the fox to his saddle.

"Kadal's eagle caught the fox. Why is Yasiin keeping it?" I asked.

"Yasiin is older, so he keeps the first kill of the day," said Kadal. I guessed that in a lifetime of hunting, what comes around goes around.

Yasiin's home that evening was typically quiet. Little fanfare accompanied the hunter upon his return home. He had only done his job. We sat around the dung-fueled stove warming our hands and drinking milk tea. His children hovered over worn textbooks reviewing their schoolwork. An announcer on a battered short wave radio provided news from the far-off capital. And Yasiin set to work on the fox, knifing its limbs and peeling off its coat.

With careful detail he instructed his eight-year-old son in this art. Nusaltan stroked the soft pelt, turned it inside out and hung it on the wall to dry.

"What do you want to be when you grow up?" I asked him

He peered out from under his fur hat and smiled.

"A hunter!" he said, and started to stroke the long brown feathers of his father's eagle, longing for the day when he too could master this ancient sport.

I thought about the Turkestan wars that pushed the brave Kazakhs into these mountains 150 years ago. I considered how Stalin's pogroms had taken the lives of their parents and grandparents, and how communism had threatened their culture and dignity. But they had survived and now hold a rich cultural legacy that could not even be found among the Kazakhs living in Kazakhstan. This little boy was proof. Whatever comes to the people of Bayan-Ölgii, I doubted that it would be able to take away their eagles.

~ 20 ~

OVER THE GREAT WALL

EVERY FRIDAY NIGHT the staff at the British Embassy opened up a private bar located at the back of the embassy compound. The walls inside were strewn with photos of snow-shoeing bankers and beer-guzzling English teachers. British diplomats or the odd Australian mining executive stood behind the bar and sold cocktails and Carlsberg beer. Everything was paid for with US dollars. Foreigners went to the "Steppe Inn" to network and trade gossip. They exchanged notes on Ulaanbaatar's newest restaurants, commiserated in the latest failed government and warned newcomers about dangers of falling into open manholes. In summer they recounted the some endless jeep journey to the Gobi and the numerous breakdowns that came with it. In winter it was inevitably the cold that became a fashionable point of discussion.

One of many popular topics was fame and how foreigners seemed to so easily garner it. It was the big fish/little pond syndrome. The US ambassador for example, simply by donating wheat or lecturing at a university, appeared almost nightly on television newscasts. Chris, my old friend from the radio station, earned notoriety through local TV endorsements—he nearly broke a tooth in an advertisement for a bread company when he was asked to bite into their latest product. *"Ogoochh!"* said Chris, and he never heard the end of it. And then there were the UN volunteers who, through their promotion of benefit rock concerts, were all on a first name basis with the pop diva "Eros" Ariuna—the Mongolian Madonna.

In Ulaanbaatar, the ultimate small town atmosphere made run-ins with the rich and famous a common occurrence. It was the kind of place where you could easily end up dining on the president's leftovers, which is exactly what happened to a friend of mine. Rik, a lanky Dane with an irrepressible laugh, had been hanging around the German bakery one evening when the US ambassador arrived out of the cold. The ambassador had just come from the Taj Mahal Indian restaurant, where he and his wife had dined with President Bagabandi. Apparently there had been too much food, and the ambassador was carrying the president's leftovers in a doggie bag. But the ambassador was stuffed and offered the food to the German baker. When she declined, it was Rik, sitting by himself in the bakery, who ended up polishing off the president's lukewarm beef curry and nan.

Even I managed to achieve mild notoriety. It began with the *Gray, Short, Curly and Glasses Hour* the weekly radio show I hosted with David, Chris and Jill. I later moved onto a stint with Eagle TV, where I read the news on Sundays. I kept my reports varied, making sure to include current events (livestock figures), entertainment (theater dates), sports (wrestling results) and my personal favorite, the weather (each week I used a different adjective for cold). In autumn I read the bubonic plague report, for which the editors rolled a clip of a hunter gutting a marmot.

The weekly reports must have caught the eye of somebody in the entertainment industry because one day a young movie director came to the TV studio and asked if I wanted to play a role in his latest film. It was a low budget affair (he offered me $5 per day compensation) but I agreed to partake for the experience. The plot, a sort of tragic love affair, begins in New York where I play the role of an avaricious

American business tycoon. I am seeing a woman (played by a well-endowed, heavily made up Russian) and contemplate marriage but later I decide that she simply does not have the upper class standing and financial means to become my wife. Despite my wealth, my character is so greedy that he needs a bank-rolled bride. I decide to leave her for a wealthier woman. I tell her my plans in a bar scene and following our argument (my English, her Russian, dubbed into Mongolian) she unceremoniously smashes a cake in my face. In the next scene, she happens to be at a library where she comes across a map hidden inside a dusty old book. Upon inspection, it seems that the map gives directions to a cache of gold buried in the Mongolian outback. When she calls to announce her travel plans I warn her: "You can't go to Mongolia! Don't you know there are cannibals there? They ate our ambassador!"

Despite my admonishment, she goes to Mongolia and finds that it is not such a bad country after all. At first she lives in fear of being robbed, kidnapped, murdered, or worse, but when such maladies do not happen, she is surprised by kindness of the people she meets.

To sum up the plot; she falls in love with her hunky guide, but has no luck uncovering the gold, which turned out to be a hoax. No matter, she decides to settle down in a *ger* with her guide, a bronzed Mongolian cowboy. The movie, however, ends tragically. In the final scene a helicopter appears out of the blue and lands in an open field. I pop out of the hatch and scoop up my former girl, telling her that she is to be mine. Against her cries for help I push her into the helicopter and we fly away. The heartbroken Mongolian cowboy claws at the sky and then collapses on the ground in utter grief.

The film, strangely called *Stupid Country,* got plenty of airtime on local TV and in the theaters, and soon people were stopping me on the street to comment on my performance. It wasn't pretty I assure you, but simply being a foreigner had guaranteed my star status. (Despite this, my career in the Mongolian film industry has progressed no further).

* * *

Among the many well-known expats in Mongolia, one of the more infamous had to be Sammy. His real name was Segun Sfuwape Bamyoko Adebanjo and he came from Lagos, Nigeria. How and why he ended up in Mongolia remains a mystery, but the seventeen months he spent there—all in jail—is a tale worth recounting.

It all began when one of my wayward journeys landed me in Zamyn-Uud, a small desert town on the border with China. Consummate train traveler Paul Theroux passed by here in 1986 and described it as "a wreck of a town set on glaring sand and so lacking events that when a camel walked by everyone watched it."

While waiting around for my train to take me back to Ulaanbaatar, I suddenly remembered the story of a stranded Nigerian. Two years earlier, I recalled, he had violated a visa law trying to cross the border and had been arrested. We assumed the poor fellow had been let out.

I was curious to know how the incident had ended so I went out to the sweltering streets to find someone who might shed light on this question. I spotted a policeman squatting in the shade of a storefront. We exchanged the normal pleasantries and then I asked him about the Nigerian.

"You mean Sammy?" he said without hesitation.

"Yeah, Sammy . . . The Nigerian. Do you know when he left?"

"He didn't leave, he's over there." The policeman pointed to a high walled cement fort across a field of sand and abandoned car parts.

"Still *here?*"

"Yeah, he's still here. He's been here for nearly two years. Do you want to meet him?"

I nodded. *"Tzaaa, yo-ee,"* ("Okay, Let's go") he said, and we were off to the barracks.

A sturdy looking woman with large square glasses manned the guardhouse, which itself was furnished with two chairs, one desk and a buzzing bakelite telephone. I asked for a meeting with Sammy; the Station General was skeptical at first, but finally agreed.

"Do not take photos and do not write anything down," the General ordered.

Sammy arrived dressed in a blue shirt, black pants and an old golfer's cap. He casually sat down in the chair opposite me. My immediate impression was one of awe. How could a man, stranded for a year and a half in a wretched Mongolian prison, without any contact to the outside world, be so relaxed?

"So, what's it like to be here?" I asked shyly, not quite knowing where to begin. I tapped my pen against my notebook uneasily.

"It's tough," he said. "I am trapped. I got a wife and kid who probably think I am dead and there is nobody here to help. You are the first English-speaking person I have met since I have been here."

In all this time not a soul had come to visit? Surely someone at the UN, Amnesty International or an embassy had paid a courtesy call.

"No. I wasn't even sure if anyone knew I was here. You see, *he* doesn't let me send letters." Sammy nodded his head in the direction of the *darick* (boss). "I've tried explaining myself to them but it's too complicated. If you'd like to hear my story, I'd be happy to tell it. Maybe it will make a good article for your paper?" he said, cracking a slight smile.

Sammy had a tale filled with hope, misery, persecution and a lot of bad luck. It all started back home, in the mid-1990s, when he joined political protests against the Nigerian military strongman, General Sani Abacha. When he learned the government had targeted him for arrest he packed his bags and fled to Benin, using a friend's passport to get across the border.

"I laid low in Benin for a few months, but there was no work there, so I decided to do some business elsewhere."

This is where the plot thickened. I think the *darick* realized this because he didn't stop me when I started jotting down notes to keep up. Electronics trading, Sammy said, was an up and coming business in Africa, and Sammy decided to get in on the act—he bought a plane ticket for Beijing. Once in China he decided to visit Mongolia for a week. Before reaching Mongolia, he explained, his family mailed him his "real" passport. (Sammy said he had a Zimbabwean passport because this was his mother's native country). Dual documents in hand, he took the train north and was stamped *out* of Erlian (the Chinese border post) on his friend's Nigerian passport. Then he entered Mongolia at Zamyn-Uud and was stamped *in* using his own Zimbabwe passport. After reaching Ulaanbaatar, he mailed the Nigerian passport back to his friend in Lagos. He was back on the next available train south, returning to Erlian with his Zimbabwe passport.

"That is when my troubles began," he said with a heavy sigh and folded hands. "I was confronted by the same border guard who had stamped me out a week before. He recognized me and asked why I was using a different passport. I tried to convince him that *must* have been someone else. But they didn't buy it."

Sammy was sent back to Mongolia but his sudden return made the Mongolian border guards very suspicious. He was arrested and thrown into a concrete holding cell the size of a walk in closet.

"You start to go crazy in a room like that. You stare at the blank walls and you feel your head blowing up!"

Sammy stayed in his little cell all winter and spring, held without charges. Finally he got in contact with the Nigerian Embassy in Beijing. He was told that the political situation in Nigeria had changed: Sani Abacha had been dead for a year and there was a new democratically-elected president. It appeared that Sammy could safely return home—that was the good news. The bad news was that he would need to buy the plane ticket.

"I had no money and couldn't contact anyone for help. There was no way I could get a plane ticket on my own," he sighed again and buried his face in his hands. "And winter in Mongolia is no place for an African."

His passport fiasco was clearly illegal; but I did see that it warranted all this trouble. The guards seemed sympathetic too. One asked me to help get him out of there; they seemed to take me for some sort of diplomat. I told them I would do what I could, but the least I could do that day was to get him some decent food. So for the first time in 16 months, the guards let him out of the compound so that I could take him to a restaurant for a cooked meal.

"Can't you just escape?" I asked him, over a cutlet and mashed potatoes. His two (non-English speaking) guards quietly sat next to us, sipping grape Fantas.

"Yeah, I've thought about it. But where would I go? I stick out like a sore thumb in this country. I would be caught and that would destroy the relationship I have with these people. They trust me now."

Sammy asked me for news of the world. I realized that half the planet could have been set alight in nuclear flames and Sammy would have been none the wiser. I filled him in as best as I could; the NATO war in Bosnia, the Y2K panic, the WTO protests in Seattle and the upcoming Olympics in Sydney. It was all fresh news to him.

"I would love to watch the Olympics on TV," he said dreamily, "at home."

"Let me see what I can do," I said, suddenly feeling a bit of responsibility on my shoulders. I paid for the bill at the restaurant and the two guards led Sammy away. He didn't look back but I watched until they disappeared behind the crumbling blocks of Zamyn Uud.

When I returned to Ulaanbaatar I made an issue of Sammy's case by writing up an article for *The Mongol Messenger*. My colleagues were sympathetic, but had little to offer in the way of help.

"Oh, it's just Mongolia," was Ariunbold's response.

After the article was published, I hand delivered the paper to the British Embassy, the UNDP and the Foreign Ministry. I spoke with aid organizations and diplomats, trying to rally them behind Sammy's cause. Little came of it. One from the American contingent cynically asked if Sammy had "tried to sell me property."

The British Embassy confirmed that his Zimbabwean passport was stolen. There was a chance that I was aiding a criminal, but I failed to see the point of keeping him locked up in Zamyn Uud. At the very least, his release would take the burden off the underpaid soldiers in Zamyn Uud, who were sustaining Sammy's life out of their own pockets. The Foreign Ministry seemed to agree with that rationale.

"We would like to help this African," said the young bureaucrat assigned to resolve this case. "But we don't know what to do. The Nigerian Embassy in Beijing doesn't respond to our phone calls. Can you help?"

There it was again; the Mongolian officials thinking I had the power to get Sammy home. I realized he wasn't talking about my non-existent diplomatic status, but money. They figured I might be able to come up with the $1300 it would cost to buy Sammy a one-way ticket to Lagos. Well, I assured them I was on their side but suggested that the ministry front all the cash and wash their hands of it. Perhaps realizing that this was indeed the only option, the bureaucrat agreed to try. Several petitions were sent to the people who held the ministry purse strings. I would pop into his office every week to see how things were progressing.

"Still no approval," the bureaucrat said each time. "I'll keep trying."

Several weeks of petitioning went by until finally the young bureaucrats' efforts stirred results. At last, he told me on my fourth visit, the money for the air ticket had been allocated. With the ticket confirmed the Chinese embassy provided an emergency travel permit to get him to Beijing International Airport, from where he caught his flight home. After nearly two years, Sammy was finally free.

The end of Sammy's ordeal went largely unnoticed. Like so many other names to pass across the pages of *The Mongol Messenger*, he vanished into the realms of the unknown.

My own departure was even less dramatic than Sammy's. Just like

Jenni before me, I hired a foreigner (a young English woman named Lucy) to take over at The Mongol Messenger, cleaned out my apartment and collected my final tögrögs at Montsame. I even went to visit Zorig one last time at Altan-Ölgii Cemetery. One thing I never did was ask for a tour of the Sükhbaatar and Choibalsan Mausoleum on the Square. I thought I might save it for another trip; perhaps as an excuse to come back. My goodbyes were not dramatic because I knew I would come back.

I had stayed for three years, longer than I intended. It was like that for many expats. English teachers, miners, aid workers and diplomats usually extended their contracts by a year or two. Investors and entrepreneurs stuck it out in Mongolia's small economy simply because it was a nice place to live. It was something about the clean air, all that space, and the friendly people—priceless objects to be sure—that offered greater worth than any big money, multi-national contract they could have signed elsewhere. Mongolia was subtly seductive; its charm not in tropical beaches, but in the simple life of born nomads. This made it a great place to live for refugees from consumerism and lovers of the unknown and obscure.

I had only signed on at The Messenger for a year. Back in 1997, while home in San Francisco, I guessed that boredom would come quickly in Mongolia. I imagined myself sitting in a felt tent playing solitaire for months on end, waiting for the ice to melt away from my door. What could there possibly be to report about? Livestock births and mining figures seemed to be the only information in The Mongol Messengers Jenni had sent before my arrival. Perhaps it was just good timing, but during my three years, the news was irresistible, a reporter's dream. Like many others who visited Mongolia, I had come under its seductive spell.

It was cold the day I decided to leave, exactly three years to the day after I had arrived. And once again the steaming platform was crowded with bodies pushing bags and boxes into the hulking train. Indra and Amarbat were there, as was Baigal. She had become my closest friend and it was a tearful departure. I had tried to get her a visa to come with me to the US, but her application was rejected by the consular, who believed that she did not have "sufficient reason" to return to Mongolia and would therefore overstay her visa (as many young Mongolians had done in recent years).

We said *"bayartai,"* goodbye—a word rarely used in Mongolia except when someone is going far from home. Baigal's extraordinarily large, heavy-lidded eyes held mine for a moment. Then we sniffed each other's cheeks (a "Mongolian kiss") and a tear nearly froze on her face. We didn't know when, or if, we'd meet again.

I boarded the train and peered out the misty window as my friends huddled on the platform. Then, as *del*-wrapped women blessed the train with spoonfuls of milk, we rolled away. The passengers remained quiet as we passed through Ulaanbaatar, reflecting the mood of the somber winter day. We watched as anonymous concrete buildings streaked past our windows. Then the city was gone, replaced by snowy fields, hills, and the occasional *ger*. As Mongolia's emptiness passed by, passengers turned to one another, engaging in idle conversation. The train became our own little world and our lives began anew.

I was riding alongside an eclectic group of travelers. A longhaired Canadian named Eldo from an Inuit village near the Arctic Circle sat nearby. He came to Mongolia on a lark and was swept up by a family who took him to their countryside home to ride horses. A young married couple from Belgium looked like twins—both skinny, pale and sporting brown ponytails of equal length. A Mongolian trader gave me his phone number and told me to call him the next time I was in Ulaanbaatar. A Swede on board, who had been riding the rails all the way from Stockholm, was busy guessing people's astrological signs and then divining their fortunes. Nafi, a Sierra Leonian, was my cabin mate. She told me hair-raising stories of the civil war in her country—personal accounts of dodging gunfire and witnessing children having their arms hacked off. She had been in Ulaanbaatar for a year,

324

working at a French-African restaurant, and was returning to Beijing where she had been a performer in an African dance troupe.

We rolled through the remote Gobi Desert, gathering in the hallway or in the dining car. We ate instant soup and drank tea delivered by the slightly hunched over, recalcitrant Chinese attendant. And then at midnight the train jolted to a halt.

"Where are we?" Nafi asked.

"Zamyn Uud," I said. "The border."

"I know they will give me trouble here," she hissed. "All Africans have trouble crossing this border."

"Oh, why is that?" I asked, thinking of Sammy.

"Do you know about the Nigerian?"

"Yeah, actually I do. I met him last summer."

"Well because of him they check all of us," she said testily. "They always give us problems."

Nafi managed all right in Zamyn Uud, but sure enough, when we crossed into China, she was promptly hauled off the train and led into the station by two unblinking soldiers. Meanwhile, our train was sent into a shed and raised up on massive jacks. Blue and yellow uniformed Chinese laborers scurried around the train like ants, efficiently rolling the bogies (wheel chassis) out from under the train and replacing them with wheels that would fit Chinese rails. This was necessary because the Russians, who feared invasion by train, had made their rails a slightly different gauge. The cars were fitted back together and we returned to find Nafi waiting, and fuming, on the platform.

"You see! They always do this!" she yelled.

"Did you give them a bribe?" I asked.

"Of course not! I have a visa! I can go to China!"

She was furious and I did not envy those Chinese soldiers who had confronted her. Nafi settled back into her berth, still seething with anger, as the train lurched forward.

We rolled away from the station and I fell asleep to the soothing rhythm of the steel wheels clacking along the rails. In the morning I pulled back the shade to reveal a brown world. Narrow dirt roads and mud brick homes occasionally broke up the fallow fields. Grimy trucks sometimes passed carts pulled by shaggy burrows. Nafi was up and we looked out upon China.

"No snow," she said, as if China wouldn't allow it.

But there were signs of life. We saw a paved road. It had no potholes and the cars drove along it smoothly, without swerving, bounding or dodging. And there were road signs. We went to the Chinese dining car that had replaced the Mongolian unit. The larger Mongols were easily spotted among the newly arrived rural Chinese passengers. A Chinese waiter with greasy hair, a white undershirt and black slacks guffawed with his countrymen and then shooed Nafi and me into a booth with three Mongols: a young, rough-looking architect and two factory workers. The Mongols ordered a round of beer and eyed the plates of food set before them, not entirely sure what to make of their colorful contents.

"Do you like it?" I asked them.

One of the factory workers tried a piece of celery and cringed.

"It's like grass!" he said. "We Mongols like meat."

The others nodded.

I told him Chinese food was healthy and said the celery was good for his liver. I made that up on the spot, but it cheered him up nonetheless and he managed to put away half the celery on his plate.

The hours went by and desert farms turned to wooded hills. Then we passed chunks of the Great Wall of China and the passengers pressed their faces against the windows for a better look. The sheer size was humbling but the fact that it was built at all was as much a testament to Mongol military might as it was to Chinese ingenuity.

The train veered off course at a rebuilt section of the Great Wall to allow us to take photos. It was a tourist stop now, inhabited by a few bundled up vendors selling plastic panda bears and ice cream. But this was once the ancient dividing line between the cultivated Chinese and the barbaric nomads. When we left again, trundling down a steep grade, Mongolia, historic Mongolia, was truly behind us.

In the 1937 Hollywood movie *Lost Horizon,* a British diplomat named Robert Conway is flying over China when his plane is hijacked and taken to Shangri-La. Conway is skeptical of this mountainous paradise and an old monk says to him, "You have dreamed and written about better worlds. Is it that you fail to recognize one of your own dreams when you see it?"

I thought about this upon my arrival in Beijing. I was near the Friendship Store and felt lost—consumed by pavement, cars, bicycles, signs, skyscrapers and choking brown air. I had entered a city. A real city. I wondered if I had indeed left a better world.

A memory stuck with me as I milled about that tangle of cement and smoke. It was a memory of a walk home from Montsame one cold December night, when I came across a herd of forty horses, trotting down Trade Street near Millie's Cafe. Ice, clinging to their fur, sparkled in the orange glow of a streetlight. Then they disappeared between the apartment blocks and I was left in the silence of a frozen wonderland. The air was so crisp and clear at that moment, and the vision of the horses so strange, I felt as if I was dreaming. Ulaanbaatar was an ugly, scabby town. But it had its moments. This was one of them. No doubt there were other "garden spots" in Mongolia—the grassy fields of Dornod and the mountains of the Altai to name two—but my "horses on Trade Street" image was more powerful. Perhaps not everyone's Shangri-La, but mine.

Later in the film, Conway starts to believe that he has found what has been eluding him for a lifetime and he is asked to take over this utopia from a 200-year old Belgian friar. But in a final moment of doubt he leaves Shangri-La and heads over the treacherous mountains only to later learn that the pleasures of the valley were real. He struggles for over a year through the snow and Himalayan passes to return to the paradise lost.

* * *

In Beijing I met up with some of my journalist friends. An American photographer, who I will call Charlie, had a keen eye for parties and fast women. He said if I missed Mongolia he would take me and Eldo (the Canadian from the train) to meet some Mongolians that night. He knew bars where they gathered.

The first haunt we visited was Henry J. Beans, a surreal American brew-pub chain restaurant, right down to the hokey, junk strewn walls and burger heavy menu. I felt as if I had already arrived home. Rare Occasion was playing—a duet from Edmonton. Performers Chico and Dawn were B-52s look-alikes, right down to Chico's pink leather jacket and Dawn's vinyl top.

"I bet the fella from the Yukon can line dance!" Dawn sang, winking toward Eldo.

We ordered some beer—amber and foamy unlike the cheap Chinese *pijo* that normally ends up in Ulaanbaatar—and Charlie pointed out a girl sitting alone at the bar.

"There's a Mongolian," he said with certainty. "She's working."

"A Mongolian prostitute?" I asked.

"Yeah, sure. There's plenty of 'em."

"Here?" I looked around for others.

"No, this place attracts mostly Chinese girls, but she looks Mongolian."

I was taken aback. I had heard rumors of Mongolian girls working in other Asian cities, but never really believed them. I walked up and said, *"Sain bain uu?"*

She nearly jumped out of her barstool.

"Mongolt hilth yarj bolokh uu?" ("You speak Mongolian?") she said in a squeaky voice.

I nodded and she immediately warmed up to me like a long lost friend, wanting to hear all the latest Ulaanbaatar gossip. I dawdled through current events, and described a trip to the countryside that I had recently made.

"Oh, I miss Mongolia soooo much," she said sadly. "I am from Bulgan Province. I miss the big grassy fields, the animals..." I thought I saw her eyes mist up for a moment.

Altangerel, as she called herself, said she was 30 but looked more like 37.

She said she had worked the Asian Circuit—Singapore, Macau, Hong Kong—and had even been to Italy and Germany.

"How many other Mongolians do this sort of work?" I asked. She guessed around 500.

"How is it? You know, as a job?"

"Well, we have to make money. I have a child who lives with my parents in Ulaanbaatar. I send money home so they can get by. I just tell them I work for a company."

Altangerel saw this as a practical way to survive. Perhaps I shouldn't have been so surprised. Marco Polo tells us that Peking was home to 20,000 prostitutes when Khublai Khan was in power. He describes their main clientele.

"Whenever ambassadors come to the Great Khan on his business and are maintained at his expense, which is done on a lavish scale, (a) captain is called upon to provide one of these women every night for the ambassador and one for each of his attendants. They are changed every night and receive no payment; for this is the tax they pay to the Great Khan."

More remarkable was the situation in Huree (old Ulaanbaatar) around the turn of the 20th century. According to the Russian researcher Ivan Maiskii, any woman between the ages of 15 and 25 was a potential prostitute. People who needed their sexual desires attended to could simply find a suitable woman on the street, negotiate a price and take her to a brothel. Chinese merchants were some of the most frequent takers, but sons of Mongol officials and the odd lama were also customers.

"Near every city or major monastery there stands usually a row of yurts in which live prostitutes, often with the rest of their families," Maiskii wrote.

Prostitution was not only legal, but also respectable. Husbands would let out their wives, and parents saw to it that their daughters were involved. Just as Altangerel had noted, it was a way to support the family. Maiskii wrote:

"In her youth she enjoys all the good things of life available to her; she eats well, drinks well, and adorns herself with silks and expensive ornaments... In old age prostitutes either live out their years on the money they accumulated in their youth or, if they have children, are supported by them . . . Most often, however, prostitutes in their old age become *shabagantsa*, i.e., they take monastic vows and pray for forgiveness of the sins of their impetuous youth."

While Altangerel and I chatted I noticed that Charlie and Eldo were busy making their own contacts. Much to their chagrin every girl in the place came at a price. When they declined, the encounter would quickly fizzle and the girl would move on to any number of older, fatter, balder and richer foreigners.

"Let's go to Maggie's," Charlie said.

Maggie's, Charlie explained, was one of the liveliest late night bars in the city, and, he added, we would find more Mongolians there. I was skeptical, but couldn't pass up the opportunity to find out what Mongolians were *really* up to in China. Eldo, Charlie and I scuttled out of Henry J. Beans and into the cold night. We zipped up our jackets and hailed one of the many red taxis that own the Beijing roadways. Charlie detailed the address in Chinese to the driver and we turned up Dongdaqiao Lu toward the Worker's Stadium.

Maggie's, a little hovel set off the street, was lit up with a gaudy neon sign. Inside, it had a sticky floor, torn red leather couches, and mirrored ceilings, reminiscent of Ulaanbaatar's grittier discotheques. The first thing I noticed was that the DJ was playing Kamerton, one of Mongolia's ubiquitous boy bands. Then I saw the women, and none looked Chinese. They were all rather tall, mostly slender with square shoulders. They were all Mongolian.

"What the hell is this?"

"We call it the 'after hours Mongolian Embassy,'" Charlie said. "You said you wanted to meet Mongolians. Well, here they are." He directed his outstretched hand toward the bar. There must have been about sixty women lined up, shoulder to shoulder, and no more than fifteen men about them.

"It's still early yet; the place doesn't really get going until after midnight," Charlie informed.

I was shocked. An enclave of Mongolian sex workers living in Beijing; the surprises kept coming. Charlie and I sidled up to the bar and ordered bottles of Chinese *pijo*. A couple of Canadian back-packers were having language difficulties to our left.

"Dollar?" one said. "How much?"

"One hundreeeed," the slender girl said in heavily accented English, then turned to her friend and giggled something in Mongolian.

"How are you guys making out?" I asked the Canadian.

"They're expensive!" he said. "I didn't know Chinese girls would be so expensive."

"But they're Mongolians," I corrected.

"Same difference."

"No, you see there are Inner Mongolians who live in China and Outer Mongolians who live in Mongolia. These girls are Outer Mongolians. Maybe that's why they're expensive; they come from further away."

"Oh," he said, looking confused. I turned to the girl.

"Chi untei bain aa," ("You're a bit pricey").

The girl froze, blushed and then lit up with excitement. It took a few moments for all the accompanying Mongol camaraderie to die down. She shook my hand vigorously and implored me for details about how I acquired my Mongolian language skills. I gave her the short version.

"So what are you doing here?" I asked. Her name was Ana and she was rather pretty.

"Oh, just trying to make a little money," she said, obviously embarrassed. "I am a volleyball instructor in Ulaanbaatar, and you know how salaries are there. Very difficult. But I am having trouble meeting guys here. It's my first time."

"Oh, I am sure you tell all the guys that," I said with a nudge.

"No, really, I've just come down here with a friend; she is a student." The girl next to her, shorter and even more demure, gave me a soft handshake. "It's our winter break and we heard that girls could make good money here. But it's really expensive. We have to pay for the train and a hotel and food. We don't know if we will make any money."

"I am sure you will do fine," I said. "Don't be so nervous. I think these Canadian guys like you." They peered over my shoulder and giggled again. Then she asked me if I could negotiate for them.

"No way!" I said. "This is your deal, you figure it out."

The Canadian backpackers looked baffled. I wished them all good luck and turned back to Charlie.

"They're so innocent," I said. "They haven't a clue what they are doing."

"Yeah, but some of them are really *hot!*" he said.

It was true. A few were gorgeous. Others looked old and tired, weary from this trade. But very few appeared to be full time hookers. Most were students on their break—down here on a 30-day visa—taking a chance in an unknown world. This was the gritty underbelly of Mongolia's transition, a reflection of how desperate young people had become. As Altangerel had indicated, neither drugs nor personal problems had forced them here. They were merely doing what they could to support themselves and their families

The next day I took a red cab to the embassy district and stepped out in a biting northern wind. Wispy gray clouds floated overheard and snow looked certain. I pulled my *hurrum* (Mongolian jacket) tight around me and entered the Mongolian Embassy compound. It was a lovely brown building surrounded by patches of ice and stubby wilted grass. Khublai Khan had planted prairie grass at his palace in Beijing to remind him of home and I wondered if the ambassador had done the same. I pushed in the heavy wooden doors and introduced myself to the receptionist—a plump woman in a snug fitting purple *del*. Pleased that a representative of her national news agency had come to visit, she happily gave me a tour of the building, which included three spacious wood-paneled halls adorned with big oil paintings of Mongolia's empty steppes and craggy peaks.

One of the paintings was a "Day in the Life," the popular genre that depicts any number of daily chores for the nomad family. I studied it for a moment. A band of hunters stalked a wolf in one corner, while airag swilling nomads danced in the middle. To their right, children beat felt with sticks and below them a cowboy charged after a wild horse. I looked closely behind the dancing nomads and barely made out two naked bodies lolling in a tent.

"This is just how it is in the countryside," the receptionist said proudly. "I think you have seen how we Mongols live?"

She showed me behind the main building to a smaller one that housed the visa office, a little hotel for Mongol expats, and a restaurant for mutton-starved Mongolian travelers. We returned to the main building and she opened up a door that led to a courtyard. Flakes of snow were fluttering out of a sooty sky and into the yard, which held, believe it or not, a full sized *ger*. The *ger*, she said, was built to entertain guests, but she admitted that the staff sometimes retreated there when they were homesick—escaping the Chinese world to enter the very essence of Mongolia.

The secretary let me inside and disappeared for a moment before returning with a kettle of tea. She closed the door behind her, cutting off the chill outside, and showed off the tokens of her homeland. Brown felt rugs lined the floor. A horsehead fiddle was propped up in one corner. Silver drinking cups formed a line across the orange mantle. There was even a chess set with goats, sheep, yaks, camels, and *del*-clad herders instead of the traditional pieces. It was a bit flashy for a *ger*, but it was a *ger* nonetheless.

I sat on a little orange stool at an equally miniature table and she passed a steaming cup toward me with an outstretched arm. I held my elbow with my left hand as tradition dictates and accepted it, inhaling the steam. Maybe I imagined it, but the scent of burning dung and boiled mutton seemed close by. The secretary filled her cup, took a sip of tea, and we talked about Mongolia—about the winter mostly.

When we re-entered the main building, my host said the ambassador was in and asked if I wanted to meet him. Ambassador Tsakhilgan, a name that means "electricity," was a mountain of a man with big glasses and pale skin. It was he, I learned later, who had played a key role in Mongolia's democratic revolution. Tsakhilgan, along with another MPRP official named Lantuu (a named that means hammer), were dispatched by the government to hold the first negotiations with Zorig and the Democrats back in 1990. Skeptical Democrat supporters joked that the government had sent an "electric hammer" out to crush their movement, but in the end Tsakhilgan proved forthcoming and diplomatic, paving the way for the young dissidents to tear down communism.

"Please sit," he ordered with a wide smile and outstretched hand. I settled into a large leather couch. His secretary brought us some tea. It was black, not *suutei tsai,* called for under diplomatic protocol. I asked about him—where he was from and how he ended up becoming ambassador to China. But he was more interested in lecturing me on Sino-Mongol relations.

"We must have a balanced relationship with our two great neighbors," he began. "We have had diplomatic relations with the PRC since 1949, but our relations only normalized in the late 1980s."

In the 1960s, after the Sino-Soviet split, thousands of Chinese were kicked out of Mongolia and the country became a potential battlefield when the Soviets built up their troops in the Gobi Desert. As long as we were going to talk politics, I asked him if the Cold War between Mongolia and China was really over.

"Officially, we do not look to the past, we hold no grudge."

Unofficially, I thought, there was a different story. To say that relations between China and Mongolia have always been cool would be an understatement. Indeed the two cultures have little in common except a shared history of warfare and occupation. The irony, I always thought, was that the outside world usually lumped the Mongols together with the Chinese in the same ethnic category. Two peoples could not be more different.

As we furthered the interview on the long-time political and economic tie up between the two countries, I took a moment to look around his office. There were little mementos of Mongolia all over the place; from wood-carved camels to paintings of multi-armed Buddhist deities. There was little to indicate that we were actually in China.

"Your embassy is like a little island of Mongolia in Beijing," I commented, and asked him if he planted Mongolian grass as Khublai had done. He raised his eyebrows.

"Actually yes, we do have Mongolian grass here. Some former ambassadors planted it in the compound. And years back, wild berry bushes and apple trees were transplanted here from Selenge province."

Until now he had played the consummate diplomat. But now he was wistful. He took another sip of his tea.

"The staff likes it that way. In late summer we can pick berries just as we would back home."

His eyes wandered away for a moment, and I saw in them his own childhood memories of collecting berries and riding horses in the tall summer grass; memories of scampering up wooded hillsides to rocky peaks, and long winter nights playing with sheep ankle-bones on the floor of his *ger*.

"Yes, just like home."

GLOSSARY

Aksakal—eagle trainer

Arul—dried curd

Buriat—Mongol ethnic group in Siberia and northern Mongolia

Bogd Lama—Mongolia's spiritual leader. Also known as Bogd Gegeen, Jebtzun Damba or Bogd Khan

Bortzig—fried bread

Buus—silk belt tied around the Mongol robe

Buuz—meat dumpling

Chingis Khan—Mongol pronunciation of Ghengis Khan

Del—traditional Mongol robe

Evenki—Ethnic group of Siberia and Manchuria

Ger—Mongol word for yurt. Traditional home of the Mongols, this felt tent is supported by a lattice framework and poles that hold up the roof

Hiimori—energy housed inside the chest cavity, similar to karma

Il Tod—Mongolian word for Perestroika

Khalkh—majority ethnic grouping

Khuushuur—fried meat pancake

Khublai Khan—grandson of Chingis Khan and founder of Yuan Dynasty

Malchin—herder/livestock breeder

Montsame—Mongolia's national news agency

MPRP—acronym for Mongolian People's Revolutionary Party, Mongolia's first political party

MUM—Mongolian United Movement, protest group opposed to corruption in government

Naadam—Games. Usually referring to a festival with horse riding, wrestling and archery

NGO—Non-Governmental Organization

Suutei tsai—tea with milk and salt
Takhilch—lama in charge of objects used during sacrifice
Tenger—sky or heaven
Toono—skylight at the top of the *ger*
Tsagaan Sar—Mongolian New Year
Urum—cream
Uyach—horse trainer
Zud—winter of heavy snow and extreme cold

Montsame staff members
Amarbat—the *Mongol Messenger* production manager
Amarsanaa—the Montsame director
Ariunbold—the *Mongol Messenger* Editor-in-Chief
Baatarbeel—a *Mongol Messenger* reporter
Baatarjav—the Montsame night watchman
Chuluun—retired Montsame editor
Davaajav—Editor of the Foreign News Desk
Indra—the *Mongol Messenger* senior journalist
Gantamor—Montsame computer technician
Moogie—a translator on the Montsame foreign news desk
Purevsambuu—Montsame Editor-in-Chief
Purevesuren—Parliament correspondent
Bayarmaa—the *Mongol Messenger* junior translator
Tsetsegay—Amarsanaa's secretary
Undrakh—the *Mongol Messenger* senior translator
Zorigt—Montsame Editor

MONGOLIA FAST FACTS

Population: 2.8 million (world rank: 135)
Life expectancy: Female 67 years. Male 62 years
Ethnic groups: Khalkh Mongol (86%), Kazakh (5%), Other minorities including Buriat, Dorvod, Dukha (8%).
Religion: Buddhism (80%), Atheist (10%), Islam (5%), Christian (5%). Many adherents of Buddhism also believe in Shamanism.
Temperature in Ulaanbaatar in . . .
January: minus 20 to 0 Fahrenheit.
July: 52 to 70 Fahrenheit.
Per Capita income: US$1840 per person
Currency: US$1 = 1200 Mongolian tögrög
Leading industries: Copper, gold, cashmere, coal, meat
Annual Budget: Revenues: $582 million. Expenditures $602 million.
Percentage of people involved in herding/agriculture: 42%.
Number of tourists to visit Mongolia per year: 30,000
Literacy: 98%

Notable Names
Chingis Khan (1162-1227). Born Temujin, this nomad boy endured adolescent hardships to win leadership within his clan. He was later crowned Chingis Khan (Universal King). In 1206, following 25 years of civil war, he united the Mongol tribes into a formidable fighting force. After destroying several kingdoms in what is now China, he conquered all of Central Asia.

Ögödei Khan (1186-1241): Succcessor to his father Chingis, Ögödei would rule the Mongol empire from 1229 to 1241. Under his reign the empire would push west to eventually reach Europe.

Subodei (1176-1248): An ethnic Tuvan, Subodei became General of the Mongol army during its European conquests. Under his leadership, the Mongols took Russia, Poland and Hungary.

Hulegu (1217-1265): Grandson of Chingis Khan, Hulegu conquered Persia and sacked Baghdad in 1258.

Khublai Khan (1215-1294). Grandson of Chingis Khan, Khublai would rule over the greatest Mongol empire. During his time the empire stretched from Korea to Hungary. This was also the empire in which Marco Polo travelled and described to the world in his book, The Travels.

Altan Khan (1507-1583): Mongolian leader who attempted to unite warring clans under one religion. To this effort, he formed an alliance with the spiritual leader of Tibet, Sodnomjampts, and declared Buddhism the state religion in 1578. In an exchange of titles, Altan conferred upon Sodnomjampts the name Dalai Lama.

Zanabazar (1635-1723): The first Bogd Gegeen (Bogd Khan) of Mongolia. Recognized at the age of three as an incarnated saint, and then sent to Tibet at the age of 14 to study under the Dalai Lama. Zanabazar soon developed skills as a master artist and sculptor and led a renaissance in Mongolian arts. He invented the soyombo, Mongolia's national symbol and developed a new script for translating Tibetan texts into Mongolian. He also founded Mongolia's new capital, Örgöö, which would eventually become Ulaanbaatar.

Roy Chapman Andrews (1884-1960): Wisconsin-born American Zoologist who led the Central Asiatic Expeditions, funded by the Natural History Museum in New York. During five trips to Mongolia's Gobi Desert in the 1920s, Andrews' team uncovered a wealth of dinosaur fossils and put Mongolia on the map as a major study area for palaeontology. Andrews chronicled his adventures to Mongolia in several books, and is believed to be the prototype for Steven Spielberg's character, Indiana Jones.

Eighth Bogd Khan (1869-1924): Born in Tibet, the Eighth Jebtzun Damba (Lord of Refuge) was the last religious leader to rule Mongolia. He encouraged revolutionaries to oust the Chinese in 1911 and again in 1921. An eccentric figure, he collected a variety of trinkets and animal trophies from around the world, keeping them in his mansion south of Ulaanbaatar. He was also renowned for his sexual predations, which led to syphilis and blindness.

Sükhbaatar (1893-1923): Soldier and leading figure in Mongolia's fight for independence. After a stint as a typesetter in Huree (Ulaanbaatar), he went to Irkutsk to study at a military academy. Sükhbaatar went on to lead the Regular Mongolian People's Army and was part of an underground resistance founded in 1920 called the Mongolian People's Party (MPP), which later became the Mongolian People's Revolutionary Party (MPRP). The MPP established links with Soviet Russia with its help, liberated Mongolia from White Russian occupation. Sükhbaatar declared Mongolia's independence on July 11, 1921. He was named Mongolia's first Minister of War. He died in February 1923, allegedly poisoned.

Genden (1892-1937): An uneducated horse thief, Genden moved to Ulaanbaatar, joined the MPRP and quickly gained power until he was named prime minister. In 1932, following a bloody civil war between the army and the monastic class, Genden attempted to seek peace with the monks under his "New Reform Policy." Constantly at odds with Stalin, and refusing to purge the monks, Genden was eventually accused of aligning with Japan. He was shot on November 26, 1937.

Choibalsan (1895-1952): An original member of the MPP, Choibalsan slowly rose to power under direction of his mentor, Joseph Stalin. In

1934 he was appointed Deputy Prime Minister. In 1935, Stalin sent him a gift of 20 Gaz limousines, indicating his favor to the young leader. In 1936, the Soviets awarded him with the title of "Marshal." That same year, Choibalsan, now minister of Internal Affairs, receives another gift from Stalin—four rifles and 30,000 bullets. He is next named Premier and launches a purge on Mongolia's monastic class. In the end, nearly 30,000 people are dead or missing, most of them lamas.

Tsedenbal (1916-1991): Mongolian leader from 1952 until 1984. Over saw the elimination of Mongolian culture and the Russification of society. Ousted from power and died in Moscow in 1990.

Tumor-Ochir: Polituburo member during the 1950s and 1960s, but exiled after an attempt to rehabilitate victims of the purge and resurrect the name of Chingis Khan. He was assassinated in his apartment on October 2, 1985.

Batmönkh: Mongolia's Gorbachev, Batmönkh oversaw the transition of Mongolia from isolated Soviet client to an open and free society with multi-party elections and relations with Western countries.

Zorig (1962-1998): Dissident leader during the 1990 demonstrations that led to the end of Communism in Mongolia. Voted to Parliament twice and the Minister for Infrastructure, he was assassinated in his apartment on October 2, 1998.

Elbegdorj (b. 1963): Dissident leader turned politician, Elbegdorj has served as prime minister of Mongolia twice. He also earned a degree in public policy from Harvard School of Law.

Enkhbayar (b. 1958): Former head of the Mongolian People's Revolutionary Party, Enkhbayar served as Prime Minister from 2000 to 2004. He is currently serving as President of Mongolia.

Timeline of Mongolian History

1162: Temujin is born.

1181: Temujin and Borte are married.

1195: Temujin is renamed Chingis Khan (Universal King).

1206: Chingis Khan unites all Mongol tribes.

1206-09: Mongols go to war against the Tangut.

1215: Chingis Khan captures Peking.

1220-21: Chingis Khan captures Central Asia, including the former Soviet republics and Afghanistan.

1227: Chingis Khan dies.

1229: Ögödei elected grand Khan.

1230: Mongols occupy Iran.

1235: Foundation of Karakorum as the capital of the empire.

1238: Mongols capture Moscow, make incursions into Iraq.

1237-1241: Mongols crush Eastern European armies. Take Kiev, Krakow and Budapest and Zagreb.

1241: Death of Ögödei.

1245-47: John of Plano Carpini travels to Mongolia.

1258: Hulegu Khan destroyed Baghdad and creates the Ikh Khanate Dynasty in Persia.

1274: Mongols make an unsuccessful attack on Japan.

1279: Khublai Khan establishes the Yuan Dynasty in China.

1281: Mongols declare war on Vietnam.

1294: Khublai Khan dies.

1299: Mongols capture Allepo and Damascus.

1336: Collapse of Mongol power in Iran.

1368: Yuan Dynasty overthrown and Mongols retreat toward ancestral homelands. Ming dynasty established in China.

1370: Tamerlane is proclaimed Grand Emir and establishes a capital in Samarkand.

1502: End of the Golden Horde.

1586: Mongols adopt Tibetan Buddhism.

1691: Most of Mongolia falls to China.

1732: Western Mongols finally surrender to China.

1911: Mongolia proclaims its independence from China.

1921: Communist rebels gain control of Mongolia.

1924: The death of the eighth Bogd Khan spells the end for the monarchy; Mongolia proclaimed the world's second communist country.

1937: The Great Purge kills up to 30,000 monks and civilians. More than 700 monasteries are destroyed.

1961: Mongolia joins the United Nations.

1990: Peaceful protests for the Mongolian government to allow multi-party elections and a free market. Communism is abolished.

1996: Mongolian Democratic Coalition (DemUnion) trounces the Mongolian People's Revolutionary Party (MPRP) in Parliamentary elections.

1997: N. Bagabandi becomes Mongolia's second democratically elected President.

1998: In April, Prime Minister M. Enkhsaikhan resigns and is replaced by Ts. Elbegdorj.

1998: In October, Minister for Infrastructure Sanjasurengiin Zorig is assassinated by masked assailants in his home.

1998: In December, J. Naransatsralt replaces Ts. Elbegdorj as Prime Minister.

1999: In July, R. Amarjargal replaces J. Naransatsralt as Prime Minister

2000: The Mongolian People's Revolutionary Party (MPRP) wins 72 of 76 seats in Parliamentary elections. Party leader N. Enkhbayar becomes Prime Minister.

2001: President N. Bagabandi is re-elected to a second term in office.

2004: In Parliamentary elections, The MPRP wins 34 seats and the Democrats win 36 seats. A national government is formed with Ts. Elbegdorj serving as Prime Minister.

2005: N. Enkhbayar becomes Mongolia's third democratically elected president.

2006: Mongolia celebrates 800 years of statehood.

RECOMMENDED READING

Andrews, Roy Chapman. *Across Mongolian Plains*. New York: D. Appleton and Company, 1921.

Andrews, Roy Chapman. *On the Trail of Ancient Man*. New York: G.P. Putnam's Sons, 1922.

Baabar. *Twentieth Century Mongolia*. Cambridge: The White Horse Press, 1999.

Bawden, Charles R. *The Modern History of Mongolia*. New York: Kegan Paul International, 1989.

Chambers, James. *The Devil's Horsemen*. New York: Atheneum, 1985.

Gilmour, James. *Among the Mongols*. New York: American Tract Society, publishing date unknown.

Huc, Abbe. *Travels in Tartary and Tibet*. Geneva: Heron Books, 1970

Lattimore, Owen. *Mongol Journeys*. New York: Doubleday, Doran and Co. Inc., 1941

Lattimore, Owen, and Eleanor Lattimore. *Silks, Spices and Empire*. New York: Delacorte Press, 1968.

Ossendowski, Ferdinand. *Beasts, Men and Gods*. New York: E.P. Dutton & Company, 1922.

Polo, Marco. *The Travels*. London: Penguin Books Ltd. Translated by Ronald Latham, 1958.

Prejevalsky, N. *Mongolia, The Tangut Country, and the Solitudes of Northern Tibet*, Translated by E. Delmar Morgan, vol. 1. London: Sampson Low, Marston, Searle & Rivington, 1876.

Sarangerel. *Riding Windhorses*. Vermont: Destiny Books. 2000.

Yeshe, Lama. *Introduction to Tantra*. Boston: Wisdom Publications. 1987.

Weatherford, Jack. *Ghengis Khan and the Making of the Modern World*. New York: Three Rivers Press. 2004.

ACKNOWLEDGEMENTS

There are so many people who helped bring this story to life and I apologize that I cannot name them all. Many were people on the streets of Ulaanbaatar or nomads in the countryside who lent me their opinions and shared their thoughts on the changing face of Mongolia. My thoughts are still with you.

This book certainly would not have been possible without my colleagues at The *Mongol Messenger* and Montsame. Special thanks to: Ariunbold, Indra, Undrakh, Baatarbeel, Bayarmaa, Amarbat, Ooloon, Maidar, Batbayar, Chuka, Amarsanaa and the indefatigable Moogie.

My many friends in Ulaanbaatar added to the spice of life. My experience would not have been so rewarding without Jill, Dave, Chris, Susan, Pierre-Yves, Julie, Ishbel, Andy, Alison, Ben, Guido, Tjalling, Uli, Lucy, Darren, Batbold, Zaya, Gyatso, Alan, Rogier and Keith. Thanks also to the always-welcoming staff at the UK embassy, the VSO crew in Ulaanbaatar and the many Peace Corps volunteers that put me up when I visited the countryside.

In Mongolia and Beijing, I was fortunate to meet a number of experienced journalists and photographers who showed me the ropes. Thanks especially to Associated Press staffers John Leicester, Jill Hazelton, Joe Coleman, Greg Baker, Joe McDonald and Charles Hutzler. Thanks also to Alice Donald at the BBC. At RDR books, thanks to Roger Rapoport and Richard Harris.

Thank you to my parents, Susan and Stephen Kohn, and family members Lori, Cliff, Brooke, Jake, Jeff, Valerie, Max and Erin. Most of all, *bayarlalaa* and *hairtai* to my wife Baigal.

ABOUT THE AUTHOR

Michael Kohn lived and worked in Mongolia from 1998 to 2000 and frequently returns to cover news stories and sample the mares' milk. A writer for Lonely Planet, Michael has also worked in Israel, Colombia, Uzbekistan, South Africa and Tibet. He can be located in cyberspace at: www.michaelkohn.us